High Availability MySQL Cookbook

Over 50 simple but incredibly effective recipes focusing
on different methods of achieving high availability
for MySQL databases

Alex Davies

[PACKT] open source*
PUBLISHING   community experience distilled

BIRMINGHAM - MUMBAI

High Availability MySQL Cookbook

First published: April 2010

Production Reference: 1220410

Published by Packt Publishing Ltd.
32 Lincoln Road
Olton
Birmingham, B27 6PA, UK.

ISBN 978-1-847199-94-2

www.packtpub.com

Cover Image by Vinayak Chittar (vinayak.chittar@gmail.com)

Credits

Author

Alex Davies

Reviewers

Marc Delisle

Kai 'Oswald' Seidler

Acquisition Editor

Sarah Cullington

Development Editor

Darshana D. Shinde

Technical Editors

Charumathi Sankaran

Vishal Wadkar

Copy Editor

Leonard D'Silva

Indexer

Rekha Nair

Editorial Team Leader

Aanchal Kumar

Project Team Leader

Priya Mukherji

Project Coordinator

Prasad Rai

Proofreader

Lynda Sliwoski

Graphics

Geetanjali Sawant

Production Coordinator

Aparna Bhagat

Cover Work

Aparna Bhagat

About the Author

Alex Davies was involved early with the MySQL Cluster project and wrote what, at the time, was the first simple guide for MySQL Cluster after working with MySQL for many years and routinely facing the challenge of high availability. Alex has continued to use MySQL Cluster and many other high-availability techniques with MySQL. Currently employed as a system and virtualization architect for a large e-Gaming company, Alex has also had the fortune to work for companies of all sizes ranging from Google to countless tiny startups.

In writing this book, I owe an enormous debt of gratitude to the developers and members of the wide MySQL community. The quality of the freely-available software and documentation is surpassed only by the friendliness and helpfulness of so many members of the community and it's always a pleasure to work with MySQL.

I am deeply grateful to my colleague Alessandro Orsaria who spent an enormous amount of his valuable time offering suggestions and correcting errors in the drafts of this book. The final version is much stronger as a result and any remaining errors are entirely my own.

About the Reviewers

Marc Delisle is a member of the MySQL Developers Guild, which regroups community developers because of his involvement with phpMyAdmin. He started contributing to this popular MySQL web interface in December 1998, when he made the first multi-language version. He has been actively involved with this software project since May 2001 as a developer and project administrator.

Marc has worked at Cegep de Sherbrooke, Québec, Canada, as an application programmer and network manager since 1980. He has also been teaching networking, security, and PHP / MySQL application development. Marc lives in Sherbrooke with his wife and they enjoy spending time with their four children.

Marc authored the first ever Packt Publishing book, *Mastering phpMyAdmin for Effective MySQL Management*, and its revised editions. He also wrote *Creating your MySQL Database*: *Practical Design Tips and Techniques*, again with Packt Publishing.

I would like to thank the fine team at Packt for the support in reviewing this book.

Kai 'Oswald' Seidler was born in Hamburg in 1970. He graduated from Technical University of Berlin with a Diplom Informatiker degree (Master of Science equivalent) in Computer Science. In the 90s, he created and managed Germany's biggest IRCnet server, `irc.fu-berlin.de`, and co-managed one of the world's largest anonymous FTP servers, `ftp.cs.tu-berlin.de`. He professionally set up his first public web server in 1993. From 1993 until 1998, he was member of Projektgruppe Kulturraum Internet, a research project on net culture and network organization. In 2002, he co-founded Apache Friends and created the multi-platform Apache web server bundle XAMPP. Around 2005, XAMPP became the most popular Apache stack worldwide. In 2006, his third book, *Das XAMPP-Handbuch* was published by Addison Wesley.

Currently, he's working as Technology evangelist for web-tier products at Sun Microsystems.

Table of Contents

Preface

High availability is a regular requirement for databases, and it can be challenging to get it right. There are several different strategies for making MySQL, an open source **Relational Database Management System** (**RDBMS**), highly available. This may be needed to protect the database from hardware failures, software crashes, or user errors.

Running a MySQL database is fairly simple, but achieving high availability can be complicated. Many of the techniques have out-of-date, conflicting, and sometimes poor documentation. This book will provide you with the recipes showing you how to design, implement, and manage a highly-available MySQL environment using MySQL Cluster, MySQL Replication, block-level replication with DRBD, and shared storage with a clustered filesystem (that is, the open source **Global File System** (**GFS**)).

This book covers all the major techniques available for achieving high availability for MySQL, based on MySQL Cluster 7.0 and MySQL 5.0.77. All the recipes in this book are demonstrated using CentOS 5.3, which is a free and effectively identical version of the open source but commercial Red Hat Enterprise Linux operating system.

What this book covers

Chapter 1, High Availability with MySQL Cluster explains how to set up a simple MySQL Cluster. This chapter covers practical steps that will show you how to design, install, configure, and start a simple MySQL Cluster.

Chapter 2, MySQL Cluster Backup and Recovery covers the options available for backing up a MySQL Cluster and the considerations to be made at the cluster-design stage. It covers different recipes that will help you to take a backup successfully.

Chapter 3, MySQL Cluster Management, covers common management tasks for a MySQL Cluster. This includes tasks such as adding multiple management nodes for redundancy and monitoring the usage information of a cluster, in order to ensure that a cluster does not run out of memory. It also covers the tasks that are useful for specific situations such as setting up replication between clusters (useful for protection against entire site failures) and using disk-based tables (useful when a cluster is required, but it's not cost-effective to store the data in memory).

Chapter 4, MySQL Cluster Troubleshooting covers the troubleshooting aspects of MySQL Cluster. It contains recipes for single-storage node failure, multiple-storage node failures, storage node partitioning and arbitration, debugging MySQL Clusters, and network redundancy with MySQL Cluster.

Chapter 5, High Availability with MySQL Replication covers replication of MySQL databases. It contains recipes for designing a replication setup, configuring a replication master, configuring a replication slave without synchronizing data, and migrating data with a simple SQL dump.

Chapter 6, High Availability with MySQL and Shared Storage highlights the techniques to achieve high availability with shared storage. It covers recipes for preparing a Linux server for shared storage, configuring MySQL on shared storage with Conga, fencing for high availability, and configuring MySQL with GFS.

Chapter 7, High Availability with Block Level Replication covers **Distributed Replicated Block Device** (**DRBD**), which is a leading open source software for block-level replication. It also covers the recipes for installing DRBD on two Linux servers, manually moving services within a DRBD Cluster, and using heartbeat for automatic failover.

Chapter 8, Performance Tuning covers tuning techniques applicable to RedHat and CentOS 5 servers that are used with any of the high availability techniques. It also covers the recipes for tuning Linux kernel IO, CPU schedulers, and GFS on shared storage, queries within a MySQL Cluster, and MySQL Replication tuning.

Appendix A, Base Installation includes the kickstart file for the base installation of MySQL Cluster.

Appendix B, LVM and MySQL covers the process for using the **Logical Volume Manager** (**LVM**) within the Linux kernel for consistent snapshot backups of MySQL.

Appendix C, Highly Available Architectures shows, at a high level, some different single-site and multi-site architectures.

What you need for this book

The software applications required to run the recipes in this book are:

- CentOS or Red Hat Enterprise Linux 5.3
- MySQL 5.0.77
- MySQL and MySQL Cluster 7.0.x

This book includes the process for installing both MySQL and MySQL Cluster onto CentOS.

Who this book is for

This book is targeted at system administrators or database administrators who have basic familiarity with Linux, the shell, and MySQL. You may already have some basic MySQL experience but are looking for practical guidance for configuring high availability, as well as a reference covering all of the common options used for high availability.

Conventions

In this book, you will find a number of styles of text that distinguish between different kinds of information. Here are some examples of these styles, and an explanation of their meaning.

Code words in text are shown as follows: "The `world` sample database is provided as a `SQL` file, which includes statements to build three tables and populate them with data.".

A block of code is set as follows:

```
[mysqld]
id=20
HostName=10.0.0.10
```

When we wish to draw your attention to a particular part of a code block, the relevant lines or items are set in bold:

```
HWADDR=00:16:3E:xx:xx:xx
BOOTPROTO=none
ONBOOT=yes
MASTER=bond0
SLAVE=yes
USERCTL=no
/etc/sysconfig/network-scripts/ifcfg-eth1:
DEVICE=eth1
```

Any command-line input or output is written as follows:

```
[root@node3 ~]# iptables -F
[root@node3 ~]# iptables -L
```

New terms and **important words** are shown in bold. Words that you see on the screen, in menus or dialog boxes for example, appear in the text like this: "The maximum number of ordered indexes is low and if you reach it, it will return a slightly cryptic error, **Can't create table xxx (errno: 136)**."

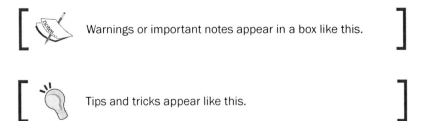

Warnings or important notes appear in a box like this.

Tips and tricks appear like this.

Reader feedback

Feedback from our readers is always welcome. Let us know what you think about this book—what you liked or may have disliked. Reader feedback is important for us to develop titles that you really get the most out of.

To send us general feedback, simply send an email to `feedback@packtpub.com`, and mention the book title via the subject of your message.

If there is a book that you need and would like to see us publish, please send us a note in the **SUGGEST A TITLE** form on `www.packtpub.com` or email `suggest@packtpub.com`.

If there is a topic that you have expertise in and you are interested in either writing or contributing to a book on, see our author guide on `www.packtpub.com/authors`.

Customer support

Now that you are the proud owner of a Packt book, we have a number of things to help you to get the most from your purchase.

Downloading the example code for the book

Visit `http://www.packtpub.com/files/code/9942_Code.zip` to directly download the example code.

The downloadable files contain instructions on how to use them.

Errata

Although we have taken every care to ensure the accuracy of our content, mistakes do happen. If you find a mistake in one of our books—maybe a mistake in the text or the code—we would be grateful if you would report this to us. By doing so, you can save other readers from frustration, and help us to improve subsequent versions of this book. If you find any errata, please report them by visiting http://www.packtpub.com/support, selecting your book, clicking on the **let us know** link, and entering the details of your errata. Once your errata are verified, your submission will be accepted and the errata added to any list of existing errata. Any existing errata can be viewed by selecting your title from http://www.packtpub.com/support.

Piracy

Piracy of copyright material on the Internet is an ongoing problem across all media. At Packt, we take the protection of our copyright and licenses very seriously. If you come across any illegal copies of our works, in any form, on the Internet, please provide us with the location address or web site name immediately so that we can pursue a remedy.

Please contact us at copyright@packtpub.com with a link to the suspected pirated material.

We appreciate your help in protecting our authors, and our ability to bring you valuable content.

Questions

You can contact us at questions@packtpub.com if you are having a problem with any aspect of the book, and we will do our best to address it.

1
High Availability with MySQL Cluster

In this chapter, we will cover:

- ▶ Designing a MySQL Cluster
- ▶ Creating an initial cluster configuration file—`config.ini`
- ▶ Installing a management node
- ▶ Starting a management node
- ▶ Installing and starting storage nodes
- ▶ Installing and starting SQL nodes
- ▶ Creating a MySQL Cluster table
- ▶ Restarting a MySQL Cluster without downtime
- ▶ Recovering from a cluster shutdown

Introduction

MySQL Cluster is the leading open source high availability database available today and is being used in many environments to achieve low cost "carrier grade" high availability and scalability. MySQL Cluster originates from a product called **Network DataBase,** which was known as **NDB**. This name has also stuck in the current software, so there are many references to NDB. For example, the name of the MySQL Cluster storage engine is NDB (instead of MyISAM or InnoDB). In general, wherever you see NDBCLUSTER (sometimes abbreviated as just NDB), you can think of it as "MySQL Cluster".

In this chapter, we will introduce MySQL Cluster as a technology and explain how to set up a simple cluster. This chapter will cover practical steps that will show you how to design, install, configure, and start a simple MySQL Cluster. We'll delve deeper into more advanced tasks in the later chapters.

Designing a MySQL Cluster

In this recipe, we will explain how to design a MySQL Cluster correctly. MySQL Cluster is an extremely powerful technology and this recipe will outline and briefly discuss some of the factors that you should consider while designing a MySQL Cluster.

We start with a high-level description of how a MySQL Cluster works in the *How to do it...* section. The *How it works...* section explores the bits that make up a cluster in more detail and the *There's more...* section discusses the way that a MySQL Cluster stores and retrieves data.

How to do it...

MySQL Clusters are built from three different types of *node*. These three types of node, when connected together, allow a cluster to provide a cluster storage engine on MySQL servers for clients to connect to. To build a cluster, you must select the hardware on which you can run at least one type of each node. We now discuss these types of node and how they connect together.

 A node does not mean a single physical machine but a process that forms a part of a cluster. It is quite possible to run multiple nodes (that is, processes) on the same physical machine. For example, it is common to run a management node on the same host as the SQL node.

The three kinds of nodes that make up a MySQL Cluster are:

1. **Management node**—these are the nodes that control information about the makeup of the cluster, provide a central point to collect the information such as logs and also to control other nodes. A management node must be started before any other node.

2. **Data or storage node**—this is the ndbd process that holds the data in the cluster and does the low-level work of answering queries in conjunction with the other storage nodes in the cluster.

3. **API nodes**—these are the nodes that connect to the cluster to extract the data—the most common example of this type of node is a mysqld process that is compiled to support MySQL Cluster which is commonly known as a *SQL node*. In this book, we use the term API and SQL node interchangeably except when referring to an API node that specifically is not a mysqld process.

To design a cluster with redundancy of operations (in other words, one that is highly available), you require at least one management node, two storage nodes, and two SQL nodes. A management node is only required when starting another node in your cluster—a cluster that is running will happily run even without a management node. Note that when there is no management node running in a cluster, there is no central point to control your cluster, view logs, and critically if another node fails, it will not be able to restart.

If you were building the simplest possible cluster, it would consist of:

- Two similar servers, each running a storage and SQL node
- One small server, running a management node

Three physical pieces of hardware are required to handle the case where a cluster is cut clean down the middle (for example, in a two-node cluster, one node's network cable is unplugged). This is called a **split brain** problem and is explored in more detail in the *How it works...* section that follows. In short, with only two nodes, in the event of nodes being unable to communicate (for example, when one node fails) both nodes must shut down to protect data consistency—which makes for a rather pointless cluster.

When it comes to calculating how many storage nodes you actually require, the recipe *Calculating* `DataMemory` *and* `IndexMemory` in *Chapter 3, MySQL Cluster Management* will tell you the total amount of memory required for your cluster. From a function of this number, the desired level of redundancy (see the following information box), the most cost-efficient amount of RAM to fit per server, and the performance required it is possible to calculate the optimum number of servers required for storage nodes and the RAM requirement for each. For a simple test cluster of two nodes, you simply require enough spare RAM per storage node to carry all of the data that you plan to store in the cluster, plus a little more space (approximately 20 percent) to handle overheads and indexes.

> The *level of availability* refers to the number of servers that you wish to store each fragment of data on for redundancy. This is known as `NoOfReplicas` and is difficult to change in the future—often it is set to 2 or 4. Your number of data nodes must be a multiple of `NoOfReplicas`.

It is an extremely good practice to keep SQL nodes and storage nodes on different servers in order to prevent a large query swapping and crashing the storage node located on the same server, so in practice a cluster size of 3 is unusual.

The nodes in your cluster absolutely require uninterrupted and private network connections between them. If this is not the case, there are the following three problems:

1. Firewalls can cause bizarre behavior as MySQL Cluster daemons use a wide range of ports.
2. Data sent between nodes in a cluster is not encrypted. Therefore, anyone with access to that network can access all data stored in the cluster.
3. No form of security exists in communication between nodes, so anyone with access to the storage or management nodes can, for example, shutdown the cluster or inject their own data.

To avoid this, connect your cluster nodes to a private, non-firewalled network and dedicated switch, and protect the public interface with a good firewall.

MySQL Clusters must be built with nodes having very low latency connections—generally, just a pair of Ethernet switches. It is not possible to build a cluster over a higher-latency link (such as the Internet), although replication between MySQL Clusters is covered in *Chapter 3*.

How it works...

MySQL Cluster sits at the *storage engine* layer of a MySQL database server, with a storage engine known as NDBCLUSTER. This means that for clients connecting to that MySQL server, a MySQL Cluster table is exactly the same as a local InnoDB or MyISAM table. It is also quite conventional to only have some tables configured to use MySQL Cluster, as the following diagram demonstrates with a single MySQL server (mysqld process) running one database (database1) with three table types—MyISAM tables, InnoDB tables, and MySQL Cluster tables (NDBCLUSTER).

All of the cluster magic that allows physical servers holding parts of your database to fail without causing downtime is handled below the level of the MySQL server on which an incoming query is processed. The following diagram shows a MySQL Server (mysqld) connecting to a four-storage node MySQL Cluster, a local MyISAM table, and an InnoDB table stored on an external disk array. The client cannot tell the difference between these three types of tables.

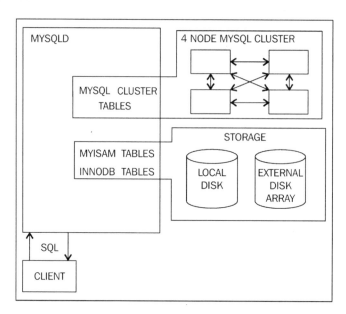

MySQL Cluster has a *shared nothing* property, which means that unlike most clustering solutions, there is genuinely no single point of failure. On the other hand, in many other systems including some that we will cover later in this book, there is what can be considered a very reliable single point of failure—often a *redundant* shared disk system which can still fail as a result of a single event, such as a physical problem with the unit.

To achieve this *no single point of failure* architecture, MySQL Clusters store all of the data in the cluster on more than one node, which obviously has a performance impact. To mitigate this potential impact, most production clusters store both data and indexes in storage node memory (RAM).

Storing data in memory sounds scary and it is possible to configure tables to be stored on the disks of the storage nodes (covered in a later recipe). However, RAM-based storage provides significantly greater performance. By ensuring that data is stored on at least two different physical servers at a time it is unlikely that a failure (such as a disk drive or PSU) will occur in all the nodes holding a fragment of data at the same time.

However, it is still of course possible that all the nodes could fail (for example, in a data center-wide power failure). In order to ensure that this does not result in a loss of all data in the cluster, running storage nodes are constantly check pointing the data stored in the memory to a persistent storage on the disk.

In clusters consisting of more than two storage nodes, it is possible for all the servers holding a single fragment of data to fail. In this case, the cluster shuts itself down to ensure data consistency—this process is covered in more detail in the following *There's more...* section.

There's more...

In the background, a MySQL Cluster works by chopping up (also known as partitioning) your data into chunks (known as partitions, or by the preferred MySQL Cluster term **fragments**) and storing each fragment on as many different servers (data nodes) as you have selected. In this section, this process is explained in more detail. This is important to understand for anything other than the most superficial use of MySQL Cluster.

This process is shown in the following diagram, which shows a cluster design for two data nodes and two copies of each fragment of data to be held within the cluster. The MySQL Cluster has automatically worked out that it needs to partition our data into four partitions. Given this, it will ensure that each node has two fragments of data and that any single node does not have two identical chunks. It can be shown as follows:

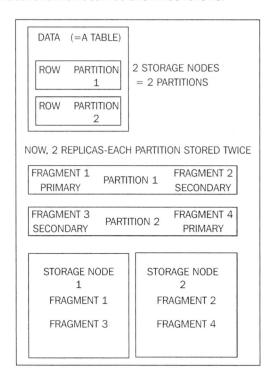

In clusters where there are more storage nodes than the number of copies of each piece of data (which in many clusters is two, that is, each fragment is stored on two separate nodes), the cluster must further split the storage nodes into nodegroups. **Nodegroups** are groups of storage nodes that store the same fragments of data, and as long as one node in each nodegroup remains available, the cluster will have an entire copy of the data.

While each node in a nodegroup has the same data, each fragment within the cluster has a *primary* copy and one or more replicas (the number depending on `NoOfReplicas` again). The primary copy ("*fragment replica*") for each fragment or partition will be moved around automatically by the cluster to be spread out among the nodes for performance reasons. In the case of two nodes per nodegroup, each node will have approximately 50 percent of the primary fragments.

In a MySQL Cluster, if we wish to change a piece of our data (one or more of the fragments), we must modify each copy of fragment. In other words, make the same change on every node that stores that fragment. MySQL Cluster will attempt to do this in parallel, that is, it will send the request to change the fragment simultaneously to all nodes containing the relevant fragment. However, until the change has been committed, the transaction remains uncommitted in case a node fails.

MySQL Cluster declares the transaction committed to the client once all active data nodes with the relevant fragment on them have received the request to update their fragments and a single storage node has committed all of the changes.

This process is called a two-phase commit, and while it increases data integrity significantly, it reduces performance. The speed of a cluster executing transactions is a function of the following parameters (with the first and last extremely quick, due to all the data being stored in memory rather than on disk):

- Time taken to locate all nodes involved in a transaction
- Network latency talking to all involved nodes
- Bandwidth available for transferring data between nodes
- Time taken for all nodes to retrieve and / or change relevant data

This process is almost certainly slower than just accessing data from a locally attached disk (or from a kernel cache of a disk) and therefore, MySQL Cluster will almost always be slower in terms of query execution time for low workloads. MySQL Cluster may be faster under very high load (where its near linear scalability kicks in, as the load is spread over more nodes) and is valuable at all demand levels for its high availability. When you are designing your cluster, consider how much cost and performance you are willing to trade for scalability and high availability.

When you are considering to deploy the MySQL Cluster, it is essential to have an idea of both the problems that the MySQL Cluster will not solve and its specific requirements.

 For a complete list of requirements and limitations, visit the online MySQL Cluster reference guide (accessible from `http://dev.mysql.com/doc/`).

The remainder of this section covers and explains the limitations that most commonly cause problems for a MySQL Cluster administrator.

- **Operating System requirements**: MySQL Cluster runs on several operating systems, and is specifically supported by the following:

    - Linux (Red Hat and SUSE)

    - Solaris

    - Mac OS X

    - Windows

    When considering which of the supported operating systems to use, it is worth noting that far and away the most tested is the Linux operating system.

- **Limitations using indexes**: There are some common limitations related to indexes inside MySQL Cluster tables as follows:

    - Full-text indexes do not work with MySQL Cluster. Consider using Sphinx (`http://www.sphinxsearch.com/`) and / or a separate table for your full-text searches, possibly using another high-availability technique such as MySQL Replication in order to run your intensive search queries against a replica without affecting performance on the master (*Chapter 5, High Availability with MySQL Replication*).

    - Text or BLOB fields cannot have indexes (however, `VARCHAR` fields can).

    - You may only have one `AUTO_INCREMENT` field per table. If your table does not already have a primary key when it was created or altered to MySQL Cluster, a hidden `AUTO_INCREMENT` primary key field will be created (and used for partitioning). If this happens, you will not be able to create another `AUTO_INCREMENT` field, even though you cannot see the one that exists. Therefore, ensure that you always define a primary key in your tables (which are often the `AUTO_INCREMENT` fields). One of the key differences between MySQL Cluster and InnoDB tables is that for clustered tables in InnoDB, foreign key constraints are simply ignored (this is the same behavior with the MyISAM storage engine).

- **Limitations using transactions**: While MySQL Cluster is transactional, in general, it does not support very large individual transactions particularly well.

    The limit is difficult to quantify and depends on node performance, network connections, and number of transactions. However, in general, applications that use larger numbers of smaller transactions are more likely to experience fewer problems with MySQL Cluster. Therefore, if you have the choice, design the application that is to use MySQL Cluster for lots of small transactions wherever possible.

- **Common "Hard Limits" to reach**: The following list of unchangeable limitations does vary significantly from release to release, but the limitations of the current version (that is, MySQL Cluster 7) are as follows:

  - The total number of **objects** (databases, tables, and indexes) cannot exceed 20320

  - The total number of **attributes** (columns and indexes) per table cannot exceed 128

  - The total size of a row cannot exceed 8 KB

  - The total number of storage nodes in a cluster cannot exceed 48

  - The total number of nodes (storage, management, and SQL) cannot exceed 255

- **Networking requirements**: MySQL Clusters require inter-cluster network traffic to have extremely low latency (small *round trip* (ping) times) and almost no packet loss.

  If this is not the case, performance will generally be extremely poor and it is possible that nodes will continually be kicked out of the cluster for not replying to heartbeat packets from other nodes quickly enough. To achieve these requirements, it is desirable for all members of the cluster to be interconnected using the same switch infrastructure, which should have a speed of at least one gigabit.

  Any network design involving a layer-3 device (such as a router) should be avoided wherever possible (although with modern wire speed, layer 3 forwarding for network devices can be as fast as layer 2). It is not recommended to attempt to get a cluster to work over a large network such as the Internet.

  While technically not truly impossible, it is strongly recommended that you do not attempt to change the timeout values to configure a cluster over a high-latency link, as this won't really work properly!

  If there is a need to replicate data across a WAN, consider replication between clusters (covered in the *Replication between MySQL Clusters* recipe in *Chapter 3*). It is possible to use high-speed cluster interconnects or Unix-like shared-memory segments, which themselves provide for extremely low-latency and high-reliability links.

- **System RAM requirements and best practice**: MySQL Cluster is extremely memory-intensive. Although, actual data can be stored both on disk and in memory (RAM), the performance of data in memory tables is, in most cases, better when compared with disk-based tables in terms of order of magnitude.

  Furthermore, even for disk-based tables, indexes (which can take up a significant amount of space) must still be stored in memory. Therefore, the RAM usage on data nodes is high, and the overall RAM requirement for a cluster is likely to be order of magnitude more than that required by a standalone MySQL server using InnoDB or MyISAM.

There are two major points to consider at an early stage:

- ❑ Firstly, 32-bit operating systems can have a problem allocating more than 2 gigabytes of RAM to a single process. They will also certainly have a problem addressing more than 4 GB RAM system-wide (even with special modifications to the 32-bit kernel to hack around this limit). Therefore, in most real-world clusters, a 64-bit operating system is likely to make more sense.

- ❑ Secondly, if a MySQL data node does not have enough physical RAM, it will either run out of it completely, in which case the kernel's *out of memory (OOM)* killer will almost certainly kill a data node process, or the operating system will begin to swap. This will likely result in a poor performance as the data node will not be able to respond to the heartbeats in a reasonable time and therefore, will be ejected from the cluster.

- ▸ **Processor architecture requirements**: MySQL will run on both 32-bit and 64-bit architectures for all supported operating systems. When we want to decide which one of these to select, it is worth to remember the limitations of 32-bit architectures on RAM and also considering that the MySQL Cluster storage node process is available in two forms—a single- and multi-threaded binary.

The single-threaded version of the storage node process has been tested significantly. However, the multi-threaded binary is simpler to use when trying to run multiple versions of the single-threaded binary on a single machine.

Operating systems can be described as little-*endian* or big-*endian* (**endianness** can be thought of as the byte ordering used by an operating system). There are two parts to this constraint:

- ❑ Firstly, all machines used in the cluster must have the same architecture. For example, you cannot have an x86 management node talking to data nodes running on PowerPC.

- ❑ Secondly, it is important to remember that the MySQL client API is not endian-sensitive. So your big-endian cluster can happily communicate with the applications running on both big- and-little-endian operating systems.

Creating an initial cluster configuration file—config.ini

In this recipe, we will discuss the initial configuration required to start a MySQL Cluster. A MySQL Cluster has a global configuration file—config.ini, which resides on all management nodes. This file defines the nodes (processes) that make up the cluster and the parameters that the nodes will use.

Each management node, when it starts, reads the config.ini file to get information on the structure of the cluster and when other nodes (storage and SQL / API) start, they contact the already-running management node to obtain the details of the cluster architecture.

The creation of this global configuration file—config.ini, is the first step in building the cluster and this recipe looks at the initial configuration for this file. Later recipes will cover more advanced parameters which you can define (typically to tune a cluster for specific goals, such as performance).

How to do it...

The first step in building a cluster is to create a global cluster configuration file. This file, called config.ini, by convention, is stored on each management node and is used by the management node process to show the cluster makeup and define variables for each node. In our example, we will store this in the file /usr/local/mysql-cluster/config.ini, but it can be stored anywhere else.

The file consists of multiple sections. Each section contains parameters that apply to a particular node, for example, the node's IP address or the amount of memory to reserve for data. Each type of node (management, SQL, and data node) has an optional default section to save duplicating the same parameter in each node. Each individual node that will make up the cluster has its own sections, which inherits the defaults defined for its type and specifies the additional parameters, or overrides the defaults.

This global configuration file is not complex, but is best analyzed with an example, and in this recipe, we will create a simple cluster configuration file for this node. The first line to add in the config.ini file is a block for this new management node:

```
[ndb_mgmd]
```

Now, we specify an ID for the node. This is absolutely not required, but can be useful—particularly if you have multiple management nodes.

```
Id=1
```

Now, we specify the IP address or hostname of the management node. It is recommended to use IP addresses in order to avoid a dependency on the DNS:

```
HostName=10.0.0.5
```

 It is possible to define a node without an IP address, in this case, a starting node can either be told which nodeID it should take when it starts, or the management node will allocate the node to the most suitable free slot.

Finally, we define a directory to store local files (for example, cluster `log` files):

```
DataDir=/var/lib/mysql-cluster
```

This is all that is required to define a single management node.

Now, we define the storage nodes in our simple cluster. To add storage nodes, it is recommended that we use the `default` section to define a data directory (a place for the node to store the files, which the node stores on the disk). It is also mandatory to define the `NoOfReplicas` parameter, which was discussed in the *There's more...* section of the previous recipe.

`[<type>_default]` works for all three types of nodes (`mgmd`, `ndbd`, and `mysqld`) and defines a default value to save duplicating a parameter for every node in that section. For example, the `DataDir` of the storage nodes can (and should) be defined in the `default` section:

```
[ndbd_default]
DataDir=/var/lib/mysql-cluster
NoOfReplicas=2
```

Once we have defined the `default` section, then defining the node ID and IP / hostname for the other storage nodes that make up our cluster is a simple matter as follows:

```
[ndbd]
id=3
HostName=10.0.0.1

[ndbd]
id=4
HostName=10.0.0.2
```

 You can either use hostnames or IP addresses in `config.ini` file. I recommend that you use IP addresses for absolute clarity, but if hostnames are used, it is a good idea to ensure that they are hardcoded in `/etc/hosts` on each node in order to ensure that a DNS problem does not cause major issues with your cluster.

Finally for SQL nodes, it is both possible and common to simply define a large number of [mysqld] sections with no HostName parameter. This keeps the precise future structure of the cluster flexible (this is not generally recommended for storage and management nodes).

It is a good practice to define the hostnames for essential nodes, and if desired also leave some spare sections for future use (the recipe *Taking an online backup of a MySQL Cluster* later in *Chapter 2, MySQL Cluster Backup and Recovery* will explain one of several most common reasons why this will be useful). For example, to define two-cluster SQL nodes (with their servers running mysqld) with IP addresses 10.0.0.2 and 10.0.0.3, with two more slots available for any SQL or API nodes to connect to on a first come, first served basis, use the following:

```
[mysqld]
HostName=10.0.0.2

[mysqld]
HostName=10.0.0.3

[mysqld]

[mysqld]
```

Now that we have prepared a simple config.ini file for a cluster, it is potentially possible to move on to installing and starting the cluster's first management node. Recollect where we saved the file (in /usr/local/mysql-cluster/config.ini) as you will need this information when you start the management node for the first time.

There's more...

At this stage, we have not yet defined any advanced parameters. It is possible to use the config.ini file that we have written so far to start a cluster and import a relatively small testing data set (such as the world database provided by MySQL for testing, which we will use later in this book). However, it is likely that you will need to set a couple of other parameters in the ndbd_default section of the config.ini file before you get a cluster in which you can actually import anything more than a tiny amount of data.

Firstly, there is a maximum limit of 32,000 concurrent operations in a MySQL Cluster, by default. The variable MaxNoOfConcurrentOperations sets the number of records that can be in update phase or locked simultaneously. While this sounds like a lot, it is likely that any significant import of data will exceed this value, so this can be safely increased. The limit is set deliberately low to protect small systems from large transactions. Each operation consumes at least one record, which has an overhead of 1 KB of memory.

> The MySQL documentation states the following:
>
> Unfortunately, it is difficult to calculate an exact value for this parameter so set it to a sensible value depending on the expected load on the cluster and monitor for errors when running large transactions (often when importing data):
>
> ```
> MaxNoOfConcurrentOperations = 150000
> ```

A second extremely common limit to increase is the maximum number of attributes (fields, indexes, and so on) in a cluster which defaults to `1000`. This is also quite low, and in the same way it can normally be increased:

```
MaxNoOfAttributes = 10000
```

The maximum number of ordered indexes is low and if you reach it, it will return a slightly cryptic error, **Can't create table xxx (errno: 136)**. Therefore, it is often worth increasing it at the start, if you plan on having a total of more than 128 ordered indexes in your cluster:

```
MaxNoOfOrderedIndexes=512
```

Finally, it is almost certain that you will need to define some space for data and indexes on your storage nodes. Note that you should not allocate more storage space than you have to spare on the physical machines running the storage nodes, as a cluster swapping is likely to happen and the cluster will crash!

```
DataMemory=2G
IndexMemory=500M
```

With these parameters set, you are ready to start a cluster and import a certain amount of data in it.

Installing a management node

In this recipe, we will be using the RedHat Package Manager (RPM) files provided by MySQL to install a management node on a CentOS 5.3 Linux server. We will be using a `x86_64` or 64-bit operating system. However, there is no practical difference between 64-bit and the 32-bit binaries for installation.

At the end of this recipe, you will have a management node installed and ready to start. In the next recipe, we will start the management node, as a running management node is required to check that your storage and SQL nodes start correctly in later recipes.

How to do it...

All files for MySQL Cluster for RedHat and CentOS 5 can be found in the *Red Hat Enterprise Linux 5 RPM* section from the download page at `http://dev.mysql.com`. We will first install the management node (the process with which every other cluster node talks to on startup). To get this, download the *Cluster storage engine management* package `MySQL-Cluster-gpl-management-7.a.b-c.rhel5.x86_64.rpm`.

> You must use the URL (that is, the address of the mirror site here that you have copied from the MySQL downloads page, which will replace `a.mirror` in the following commands). All the other instances where the command `wget` is used with the mirror site addresses as `a.mirror` should be replaced with the URL.

In the following example, a temporary directory is created and the correct file is downloaded:

```
[root@node5 ~]# cd ~/
[root@node5 ~]# mkdir mysql
[root@node5 ~]# cd mysql
[root@node5 mysql]# wget http://dev.mysql.com/get/Downloads/MySQL-
Cluster-7.0/MySQL-Cluster-gpl-management-7.0.6-0.rhel5.x86_64.rpm/from/
http://a.mirror/
--16:26:09--  http://dev.mysql.com/get/Downloads/MySQL-Cluster-7.0/MySQL-
Cluster-gpl-management-7.0.6-0.rhel5.x86_64.rpm/from/http://a.mirror/
<snip>
16:26:10 (9.78 MB/s) - `MySQL-Cluster-gpl-management-7.0.6-0.rhel5.x86_
64.rpm' saved [1316142/1316142]
```

At the same time of installing the management node, it is also a good idea to install the management client, which we will use to talk to the management node on the same server. This client is contained within the *Cluster storage engine basic tools* package—`MySQL-Cluster-gpl-tools-7.a.b-c.rhel5.x86_64.rpm`, and in the following example this file is downloaded:

```
[root@node5 ~]# wget http://dev.mysql.com/get/Downloads/MySQL-Cluster-
7.0/MySQL-Cluster-gpl-tools-7.0.6-0.rhel5.x86_64.rpm/from/http://
a.mirror/
--18:45:57--  http://dev.mysql.com/get/Downloads/MySQL-Cluster-7.0/MySQL-
Cluster-gpl-tools-7.0.6-0.rhel5.x86_64.rpm/from/http://a.mirror/
<snip>
18:46:00 (10.2 MB/s) - `MySQL-Cluster-gpl-tools-7.0.6-0.rhel5.x86_64.rpm'
saved [9524521/9524521]
```

Now, install the two files that we have downloaded with the `rpm -ivh` command (the flag's meaning `-i` for install, `-v` for verbose output, and `-h` which results in a hash progress bar):

```
[root@node5 mysql]# rpm -ivh MySQL-Cluster-gpl-management-7.0.6-0.rhel5.
x86_64.rpm MySQL-Cluster-gpl-tools-7.0.6-0.rhel5.x86_64.rpm
Preparing...                 ###########################################
[100%]
   1:MySQL-Cluster-gpl-manage###########################################
[100%]
   1:MySQL-Cluster-gpl-manage###########################################
[100%]
```

As these two RPM packages are installed, the following binaries are now available on the system:

Type	Binary	Description
Management	ndb_mgmd	The cluster management server
Tools	ndb_mgm	The cluster management client—note that it is not ndb_mgmd, which is the server process
Tools	ndb_size.pl	Used for estimating the memory usage of existing databases or tables
Tools	ndb_desc	A tool to provide detailed information about a MySQL Cluster table

To actually start the cluster, a global configuration file must be created and used to start the management server. As discussed in the previous recipe this file can be called anything and stored anywhere, but by convention it is called `config.ini` and stored in `/usr/local/mysql-cluster`. For this example, we will use an extremely simple cluster consisting of one management node (`10.0.0.5`), two storage nodes (`10.0.0.1` and `10.0.0.2`) and two SQL nodes (`10.0.0.3` and `10.0.0.4`), but follow the previous recipe (including the *There's more...* section if you wish to import much data) to create a configuration file tailored to your setup with the correct number of nodes and IP addresses.

Once the contents of the file are prepared, copy it to `/usr/local/mysql-cluster/config.ini`. The complete `config.ini` file used in this example is as follows:

```
[ndb_mgmd]
Id=1
HostName=10.0.0.5
DataDir=/var/lib/mysql-cluster

[ndbd default]
DataDir=/var/lib/mysql-cluster
NoOfReplicas=2

[ndbd]
```

```
id=3
HostName=10.0.0.1

[ndbd]
id=4
HostName=10.0.0.2

[mysqld]
id=11
HostName=10.2.0.3

[mysqld]
id=12
HostName=10.2.0.4

[mysqld]
id=13

[mysqld]
id=14
```

At this stage, we have installed the management client and server (management node) and created the global configuration file.

Starting a management node

In this recipe, we will start the management node installed in the previous recipe, and then use the management client to confirm that it has properly started.

How to do it...

The first step is to create the data directory for the management node that you defined in config.ini file as follows:

[root@node5 mysql-cluster]# mkdir -p /usr/local/mysql-cluster

Now, change the directory to it and run the management node process (ndb_mgmd), telling it which configuration file to use:

[root@node5 mysql-cluster]# cd /usr/local/mysql-cluster

[root@node5 mysql-cluster]# ndb_mgmd --config-file=config.ini

2009-06-28 22:14:01 [MgmSrvr] INFO -- NDB Cluster Management Server. mysql-5.1.34 ndb-7.0.6

2009-06-28 22:14:01 [MgmSrvr] INFO -- Loaded config from '//mysql-cluster/ndb_1_config.bin.1'

Finally, check the exit code of the previous command (with the command `echo $?`). An exit code of 0 indicates success:

```
[root@node5 mysql-cluster]# echo $?

0
```

If you either got an error from running `ndb_mgmd` or the exit code was not 0, turn very briefly to the *There's more...* section of this recipe for a couple of extremely common problems at this stage.

> Everything must run as `root`, including the `ndbd` process. This is a common practice; remember that the servers running MySQL Cluster should be extremely well protected from external networks as anyone with any access to the system or network can interfere with the unencrypted and unauthenticated communication between storage nodes or connect to the management node. In this book, all MySQL Cluster tasks are completed as `root`.

Assuming that all is okay, we can now run the MySQL Cluster management client, `ndb_mgm`. This will be the default, connecting to a management client running on the local host on port `1186`. Once in the client, use the SHOW command to show the overall status of the cluster:

```
[root@node5 mysql-cluster]# ndb_mgm

-- NDB Cluster -- Management Client -
```

And have a look at the structure of our cluster:

```
ndb_mgm> SHOW
Connected to Management Server at: localhost:1186
Cluster Configuration
---------------------
[ndbd(NDB)]    2 node(s)
id=3    (not connected, accepting connect from 10.0.0.1)
id=4    (not connected, accepting connect from 10.0.0.2)

[ndb_mgmd(MGM)]   1 node(s)
id=1    @node5    (mysql-5.1.34 ndb-7.0.6)

[mysqld(API)]   4 node(s)
id=11   (not connected, accepting connect from 10.2.0.2)
id=12   (not connected, accepting connect from 10.2.0.3)
id=13   (not connected, accepting connect from any host)
id=14   (not connected, accepting connect from any host)
```

This shows us that we have two storage nodes (both disconnected) and four API or SQL nodes (both disconnected). Now check the status of node ID 1 (the management node) with the `<nodeid> STATUS` command as follows:

```
ndb_mgm> 1 status
Node 1: connected (Version 7.0.6)
```

Finally, exit out of the cluster management client using the `exit` command:

```
ndb_mgm> exit
```

Congratulations! Assuming that you have no errors here, you now have a cluster management node working and ready to receive connections from the SQL and data nodes which are shown as disconnected.

There's more...

In the event that your cluster fails to start, a couple of really common causes have been included here:

If the data directory does not exist, you will see this error:

```
[root@node5 mysql-cluster]# ndb_mgmd
2009-06-28 22:13:48 [MgmSrvr] INFO      -- NDB Cluster Management Server.
mysql-5.1.34 ndb-7.0.6
2009-06-28 22:13:48 [MgmSrvr] INFO      -- Loaded config from '//mysql-
cluster/ndb_1_config.bin.1'
2009-06-28 22:13:48 [MgmSrvr] ERROR     -- Directory '/var/lib/mysql-
cluster' specified with DataDir in configuration does not exist.
[root@node5 mysql-cluster]# echo $?
1
```

In this case, make sure that the directory exists:

```
[root@node5 mysql-cluster]# mkdir -p /var/lib/mysql-cluster
```

If there is a typo in the configuration file or if the cluster cannot find the `config.ini` file you may see this error:

```
[root@node5 mysql-cluster]# ndb_mgmd   --config-file=config.ini
2009-06-28 22:15:50 [MgmSrvr] INFO      -- NDB Cluster Management Server.
mysql-5.1.34 ndb-7.0.6
2009-06-28 22:15:50 [MgmSrvr] INFO      -- Trying to get configuration
from other mgmd(s) using 'nodeid=0,localhost:1186'...
```

At this point `ndb_mgmd` will hang. In this case, kill the `ndb_mgmd` process (*Ctrl + C* or with the `kill` command) and double-check the syntax of your `config.ini` file.

Installing and starting storage nodes

Storage nodes within a MySQL Cluster store all the data either in memory or on disk; they store indexes in memory and conduct a significant portion of the SQL query processing. The single-threaded storage node process is called `ndbd` and either this or the multi-threaded version (`ndbdmt`) must be installed and executed on each storage node.

Getting ready

From the download page at `http://dev.mysql.com`, all files for MySQL Cluster for RedHat and CentOS 5 can be found in the *Red Hat Enterprise Linux 5 RPM* section. It is recommended that the following two RPMs should be installed on each storage node:

 ▸ Cluster storage engine basic tools (this contains the actual storage node process)—`MySQL-Cluster-gpl-tools-7.0.6-0.rhel5.x86_64.rpm`

 ▸ Cluster storage engine extra tools (this contains other binaries that are useful to have on your storage nodes)—`MySQL-Cluster-gpl-storage-7.0.6-0.rhel5.x86_64.rpm`

Once these packages are downloaded, we will show in an example how to install the nodes, start the storage nodes, and check the status of the cluster.

How to do it...

Firstly, download the two files required on each storage node (that is, complete this on all storage nodes simultaneously):

```
[root@node1 ~]# cd ~/

[root@node1 ~]# mkdir mysql-storagenode

[root@node1 ~]# cd mysql-storagenode/

[root@node1 mysql-storagenode]# wget http://dev.mysql.com/get/Downloads/
MySQL-Cluster-7.0/MySQL-Cluster-gpl-storage-7.0.6-0.rhel5.x86_64.rpm/
from/http://a.mirror/

--21:17:04--  http://dev.mysql.com/get/Downloads/MySQL-Cluster-7.0/MySQL-
Cluster-gpl-storage-7.0.6-0.rhel5.x86_64.rpm/from/http://a.mirror/

Resolving dev.mysql.com... 213.136.52.29

<snip>

21:18:06 (9.25 MB/s) - `MySQL-Cluster-gpl-storage-7.0.6-0.rhel5.x86_
64.rpm' saved [4004834/4004834]
```

```
[root@node1 mysql-storagenode]# wget http://dev.mysql.com/get/Downloads/
MySQL-Cluster-7.0/MySQL-Cluster-gpl-tools-7.0.6-0.rhel5.x86_64.rpm/from/
http://a.mirror/

--21:19:12--  http://dev.mysql.com/get/Downloads/MySQL-Cluster-7.0/MySQL-
Cluster-gpl-tools-7.0.6-0.rhel5.x86_64.rpm/from/http://a.mirror/

<snip>

21:20:14 (9.67 MB/s) - `MySQL-Cluster-gpl-tools-7.0.6-0.rhel5.x86_64.rpm'
saved [9524521/9524521]
```

Once both the files are downloaded, install these two packages using the same command as it was used in the previous recipe:

```
[root@node1 mysql-storagenode]# rpm -ivh MySQL-Cluster-gpl-tools-7.0.6-
0.rhel5.x86_64.rpm MySQL-Cluster-gpl-storage-7.0.6-0.rhel5.x86_64.rpm

Preparing...                ###########################################
[100%]
   1:MySQL-Cluster-gpl-stora########################################### [
50%]
   2:MySQL-Cluster-gpl-tools###########################################
[100%]
```

Now, using your favorite text editor, insert the following into /etc/my.cnf file, replacing 10.0.0.5:1186 with the hostname or IP address of the already installed management node:

```
[mysql_cluster]
ndb-connectstring=10.0.0.5:1186
```

 Ensure that you have completed the above steps on all storage nodes before continuing. This is because (unless you force it) a MySQL Cluster will not start without all storage nodes, and it is best practice to start all storage nodes at the same time, if possible.

Now, as we have installed the storage node client and configured /etc/my.cnf file to allow a starting storage node process to find its management node, we can start our cluster.

To join storage nodes to our cluster, following requirements must be met:

▶ All storage nodes must be ready to join the cluster (this can be overridden, if really required)

▶ A config.ini file must be prepared with the details of the storage nodes in a cluster, and then a management node must be started based on this file

- The storage nodes must be able to communicate with (that is, no firewall) the management node, otherwise, the storage nodes will fail to connect

- The storage nodes must be able to communicate freely with each other; problems here can cause clusters failing to start or, in some case, this can cause truly bizarre behavior

- There must be enough memory on the storage nodes to start the process (using the configuration in this example, that is, the defaults will result in a total RAM usage of approximately 115 MB per storage node)

When you start `ndbd`, you will notice that the two processes have started. One is an `angel` process, which monitors the other—the main `ndbd` process. The `angel` process is generally configured to automatically restart the main process if a problem is detected, which causes that process to exit. This can cause confusion, if you attempt to send a KILL signal to just the main process as the `angel` process can create a replacement process.

To start our storage nodes, on each node create the `data` directory that was configured for each storage node in the `config.ini` file on the management node, and run `ndbd` with the `--initial` flag:

```
[root@node1 ~]# mkdir -p /var/lib/mysql-cluster

[root@node1 ~]# ndbd --initial

2009-07-06 00:31:57 [ndbd] INFO      -- Configuration fetched from
'10.0.0.5:1186', generation: 1

[root@node1 ~]#
```

If you fail to create the `data` directory (`/var/lib/mysql-cluster` in our example in the previous recipe), you may well get a `Cannot become daemon: /var/lib/mysql-cluster/ndb_3.pid: open for write failed: No such file or directory` error. If you get this, run the `mkdir` command again on the relevant storage node

Once you have started `ndbd` on each node, you can run the management client, `ndb_mgm`, from any machine as long as it can talk to port `1186` on the management node with which it will work.

`ndb_mgm`, like all MySQL Cluster binaries, reads the `[mysqld_cluster]` section in `/etc/my.cnf` to find the management node's IP address to connect to. If you are running `ndb_mgm` on a node that does not have this set in `/etc/my.cnf`, you should pass a cluster connect string to `ndb_mgm` (see the final recipe in this chapter—Cluster Concepts).

The `--initial` flag to `ndbd` tells `ndbd` to initialize the `DataDir` on the local disk, overwriting any existing data (or in this case, creating it for the first time).

You should only use --initial the first time you start a cluster or if you are deliberately discarding the local copy of data. If you do it at other times, you risk losing all the data held in the cluster, if there is no online node in the same nodegroup that stays online, long enough, to update the starting node.

 Be aware that starting ndbd with --initial does not always delete all of the logfiles in the DataDir; you should delete these manually if you need to remove them.

The cluster will go through various stages as it starts. If you run the ALL STATUS command in the management client while the nodes are starting, you will see that they start off as unconnected, then go through the startup phases, and finally are marked as *started*.

Because often a node starting must apply a large number of database transactions either from other nodes or from its local disk, this process can take some time in clusters with data. Although, in the case of an initial start, this process should be relatively fast. The following output shows the management client when all the storage nodes have started:

```
[root@node5 ~]# ndb_mgm
-- NDB Cluster -- Management Client --


ndb_mgm> SHOW
Cluster Configuration
---------------------
[ndbd(NDB)]  2 node(s)
id=3 @10.0.0.1  (mysql-5.1.34 ndb-7.0.6, Nodegroup: 0, Master)
id=4 @10.0.0.2  (mysql-5.1.34 ndb-7.0.6, Nodegroup: 0)


[ndb_mgmd(MGM)]  1 node(s)
id=1 @10.0.0.5  (mysql-5.1.34 ndb-7.0.6)


[mysqld(API)]  4 node(s)
id=11 (not connected, accepting connect from 10.2.0.2)
id=12 (not connected, accepting connect from 10.2.0.3)
id=13 (not connected, accepting connect from any host)
id=14 (not connected, accepting connect from any host)


ndb_mgm> ALL STATUS
Node 3: started (mysql-5.1.34 ndb-7.0.6)
Node 4: started (mysql-5.1.34 ndb-7.0.6)
```

At this point, this cluster has one management node and two storage nodes that are connected. You are now able to start the SQL nodes.

In the case you have any problems, look at the following points:

  ▸ Cluster error log—in the `DataDir` on the management node, with a filename similar to `DataDir/ndb_1_cluster.log` (the number is the *sequence number)* MySQL Cluster has an inbuilt rotation system—when a file gets to 1 MB, a new one with a higher sequence number is created

  ▸ Storage node error log—in the `DataDir` on the relevant storage node, with a filename similar to `DataDir/ndb_4_out.log` (the number is the cluster node ID)

These two logfiles should give you a pretty good idea of what is causing a problem.

If one node remains in phase 1, when others are in phase 2, this likely indicates a network problem—normally, a firewall between storage nodes causes this issue. In such cases, double check that there are no software or hardware firewalls between the nodes.

There's more...

For convenience (particularly, when writing scripts to manage large clusters), you may want to start the `ndbd` process on all storage nodes to the point that they get configuration data from the management node and are able to be controlled by it but you may not want to completely start them. This is achieved with the `--nostart` or `-n` flag:

On the storage nodes (and assuming that `ndbd` is not already running):

```
[root@node1 ~]# ndbd -n

2009-07-09 20:59:49 [ndbd] INFO      -- Configuration fetched from
'10.0.0.5:1186', generation: 1
```

 If required (for example, the first time you start a node), you could add the `-initial` flag as you would for a normal start of the storage node process.

Then, on the management node you should see that the nodes are *not started* (this is different from *not connected*) as shown here:

```
ndb_mgm> ALL STATUS

Node 3: not started (mysql-5.1.34 ndb-7.0.6)

Node 4: not started (mysql-5.1.34 ndb-7.0.6)

Node 5: not started (mysql-5.1.34 ndb-7.0.6)

Node 6: not started (mysql-5.1.34 ndb-7.0.6)
```

It is then possible to start all the nodes at the same time from the management client with the command `<nodeid> START` as follows:

```
NDB_MGM> 3 START
Database node 3 is being started.
ndb_mgm> NODE 3: START INITIATED (VERSION 7.0.6)
NODE 3: DATA USAGE DECREASED TO 0%(0 32K PAGES OF TOTAL 2560)
```

You can start all storage nodes in a *not started* state with the command `ALL START`:

```
NDB_MGM> ALL START
NDB Cluster is being started.
NDB Cluster is being started.
NDB Cluster is being started.
NDB Cluster is being started.
```

During the start up of storage nodes, you may find the following list of phases useful, if nodes fail or hang during a certain start up phase:

 MySQL Clusters with a large amount of data in them will be slow to start; it is often useful to look at CPU usage and network traffic to reassure you and check that the cluster is actually still doing something.

- Setup and initialization (Phase -1): During this phase, each storage node is initialized (obtaining a node ID from the management node, fetching configuration data (effectively the contents of `config.ini` file), allocating ports for inter-cluster communication, and allocating memory).
- Phase 0: If the storage node is started with `--initial`, the cluster kernel is initialized and in all cases certain parts of it are prepared for use.
- Phase 1: The remainder of the cluster kernel is started and nodes start communicating with each other (using heartbeats).
- Phase 2: Nodes check the status of each other and elect a *Master* node.
- Phase 3: Additional parts of the cluster kernel used for communication are initialized.
- Phase 4: For an initial start or initial node restart, the redo logfiles are created. The number of these files is equal to the `NoOfFragmentLogFiles` variable in the `config.ini` file. In the case of a restart, nodes read schemas and apply local checkpoints, until the last restorable global checkpoint has been reached.
- Phase 5: Execute a local checkpoint, then a global checkpoint, and memory usage check.
- Phase 6: Establish node groups.
- Phase 7: The arbitrator node is selected and begins to function. At this point, nodes are shown as *started* in the management client, and SQL nodes may join the cluster.
- Phase 8: In the case of a restart, indexes are rebuilt.
- Phase 9: Internal node's startup variables are reset.

Installing and starting SQL nodes

SQL nodes are the most common form of API nodes, and are used to provide a standard MySQL interface to the cluster. To do this, they use a standard version of the MySQL server compiled to include support for the MySQL Cluster storage engine—NDBCLUSTER.

In earlier versions, this was included in most binaries, but to use more current and future versions of MySQL, you must specifically select the MySQL Cluster server downloads. It is highly recommended to install a mysql client on each SQL node for testing.

Terminology sometimes causes confusion. A *MySQL server* is a mysqld process. A *MySQL client* is the mysql command that communicates with a MySQL server. It is recommended to install both on each SQL node, but of course, it is only required to have the server (which can be connected to by the clients on the other machines).

How to do it...

Download and install the following two files. For the sake of brevity, the process of using wget to download a file and rpm to install a package is not shown in this recipe, but it is identical to the procedure in the previous two recipes:

* Server (from the cluster section)—MySQL-Cluster-gpl-server-7.a.b-c.rhel5.x86_64.rpm
* Client (this is identical to the standard MySQL client and has the same filename)—MySQL-client-community-5.a.b-c.rhel5.x86_64.rpm

After installing these RPMs, a very simple /etc/my.cnf file will exist. We need to add two parameters to the [mysqld] section of this file to tell the mysqld server to enable support for MySQL Cluster and where to find its management node:

```
[mysqld]
# Enable MySQL Cluster
ndbcluster
# Tell this node where to find its management node
ndb-connectstring=10.0.0.5
```

The requirement to add lines to the [mysqld] section in addition to any [mysql_cluster] that may already be there is only read by the ndb_* daemons (but has a similar purpose). If you have a SQL node on the same server as a storage node you would have both.

Some modern versions of MySQL will also use a [mysql_cluster] section, but it is feasible to stick to defining the parameters in a [mysqld] section.

With these lines added, start the SQL node as follows:

```
[root@node1 ~]# service mysql start
Starting MySQL.                                    [  OK  ]
```

At this point, even if there is an error connecting to the cluster, it is unlikely that you will get anything other than okay here. However, if you see the following error in the standard `mysql` log (often `/var/lib/mysqld.log` or `/var/lib/mysql/hostname.err`), you should go and check that you have installed the correct server (the cluster server and not the standard server):

```
090708 23:48:14 [ERROR] /usr/sbin/mysqld: unknown option '--
ndbcluster'
090708 23:48:14 [ERROR] Aborting
```

Even if your SQL node (MySQL server) starts without an error, it is important to verify that it has successfully joined the cluster. There are three tests to carry out:

On the management node, run the SHOW command and ensure that this node is now connected:

```
ndb_mgm> SHOW
Cluster Configuration
---------------------
[ndbd(NDB)]   4 node(s)
id=3   @10.0.0.1   (mysql-5.1.34 ndb-7.0.6, Nodegroup: 0, Master)
id=4   @10.0.0.2   (mysql-5.1.34 ndb-7.0.6, Nodegroup: 0)
id=5   @10.0.0.3   (mysql-5.1.34 ndb-7.0.6, Nodegroup: 1)
id=6   @10.0.0.4   (mysql-5.1.34 ndb-7.0.6, Nodegroup: 1)

[ndb_mgmd(MGM)]   1 node(s)
id=1   @10.0.0.5   (mysql-5.1.34 ndb-7.0.6)

[mysqld(API)] 4 node(s)
id=11   @10.0.0.1   (mysql-5.1.34 ndb-7.0.6)
id=12   @10.0.0.2   (mysql-5.1.34 ndb-7.0.6)
id=13   @10.0.0.3   (mysql-5.1.34 ndb-7.0.6)
id=14   @10.0.0.4   (mysql-5.1.34 ndb-7.0.6)
```

Now that you have confirmed that the SQL node is connected to the management node, in the `mysql` client on the SQL node confirm the status of the `NDB` engine:

```
[root@node1 ~]# mysql
Welcome to the MySQL monitor.  Commands end with ; or \g.
Your MySQL connection id is 4
Server version: 5.1.34-ndb-7.0.6-cluster-gpl MySQL Cluster Server (GPL)


Type 'help;' or '\h' for help. Type '\c' to clear the current input
statement.


mysql> SHOW ENGINE NDB STATUS;
+------------+----------------------+------------------------------------
---------------------------------------------------------------------
-------------------------------------------------------+
| Type       | Name                 | Status
                                                       |
+------------+----------------------+------------------------------------
---------------------------------------------------------------------
-------------------------------------------------------+
| ndbcluster | connection           | cluster_node_id=11, connected_
host=10.0.0.5, connected_port=1186, number_of_data_nodes=4, number_of_
ready_data_nodes=4, connect_count=0                    |
```

Also check the output of the SHOW ENGINES command:

```
mysql> SHOW ENGINES;
+------------+----------+------------------------------------------------
----------------+---------------+------+-------------+
| Engine     | Support  | Comment
| Transactions | XA      | Savepoints |
+------------+----------+------------------------------------------------
----------------+---------------+------+-------------+
| ndbcluster | YES      | Clustered, fault-tolerant tables
| YES          | NO      | NO         |
```

If the node is not connected, the status from the first command, SHOW ENGINE NDB STATUS, will typically be something like:

```
cluster_node_id=0, connected_host=(null), connected_port=0, number_of_
data_nodes=0, number_of_ready_data_nodes=0, connect_count=0
```

Otherwise, the command will fail with `ERROR 1286 (42000): Unknown table engine 'NDB'`. If the second command does not have a `YES` in the supported column for `ndbcluster` there is a problem.

If any of these commands fail, check the following:

- ▶ `/etc/my.cnf [mysqld]` section
- ▶ That you have installed the cluster-specific `mysqld` binary

If the commands work, follow the steps in the next recipe to create a test MySQL Cluster table and ensure that your cluster is working correctly.

Creating a MySQL Cluster table

In this recipe, we will create a simple table in the cluster, and we will both insert and select data on this new table on two nodes in the example cluster created earlier in this chapter.

How to do it...

A **MySQL Cluster table** is a table of type `NDBCLUSTER` accessible from your storage nodes and can be created in the normal way—with the only difference being an explicit `TYPE` in the `CREATE TABLE` statement.

In older versions of MySQL Cluster, it was necessary to create databases on all nodes. This is no longer the case.

In this example, we will create a very simple table, `cluster_test` on `node1` and insert some data into it:

```
[root@node1 ~]# mysql
Welcome to the MySQL monitor.  Commands end with ; or \g.


Your MySQL connection id is 2
Server version: 5.1.34-ndb-7.0.6-cluster-gpl MySQL Cluster Server (GPL)


Type 'help;' or '\h' for help. Type '\c' to clear the current input
statement.


mysql> CREATE DATABASE cluster_test;
Query OK, 1 row affected (0.43 sec)
```

```
mysql> USE cluster_test;
Database changed


mysql> CREATE TABLE ctest (i INT) ENGINE=NDBCLUSTER;
Query OK, 0 rows affected (0.84 sec)


mysql> INSERT INTO ctest () VALUES (1);
Query OK, 1 row affected (0.04 sec)


mysql> SELECT * FROM ctest;


+------+
| i    |
+------+
|    1 |
+------+


1 row in set (0.00 sec)
```

The next step is to select this row from the other SQL node in the cluster (node2), and then insert another row from the second node:

```
[root@node2 ~]# mysql
Welcome to the MySQL monitor.  Commands end with ; or \g.


Your MySQL connection id is 2
Server version: 5.1.34-ndb-7.0.6-cluster-gpl MySQL Cluster Server (GPL)


Type 'help;' or '\h' for help. Type '\c' to clear the current input
statement.


mysql> SHOW DATABASES;
+--------------------+
| Database           |
+--------------------+
| information_schema |
| cluster_test       |
| mysql              |
```

```
| test                 |
+---------------------+
```

4 rows in set (0.03 sec)

mysql> use cluster_test;

Reading table information for completion of table and column names

You can turn off this feature to get a quicker startup with -A

Database changed

mysql> show tables;

```
+-----------------------+
| Tables_in_cluster_test |
+-----------------------+
| ctest                 |
+-----------------------+
```

1 row in set (0.04 sec)

mysql> SELECT * from ctest;
```
+------+
| i    |
+------+
|    1 |
+------+
```

1 row in set (0.00 sec)

mysql> INSERT INTO ctest () VALUES (2);
Query OK, 1 row affected (0.01 sec)

Finally, we return to the first node and check that the data inserted on `node2` is visible.

```
mysql> SELECT * FROM ctest;


+------+
| i    |
+------+
|    2 |
|    1 |
+------+


2 rows in set (0.00 sec)


mysql>
```

Congratulations! The cluster works, and you have created a table in it. You can repeat these tests while powering off the storage nodes and watch the cluster continue to work. With a single-cluster storage node powered off, everything will continue to work (except for the SQL node that was previously running on the powered-off mode, of course!).

Restarting a MySQL Cluster without downtime

One of the key aspects of a highly-available system is that routine maintenance can be carried out without any service interruption to users. MySQL Cluster achieves this through its *shared nothing* architecture, and in this recipe we will show how to restart the three types of nodes online (without taking the cluster down as a whole).

Getting started

For this recipe, we will be using the following cluster setup:

- ▶ Four storage nodes
- ▶ One management node
- ▶ Two SQL nodes

The output of the SHOW command on the management client for this cluster is as follows:

```
ndb_mgm> SHOW
Cluster Configuration
---------------------
[ndbd(NDB)]  4 node(s)
id=3 @10.0.0.1   (mysql-5.1.34 ndb-7.0.6, Nodegroup: 0)
id=4 @10.0.0.2   (mysql-5.1.34 ndb-7.0.6, Nodegroup: 0)
id=5 @10.0.0.3   (mysql-5.1.34 ndb-7.0.6, Nodegroup: 1, Master)
id=6 @10.0.0.4   (mysql-5.1.34 ndb-7.0.6, Nodegroup: 1)

[ndb_mgmd(MGM)]  1 node(s)
id=1 @10.0.0.5   (mysql-5.1.34 ndb-7.0.6)

[mysqld(API)]  4 node(s)
id=11 @10.0.0.1   (mysql-5.1.34 ndb-7.0.6)
id=12 @10.0.0.2   (mysql-5.1.34 ndb-7.0.6)
id=13 (not connected, accepting connect from any host)
id=14 (not connected, accepting connect from any host)
```

How to do it...

In this section, we will show how to restart each node using our example cluster.

> ▶ **Restarting a storage node**
>
> There are two ways to restart a storage node. For both the methods, the first step is to check the output of SHOW command in the management client to ensure that there is at least one other online (not starting or shutdown) node in the same nodegroup.

 In our example cluster, we have storage node ID 3 and 4 in nodegroup 0 and storage node ID 5 and 6 in nodegroup 1.

The two options for restarting a node are as follows: Firstly, from the management client a node can be restarted with the `<nodeid> RESTART` command:

```
ndb_mgm> 3 status
Node 3: started (mysql-5.1.34 ndb-7.0.6)

ndb_mgm> 3 RESTART
Node 3: Node shutdown initiated

Node 3: Node shutdown completed, restarting, no start.
Node 3 is being restarted

ndb_mgm> 3 status
Node 3: starting (Last completed phase 4) (mysql-5.1.34 ndb-7.0.6)
Node 3: Started (version 7.0.6)

ndb_mgm> 3 status
Node 3: started (mysql-5.1.34 ndb-7.0.6)
```

Secondly, on the storage node itself the `ndbd` process can simply be killed and restarted:

Remember that `ndbd` has two processes—an `angel` process in addition to the main process. You must kill both these processes at the same time.

```
[root@node4 ~]# ps aux | grep ndbd
root       4082  0.0  0.4  33480   2316 ?        Ss    Jul08   0:00
ndbd --initial
root       4134  0.1 17.4 426448  91416 ?        Sl    Jul08   0:02
ndbd --initial
root       4460  0.0  0.1  61152    720 pts/0    R+    00:11   0:00
grep ndbd
[root@node4 ~]# kill 4082 4134
[root@node4 ~]# ps aux | grep ndbd | grep -v grep | wc -l
0
```

Once we have killed the `ndbd` process, and ensured that no processes are running with the name `ndbd`, we can restart the `ndbd` process:

```
[root@node4 ~]# ndbd
2009-07-09 00:12:03 [ndbd] INFO     -- Configuration fetched from
'10.0.0.5:1186', generation: 1
```

If you were to leave a management client connected during this process, you can see that the management node picks up on the dead node and then allow it to rejoin the cluster:

```
ndb_mgm> Node 6: Node shutdown completed. Initiated by signal 15.

ndb_mgm> Node 6: Started (version 7.0.6)

ndb_mgm> 6 status

Node 6: started (mysql-5.1.34 ndb-7.0.6)
```

Remember that you can restart more than one node at a time, but you must always have one node fully started in each nodegroup or your cluster will shut down.

► **Restarting a management node**

Restarting a management node is best done by simply killing the `ndb_mgmd` process and restarting it.

When there is no management node in the cluster, there is no central logging for the cluster, and the storage and the API nodes cannot start or restart (so if they fail they will stay dead). In addition, processes that are initiated from the management client (such as hot backups) cannot be run.

Firstly, we will pass the process ID of the `ndb_mgmd` process to the `kill` command:

```
[root@node5 mysql-cluster]# kill $(pidof ndb_mgmd)
```

This will kill the management node, so now start it again:

```
[root@node5 mysql-cluster]# ndb_mgmd --config-file=config.ini

2009-07-09 00:30:00 [MgmSrvr] INFO      -- NDB Cluster Management
Server. mysql-5.1.34 ndb-7.0.6

2009-07-09 00:30:00 [MgmSrvr] INFO      -- Loaded config from '//
mysql-cluster/ndb_1_config.bin.1'
```

Finally, verify that the management node is working:

```
[root@node5 mysql-cluster]# ndb_mgm

-- NDB Cluster -- Management Client --

ndb_mgm> 1 status

Node 1: connected (Version 7.0.6)
```

▸ **Restarting a SQL node**

Restarting a SQL node is trivial—just restart the `mysqld` process as normal, and carry out the checks mentioned earlier to ensure that the node restarts correctly.

```
[root@node1 ~]# service mysql restart
Shutting down MySQL..                                    [  OK  ]
Starting MySQL..                                         [  OK  ]
```

Recovering from a cluster shutdown

This recipe will cover the procedure to follow in case of a cluster shutdown. We discuss the *split brain* problem and also explain how to start a cluster without all storage nodes.

How to do it...

This section covers the procedure to follow—both for a partial failure (some nodes fail, but the cluster remains operational) and a complete failure (all nodes fail!).

▸ **Partial cluster failure**

In the event of a single node failing, you will notice the following:

- ❑ If the node that fails is a management node—no immediate problem occurs, but other nodes cannot restart and activities requiring a management node (online backups, centralized logging) will not take place

- ❑ If the node that fails is a storage node—assuming one node remains in each nodegroup, there will be no immediate action (but there is the possibility of a small number of transactions being rolled back)

- ❑ If the node that fails is a SQL node—any clients connected to that SQL node clearly will either have to use another SQL node or will fail, but no effect on the cluster

To recover from a partial shutdown, carry out the restart procedure in the previous recipe—*Restarting a MySQL Cluster without downtime*; however, it may not be necessary to kill the existing process.

 If you do find a zombied (crashed) process remaining, you should first kill that process and then restart the node.

▶ **Complete cluster failure**

The following errors can cause a total cluster shutdown:

- ❑ Catastrophic software bug that causes multiple cluster nodes to fail

- ❑ Every node in the cluster loosing power (an entire facility failing for example), *split brain* condition (that will be discussed shortly)

- ❑ Malicious or mistaken users gaining access to the management node or any storage node

A *split brain* problem refers to the problem of cutting a cluster suffering some communication problems between nodes. If we have four nodes and split them into two groups of two nodes each (perhaps, through the failure in a switch), there is absolutely no way for either of the pairs to tell if the other node is working or not. In this case, the only safe thing to do is to shut down both the nodes, even though both pairs could have all the data required to carry on working.

Imagine what would happen if your four-data nodes, two-storage nodes cluster continued working as two separate clusters—and then you had to attempt to reconcile two completely different databases!

MySQL Cluster gets around this with the concept of an **arbitrator**—put simply, the cluster nodes elect a single node to act as the arbitrator while all nodes can still communicate.

In the event of nodes loosing each other's contact, they (as a new group) ask the following questions:

- ❑ Do we (nodes I can now talk to) have enough nodes to remain viable (one storage node per nodegroup)?

- ❑ Can I see the previously agreed arbitrator?

Unless the answer is yes for each node, the cluster will shut down with an error similar to the following appearing in the log:

```
Forced node shutdown completed. Caused by error 2305: 'Node
lost connection to other nodes and cannot form a unpartitioned
cluster, please investigate if there are error(s) on other
node(s)(Arbitration error). Temporary error, restart node'.
```

The arbitrator is typically the management node, but can be a SQL node and you can specify `ArbitrationRank=1` in `config.ini` file to make a node of high priority to become the cluster arbitrator.

Recovery of a full cluster shutdown is conceptually simple—we need to start all storage nodes. It is likely that storage nodes would have killed themselves or had been killed by whatever caused the outage. So the procedure is identical to the rolling cluster restart without killing the existing processes. In other words, start the management node (`ndb_mgmd`), start all storage nodes (`ndbd`), and start all SQL nodes (start or restart `mysqld`).

How it works...

During a full-cluster start up, the storage nodes will start and will have to use their local copies of data that they stored to disk (It is likely that there will be some data loss after a total cluster shutdown). By default, a running MySQL Cluster will commit a **Local Checkpoint** (**LCP**)—a copy of all the local data held on disk—every time 4 MB of changes are made to the cluster (since the previous LCP).

A MySQL Cluster will also take a global checkpoint (all transactions that have occurred since the last LCP) to disk every two seconds. A storage node when starting from a full shutdown will apply all local transactions up to the last LCP, and then apply them up to two seconds of transactions from the latest global checkpoint to get data that is as up-to-date as possible. Because global checkpoints are made consistently across the cluster, this allows for consistent recovery of all nodes.

There's more...

In the case of a total cluster shutdown, it may happen that a storage node is damaged and cannot be repaired quickly. It is possible to start your cluster with only one storage node per nodegroup. To do this, pass the `--nowait-nodes=<NODES>` where `<NODES>` is a comma-separated list of nodes not to wait for. For example, in this example cluster:

```
[ndbd(NDB)]  4 node(s)
id=3 @10.0.0.1   (mysql-5.1.34 ndb-7.0.6, Nodegroup: 0)
id=4 @10.0.0.2   (mysql-5.1.34 ndb-7.0.6, Nodegroup: 0, Master)
id=5 @10.0.0.3   (mysql-5.1.34 ndb-7.0.6, Nodegroup: 1)
id=6 @10.0.0.4   (mysql-5.1.34 ndb-7.0.6, Nodegroup: 1)
```

We could potentially start with nodes [(3 or 4) and (5 or 6)]. In this example, we will start without `node3`:

This example assumes that your cluster is already shut down.

Run the following command on the nodes that you want to start:

```
[root@node4 ~]# ndbd --nowait-nodes=3
2009-07-09 23:32:02 [ndbd] INFO        -- Configuration fetched from
'10.0.0.5:1186', generation: 1
```

The cluster should start without node3:

```
ndb_mgm> ALL STATUS
Node 3: not connected
Node 4: started (mysql-5.1.34 ndb-7.0.6)
Node 5: started (mysql-5.1.34 ndb-7.0.6)
Node 6: started (mysql-5.1.34 ndb-7.0.6)
```

Clearly, at this point, the cluster no longer has a single point of failure and as quickly as possible node3 should be repaired and started.

2
MySQL Cluster Backup and Recovery

In this chapter, we will cover:

- ▶ Importing SQL files to a MySQL server and converting them to MySQL Cluster
- ▶ Taking an online backup of a MySQL Cluster
- ▶ Restoring the cluster from a MySQL Cluster online backup
- ▶ Restricting write access to a MySQL Cluster with single-user mode
- ▶ Taking an offline backup with MySQL Cluster

Introduction

When designing a MySQL Cluster, it is unlikely that backups will be at the forefront of your mind. However, it is important that they are considered at an early stage. In this chapter, we will discuss the options available for backing up a MySQL Cluster and the considerations to be made at the cluster-design stage.

There are two main ways to back up a MySQL Cluster:

- ▶ First is the `mysqldump` command that is commonly used with all other storage engines
- ▶ Second is a hot backup facility provided within the MySQL Cluster kernel

Both of these options take a backup of both schema (table information) and data, and allow this backup to be restored elsewhere. A MySQL Cluster hot backup must be imported to another MySQL Cluster. A `mysqldump` backup may be imported to any MySQL server of a similar version.

Backups require early consideration during the design of a MySQL Cluster for two reasons:

1. Firstly, because MySQL Cluster offers some fantastic backup features far superior to those available with other storage engines (even with third-party tools).

2. Secondly, because you may need to make small changes to your intended cluster design to ensure that backups are easy and quick to both take and restore from in future.

Backups are particularly important with a MySQL Cluster because generally all the data is stored in memory (across multiple nodes). In most applications and database solutions memory is used only to store temporary data due to the lack of persistence in the event of a server crashing or rebooting. Due to the "shared-nothing high availability" architecture of a MySQL Cluster, a correctly designed and operated in-memory cluster can be extremely reliable as explained in *Chapter 1, High Availability with MySQL Cluster*.

However, the "No single point of failure" architecture, even when properly designed and implemented, does not however guarantee absolute availability. It is, of course, possible for all nodes in a cluster's nodegroup to fail at the same time (due to, for example, power outages or software bugs). In this case, storage nodes will use the local and global checkpoints that they automatically store to the local disk in the `BackupDir` to start up again with minimal loss of data. However, it is important not to rely solely on the working of this process and is essential, for several reasons, that every MySQL Cluster has regular and secure backups (that is, not stored on the storage nodes!). Some reasons include:

- Human error: Databases are managed and used by humans who make mistakes. This is one reason that a *replica* is not the same as a backup; a replica will immediately update to take account of any change, even if that change is an accidental `DROP TABLE` command.

- Application error: Applications are written by humans and may contain bugs. Furthermore, applications may be attacked by crackers. In either case, the result can be that the application sends queries that are damaging to a database and a backup must be used to restore the data in the cluster to how it was at a previous point in time.

- Disaster recovery: MySQL Cluster requires low-latency connections between nodes, and this almost certainly means that all your nodes will be in the same data center, possibly, in the same rack. Clearly, a natural disaster or even small fire could destroy all the nodes and all local backups, so a full backup that has been stored elsewhere is vital.

 It must be remembered that disk-based databases are also not immune to disaster and can suffer from all of these problems in addition to being more vulnerable to a single node crash. In some ways, storing data in memory will make administrators more aware of its vulnerability and encourage good backup practice!

When designing a cluster, it is important to consider the following options:

- If backups are initially to be stored on the same machines on which the storage node processes are running, local disk space should be enough to store backups regardless of how the backups are taken. This ideally will be on a block device (disk) separate from the `DataDir` to ensure that `DataDir` I/O performance is unchanged during the backup.

- To restore a MySQL online backup, the binary `ndb_restore` must connect to an API node , once per backup file (of which there will be one per storage node in the backed up cluster). It is recommended to add these `[API]` sections to `config.ini` file (one per `ndb_restore` command that you would likely want to run) at the initial deployment of a cluster to reduce backup recovery times.

- Backups should be automatically stored away from the cluster, preferably on read-only media in an offsite location.

Importing SQL files to a MySQL server and converting them to MySQL Cluster

It will often be required to import data from an SQL file and then convert this freshly installed data to have a storage engine of `NDB` (MySQL Cluster's storage engine). This may be required for the following reasons:

- Importing `mysqldump` backup files in the case of a recovery

- Importing data from a non-clustered system into a cluster, for example, a `mysqldump` from an old system into a new cluster

In this recipe, we will follow an example that uses the `world` sample dataset provided by MySQL for testing use. We will import it to MySQL, convert it from the default table engine (in our case, `MyISAM`) to MySQL Cluster (`NDBCLUSTER` storage engine), and then check that it appears on all the SQL nodes in the cluster.

This example uses a simple cluster with two SQL nodes—`node1` and `node2` (the configuration of the rest of the MySQL Cluster is irrelevant).

How to do it...

The `world` sample database is provided as a `SQL` file which includes statements to build three tables and populate them with data. The tables are defined with a table type of `MyISAM`.

In this recipe, we will use this `SQL` file to be imported, but it could just as well be the output from `mysqldump` running on another non-clustered server. The steps to do this are as follows:

1. The first step is to download the `SQL` file from the MySQL website to the temporary directory `/tmp/` as follows:

   ```
   [root@node1 ~]# cd /tmp/
   [root@node1 tmp]# wget http://downloads.mysql.com/docs/world.sql.
   gz
   --03:37:55--  http://downloads.mysql.com/docs/world.sql.gz
   Resolving downloads.mysql.com... 192.9.76.15
   Connecting to downloads.mysql.com|192.9.76.15|:80... connected.
   HTTP request sent, awaiting response... 200 OK
   Length: 91954 (90K) [application/x-gzip]
   Saving to: `world.sql.gz'

   100%[========================================>] 91,954        136K/s
   in 0.7s

   03:37:57 (136 KB/s) - `world.sql.gz' saved [91954/91954]
   ```

2. Uncompress the file using following command:

   ```
   [root@node1 tmp]# gunzip world.sql.gz
   ```

3. The next step is to create a database, `world`, to hold the new tables:

   ```
   [root@node1 tmp]# mysql
   Welcome to the MySQL monitor.  Commands end with ; or \g.
   Your MySQL connection id is 5
   Server version: 5.1.34-ndb-7.0.6-cluster-gpl MySQL Cluster Server
   (GPL)

   Type 'help;' or '\h' for help. Type '\c' to clear the current
   input statement.

   mysql> CREATE DATABASE world;
   Query OK, 1 row affected (0.20 sec)

   mysql> exit;
   Bye
   ```

Now there are two options—either import the SQL file as it is that will create MyISAM tables, and then alter the table to be of ENGINE=NDBCLUSTER type or run sed to search and replace the string ENGINE=MyISAM with ENGINE=NDBCLUSTER and import the modified set of SQL commands. The latter option is faster and simpler but requires the use of the sed utility.

The first option (which is slower and more manual), that is, importing with existing storage engine (MyISAM, in this example) and running ALTER TABLE command, is completed with the following steps:

1. Firstly, import the SQL file with the same storage engine as follows:

   ```
   [root@node1 tmp]# mysql world < world.sql
   ```

2. Secondly, enter the MySQL client, select the correct database, and check the tables that need to be converted:

   ```
   [root@node1 tmp]# mysql
   Welcome to the MySQL monitor.  Commands end with ; or \g.
   Your MySQL connection id is 8
   Server version: 5.1.34-ndb-7.0.6-cluster-gpl MySQL Cluster Server
   (GPL)

   Type 'help;' or '\h' for help. Type '\c' to clear the current
   input statement.

   mysql> USE world;
   Reading table information for completion of table and column names
   You can turn off this feature to get a quicker startup with -A

   Database changed
   mysql> SHOW TABLES;
   +-----------------+
   | Tables_in_world |
   +-----------------+
   | City            |
   | Country         |
   | CountryLanguage |
   +-----------------+
   3 rows in set (0.00 sec)
   ```

3. Now, we can see all the tables in the database that have been imported. For each table, check that the table is currently not using an engine of NDBCLUSTER:

```
mysql> SHOW TABLE STATUS FROM world LIKE 'City'\G;
*************************** 1. row ***************************
           Name: City
         Engine: MyISAM
        Version: 10
     Row_format: Dynamic
           Rows: 2076
 Avg_row_length: 92
    Data_length: 196608
Max_data_length: 0
   Index_length: 0
      Data_free: 0
 Auto_increment: 4080
    Create_time: NULL
    Update_time: NULL
     Check_time: NULL
      Collation: latin1_swedish_ci
       Checksum: NULL
 Create_options:
        Comment:
1 row in set (0.00 sec)
```

4. The final step is to convert tables that are not already in NDBCLUSTER to this storage engine. To do this, run an ALTER TABLE query (one per table) which may take some time as follows:

```
mysql> ALTER table City ENGINE=NDB;
Query OK, 4079 rows affected (1.64 sec)
Records: 4079  Duplicates: 0  Warnings: 0


mysql> ALTER table Country ENGINE=NDB;
Query OK, 239 rows affected (1.41 sec)
Records: 239  Duplicates: 0  Warnings: 0


mysql> ALTER table CountryLanguage ENGINE=NDB;
Query OK, 984 rows affected (1.41 sec)
Records: 984  Duplicates: 0  Warnings: 0
```

NDB is an alias for NDBCLUSTER, which as explained in *Chapter 1*, means a storage engine for MySQL. All MySQL Cluster tables must be of type NDBCLUSTER.

The second, faster, technique, that is "importing as NDB tables", requires the sed stream editor to be installed on the system (this is included by default with Red Hat Enterprise Linux 5 and CentOS 5). This technique changes the ENGINE=, on-the-fly with the following command:

```
[root@node1 tmp]# cat world.sql | sed -e 's/ENGINE=MyISAM/
ENGINE=NDBCLUSTER/g' | mysql world;
```

If the world.sql file contained InnoDB tables (or a mix of engines), the search regular expression should be changed to whatever is appropriate.

While this is an extremely convenient technique, if your database contains strings that might possibly contain the text ENGINE=MyISAM, this regular expression will change it, which may be bad. I've never experienced this as a likely problem, but it is worth bearing this in mind.

There's more...

By now, the data should be imported into the cluster regardless of the technique that you used. As a final check, execute a SELECT query on more than one SQL node to ensure that the data has been imported successfully.

The following example checks the number of rows in a certain table. The steps are as follows:

1. Firstly, enter the mysql client on one SQL node as follows:

```
[root@node2 ~]# mysql
Welcome to the MySQL monitor.  Commands end with ; or \g.
Your MySQL connection id is 22
Server version: 5.1.34-ndb-7.0.6-cluster-gpl MySQL Cluster Server
(GPL)


Type 'help;' or '\h' for help. Type '\c' to clear the current
input statement.
```

2. Select the `world` database and view the tables contained within it as follows:

```
mysql> USE world;
Reading table information for completion of table and column names
You can turn off this feature to get a quicker startup with -A

Database changed
mysql> SHOW TABLES;
+-----------------+
| Tables_in_world |
+-----------------+
| City            |
| Country         |
| CountryLanguage |
+-----------------+
3 rows in set (0.00 sec)
```

3. Select the number of rows in the table (you can also use the `DESC tablename` command to find the field names):

```
mysql> SELECT COUNT(ID) from City;
+-----------+
| COUNT(ID) |
+-----------+
|      4079 |
+-----------+
1 row in set (0.00 sec)
```

4. Now, repeat this identical process on another node and ensure that the number of rows are the same.

5. If there are problems, run `SHOW ENGINES` command to ensure that `NDBCLUSTER` is enabled and refer to the troubleshooting steps in *Section 1* of this recipe.

Taking an online backup of a MySQL Cluster

MySQL Cluster online backups allow administrators to take a consistent, "point in time", backup of an entire cluster. This is an extremely useful feature and this recipe will explain how these backups work and demonstrate how to take an online backup.

An online backup can only be restored into another MySQL Cluster. If you wish to take a "disaster recovery" backup, which can be restored into say a single MySQL server relatively quickly, you must use `mysqldump` (look at the previous recipe) or cluster replication (explained in *Chapter 5, High Availability with MySQL Replication*).

Getting ready

MySQL Cluster online backups cover all the tables in the cluster (that is, all the NDB tables) and are initiated with a single command issued to the management client. The management client contacts all storage nodes, which then start their backup. The resulting backup is stored in a specified directory on each storage node, and each node dumps to disk its primary fragments of the overall cluster data which consist of the following files:

- **Metadata**—the details of cluster databases and tables, stored in the file `BACKUP-backup_id.node_id.ctl`
- **Table data**—the data within each table at the time of the backup, stored within the file `BACKUP-backup_id-0.node_id.data`
- **Transaction logs**—a logfile containing records of committed transactions, stored within the file `BACKUP-backup_id.node_id.log`

 Each node only takes a backup of the fragments for which it is the primary node. There is only one storage node, primary, for each fragment. To recover from a cluster backup, you require all of the backup files from each storage node (that is, if you have four storage nodes, each will produce a backup folder, and you will require all four folders to restore the backup successfully).

As is clear from the filenames, each backup has a `backup_id` which is generated by the management client when a backup is started. This is useful for keeping track of which files are associated with which backup (this is particularly useful when backups files from all nodes end up in the same place, for example, on a single folder on a backup server or tape).

How to do it...

To initiate an online backup, you must have a connection to the management node from a management client, and run the command START BACKUP.

 You must have all data nodes and a management node started to take a backup successfully.

In this example, we will backup a fully-functioning four storage node cluster.

Firstly, check the status of the cluster (all storage nodes must be up) using the `show` command as follows:

```
ndb_mgm>SHOW
Cluster Configuration
---------------------
[ndbd(NDB)] 4 node(s)
id=3 @10.0.0.1  (mysql-5.1.34 ndb-7.0.6, Nodegroup: 0)
id=4 @10.0.0.2  (mysql-5.1.34 ndb-7.0.6, Nodegroup: 0, Master)
id=5 @10.0.0.3  (mysql-5.1.34 ndb-7.0.6, Nodegroup: 1)
id=6 @10.0.0.4  (mysql-5.1.34 ndb-7.0.6, Nodegroup: 1)

[ndb_mgmd(MGM)] 2 node(s)
id=1 @10.0.0.5  (mysql-5.1.34 ndb-7.0.6)
id=2 @10.0.0.6  (mysql-5.1.34 ndb-7.0.6)

[mysqld(API)] 4 node(s)
id=11 @10.0.0.1  (mysql-5.1.34 ndb-7.0.6)
id=12 @10.0.0.2  (mysql-5.1.34 ndb-7.0.6)
id=13 (not connected, accepting connect from any host)
id=14 (not connected, accepting connect from any host)
```

Now start the backup as follows:

```
ndb_mgm> START BACKUP
Waiting for completed, this may take several minutes
Node 4: Backup 1 started from node 1
Node 4: Backup 1 started from node 1 completed
 StartGCP: 630209 StopGCP: 630212
 #Records: 7369 #LogRecords: 0
 Data: 496720 bytes Log: 0 bytes
ndb_mgm> exit
```

The backup is now completed. Take a moment to look at the files that have now appeared on the storage nodes. There is now a new folder BACKUP-1 in the BACKUP subdirectory within the DataDir on each storage node. We can see from the output of the management client (and also the cluster log) that the backup ID is 1 and it has completed successfully.

These are the files that are on node1 (which had a nodeID of 3 according to the management client output earlier).

```
[root@node1 ~]# cd /var/lib/mysql-cluster/BACKUP/
[root@node1 BACKUP]# ls -lh
total 4.0K
drwxr-x--- 2 root root 4.0K Jul 23 22:31 BACKUP-1
[root@node1 BACKUP]# cd BACKUP-1/
[root@node1 BACKUP-1]# ls -lh
total 156K
-rw-r--r-- 1 root root 126K Jul 23 22:31 BACKUP-1-0.3.Data
-rw-r--r-- 1 root root  18K Jul 23 22:31 BACKUP-1.3.ctl
-rw-r--r-- 1 root root   52 Jul 23 22:31 BACKUP-1.3.log
```

Node2 will have exactly the same files; the only difference is the nodeID (which is 4). The same can be seen on the other two storage nodes as follows:

```
[root@node2 ~]# cd /var/lib/mysql-cluster/BACKUP/BACKUP-1/
[root@node2 BACKUP-1]# ls -lh
total 152K
-rw-r--r-- 1 root root 122K Jul 23 22:31 BACKUP-1-0.4.Data
-rw-r--r-- 1 root root  18K Jul 23 22:31 BACKUP-1.4.ctl
-rw-r--r-- 1 root root   52 Jul 23 22:31 BACKUP-1.4.log
```

The default location for backups is the BACKUP subfolder in DataDir; however, the parameter BackupDataDir in config.ini file can be specified to set this to something else and it is best practice to use a separate block device for backups, if possible. For example, we could change the [NDBD_DEFAULT] section to store backups on /mnt/disk2 as follows:

```
[ndbd default]
DataDir=/var/lib/mysql-cluster
BackupDataDir=/mnt/disk2
NoOfReplicas=2
```

There's more...

There are three tricks for the initiation of online backups:

Preventing commands hanging

The START BACKUP command, by default, waits for the backup to complete before returning control of the management client to the user. This can be annoying, and there are two other options to achieve the backup:

- START BACKUP NOWAIT: This returns control to the user immediately; the management client will display the output when the backup is completed (and you can always check the cluster management log.) This has the disadvantage that if a backup is going to fail, it is likely to fail during this brief initial period where the management client passes the backup instruction to all storage nodes.

- START BACKUP WAIT STARTED: This returns control to the user as soon as the backup is started (that is, each of the storage nodes has confirmed receipt of the instruction to start a backup). A backup is unlikely to fail after this point unless there is a fairly significant change to the cluster (such as a node failure).

Aborting backups in progress

It is possible to abort a backup that is in progress using the ABORT BACKUP <number>, which will return control immediately and display the output, once all storage nodes confirm receipt of the abort command.

All of these management client commands can be passed using the following syntax:

```
[root@node5 ~]# ndb_mgm -e COMMAND
```

For example, by adding these commands to the cron:

```
[root@node5 ~]# crontab -e
```

Add a line such as the following one:

```
@hourly /usr/bin/ndb_mgm -e "START BACKUP NOWAIT" 2>&1
```

This trick is particularly useful for simple scripting.

Defining an exact time for a consistent backup

By default, an online backup of a MySQL Cluster takes a consistent backup across all nodes at the end of the process. This means that if you had two different clusters and ran an online backup at the same time, the backup would not take place at exactly the same time. The difference between the two backups would be a function of the backup duration, which depends on various factors such as the performance of the node and the amount of data to backup. This also means that if you required a backup of a cluster at an exact time, you can only guess how long a backup will take and try to configure a backup at the right time.

It is sometimes desirable to take a consistent backup at the exact time, for example, when you have a business requirement to take a backup at midnight of all your database servers. This is most often managed by having cron execute the commands for you automatically, and using NTP to keep server time very accurate.

The command to execute in this case is the same, but an additional parameter is passed to the START BACKUP command, that is, SNAPSHOTSTART as follows:

```
root@node5 ~]# ndb_mgm -e "START BACKUP SNAPSHOTSTART"
```

Restoring from a MySQL Cluster online backup

There are several situations in which you may find yourself restoring a backup. In this recipe, we will briefly discuss common causes for recovery and then show an example of using the ndb_restore for a painless backup recovery. Later in the recipe, we will discuss techniques to ensure that data is not changed during a restore. In broader terms, a backup recovery is required when the running cluster is, for whatever reason, no longer running and the automatically created checkpoints stored in the DataDir on each storage node are not sufficient for recovery. Some examples that you may encounter are as follows:

- A disk corruption has occurred which destroyed your DataDir on all storage nodes in a nodegroup and simultaneously crashed the machines so the in-memory copy of data was lost.

- You are conducting a major cluster upgrade (which requires a backup, total shutdown, start of the new cluster, and a restore). In this case, be aware that you can generally only import a backup into a more recent version of MySQL Cluster (review the documentation in this case).

- Human error or one of the other causes mentioned earlier in this section require you to restore the database back to an earlier period in time.

The principles of backup restoration are as follows:

- The cluster is restarted to clear all the data (that is, ndb_mgmd is restarted and ndbd --initial is executed on all storage nodes)

- Each backup directory (one per existing storage node) is copied back to a server that can connect as an API node (that is, it is on the cluster network and has a [MYSQLD] section in config.ini file that it may bind to)

- A binary ndb_restore command is run once per backup folder (that is, once per node in the existing cluster)

The first `ndb_restore` process runs with `-m` to restore the metadata on all nodes, all others just run with the following options:

- ▶ `-b`—backup ID, this is the one printed by the management node during START BACKUP and is the first number in the `BACKUP-x-y*` files

- ▶ `-n`—node ID of storage node that took backups, this is the final digit in the `BACKUP-x-y* files`

- ▶ `-r`—path to the backup files to be used for recovery

When running `ndb_restore`, you have two options:

1. Run `ndb_restore` processes in parallel. In this case, you must ensure that no other SQL nodes (such as a `mysqld` process) can change data in the cluster. This can be done by stopping the `mysqld` processes. Each `ndb_restore` will require its own `[MYSQLD]` section in `config.ini` file.

2. Run `ndb_restore` processes one at a time. In this case, you can use single-user mode (see the next recipe) to ensure that only the currently active `ndb_restore` process is allowed to change the data in the cluster.

You can restore a backup into a cluster with a different number of nodes; you must run `ndb_restore` once per existing number of storage nodes, pointing it at each of the backup files created. If you fail to do this, you will not recover all of your data but you will recover some of your data and you may be misled into thinking that you have recovered all the data successfully.

How to do it...

In this recipe, we will use a simple example to demonstrate a restore using the backups generated in the example in the previous recipe (this produced a backup with an ID of 1 from a cluster consisting of four storage nodes with IDs 3,4,5, and 6). We have an API node allocated for each storage node, which is normally connected to by a `mysqld` process (that is, a SQL node). The backups have been stored in `/var/lib/mysql-cluster/BACKUPS/BACKUP-1/` on each of the four nodes.

While it is not recommended to run production SQL nodes (that is, SQL nodes that actually receive application traffic) on the same servers as storage nodes due to the possibility of `mysqld` using a large amount of memory and causing `ndbd` to be killed, I have always found it useful to configure storage nodes to run `mysqld` for testing and debugging purposes and in this case, it is extremely useful to have an API node already configured for each SQL node.

In the following example, we are demonstrating a recovery from a backup. Firstly, ensure that you have taken a backup (earlier recipe in this chapter) and shut down all nodes in your cluster to have a realistic starting point (that is, every node is dead).

The first step in the recovery process is to stop all SQL nodes to prevent them from writing to the cluster during the recovery process. Shut down all `mysqld` processes running on all SQL nodes connected to the cluster.

Also to replicate a realistic recovery from a backup, on all storage nodes, copy the BACKUP-X (where X is the backup ID, in our example, it is 1) folder from the BACKUP subdirectory of DataDir to /tmp. In a real situation, you would likely have to obtain the BACKUP-1 folder for each storage node from a backup server:

```
[root@node1 mysql-cluster]# cp -R /var/lib/mysql-cluster/BACKUP/BACKUP-1/
/tmp/
```

Start the cluster management node as follows:

```
[root@node5 ~]# ndb_mgmd
```

Verify that `ndbd` is not already running (if it is, kill it), and start `ndbd` on all storage nodes with --initial:

```
[root@node1 ~]# ps aux | grep ndbd | grep -v grep | wc -l
0
[root@node1 ~]# ndbd --initial
2009-07-23 23:58:35 [ndbd] INFO     -- Configuration fetched from
'10.0.0.5:1186', generation: 1
```

Wait for the cluster to start by checking the status on the management node as follows:

```
ndb_mgm> ALL STATUS
Node 3: starting (Last completed phase 0) (mysql-5.1.34 ndb-7.0.6)
Node 4: starting (Last completed phase 0) (mysql-5.1.34 ndb-7.0.6)
Node 5: starting (Last completed phase 0) (mysql-5.1.34 ndb-7.0.6)
Node 6: starting (Last completed phase 0) (mysql-5.1.34 ndb-7.0.6)
ndb_mgm> ALL STATUS
Node 3: started (mysql-5.1.34 ndb-7.0.6)
Node 4: started (mysql-5.1.34 ndb-7.0.6)
Node 5: started (mysql-5.1.34 ndb-7.0.6)
Node 6: started (mysql-5.1.34 ndb-7.0.6)
```

At this point, you have a working cluster with no SQL nodes connected and no data in the cluster.

In this example, we will restore the four nodes backups in parallel by using a SQL node on each of the four storage nodes. As discussed in *Chapter 1*, it is not a good idea to expose SQL nodes running on storage nodes to production (application) traffic due to the risk of swapping. However, config.ini file should allow one to connect from each storage node because the ndb_restore binary, which does the dirty work of restoring the backup, will connect as if it was a SQL node.

 Although we are going to restore all four storage nodes backups in one go, it is important to run the first ndb_restore command slightly before the others and we'll run this with −m to restore the cluster-wide metadata. Once the metadata is restored (a very quick process), the other ndb_restore commands can be started.

Now, we are ready to restore. Triple check that no SQL nodes are connected, and that there is one API node slot available for each of the data node's IP addresses as follows:

```
ndb_mgm> SHOW
Cluster Configuration
---------------------
[ndbd(NDB)]  4 node(s)
id=3 @10.0.0.1  (mysql-5.1.34 ndb-7.0.6, Nodegroup: 0, Master)
id=4 @10.0.0.2  (mysql-5.1.34 ndb-7.0.6, Nodegroup: 0)
id=5 @10.0.0.3  (mysql-5.1.34 ndb-7.0.6, Nodegroup: 1)
id=6 @10.0.0.4  (mysql-5.1.34 ndb-7.0.6, Nodegroup: 1)

[ndb_mgmd(MGM)]  2 node(s)
id=1 @10.0.0.5  (mysql-5.1.34 ndb-7.0.6)
id=2 @10.0.0.6  (mysql-5.1.34 ndb-7.0.6)

[mysqld(API)]  4 node(s)
id=11 (not connected, accepting connect from 10.0.0.1)
id=12 (not connected, accepting connect from 10.0.0.2)
id=13 (not connected, accepting connect from 10.0.0.3)
id=14 (not connected, accepting connect from 10.0.0.4)
```

Now, start the restore of the first storage node (ID = 3)

```
[root@node1 BACKUP-1]# ndb_restore -m -b 1 -n 3 -r /tmp/BACKUP-1/
Backup Id = 1
Nodeid = 3
backup path = /tmp/BACKUP-1/
Opening file '/tmp/BACKUP-1/BACKUP-1.3.ctl'
Backup version in files: ndb-6.3.11 ndb version: mysql-5.1.34 ndb-7.0.6
Stop GCP of Backup: 0
Connected to ndb!!
Successfully restored table `cluster_test/def/ctest`
Successfully restored table event REPL$cluster_test/ctest
Successfully restored table `world/def/CountryLanguage`
Successfully created index `PRIMARY` on `CountryLanguage`
Successfully created index `PRIMARY` on `Country`
Opening file '/tmp/BACKUP-1/BACKUP-1-0.3.Data'
_____

Processing data in table: cluster_test/def/ctest(7) fragment 0
..._____

Processing data in table: mysql/def/ndb_schema(4) fragment 0
_____

Processing data in table: world/def/Country(10) fragment 0
Opening file '/tmp/BACKUP-1/BACKUP-1.3.log'
Restored 1368 tuples and 0 log entries

NDBT_ProgramExit: 0 - OK


[root@node1 BACKUP-1]#
```

> If there is no free API node for the ndb_restore process on each
> node, it will fail with the following error:
>
> ```
> Configuration error: Error : Could not allocate
> node id at 10.0.0.5 port 1186: No free node id
> found for mysqld(API).
> Failed to initialize consumers
> NDBT_ProgramExit: 1 - Failed
> ```
>
> In this case, check that there is an available [mysqld] section in
> config.ini file.

As soon as the restore gets to the line (Opening file '/tmp/BACKUP-1/BACKUP-1-0.3.Data'), you can (and should) start restoring the other three nodes. Use the same command, *without* the -m on the other three nodes ensuring that the correct node ID is passed to the -n flag:

```
[root@node2 ~]# ndb_restore -b 1 -n 4 -r /tmp/BACKUP-1/
```

Use the same command on nodes 3 and 4 as follows:

```
[root@node3 ~]# ndb_restore -b 1 -n 5 -r /tmp/BACKUP-1/
[root@node4 ~]# ndb_restore -b 1 -n 6 -r /tmp/BACKUP-1/
```

Once all the four nodes return NDBT_ProgramExit: 0 – OK, the backup is restored. Start the mysqld processes on your SQL nodes and check that they join the cluster, and your cluster is back.

If you attempt to restore the cluster with the wrong nodeID or wrong backupID, you will get the following error:

```
[root@node1 mysql-cluster]# ndb_restore -m -n 1 -b 1 -r /tmp/BACKUP-1/
Nodeid = 1
Backup Id = 1
backup path = /tmp/BACKUP-1/
Opening file '/tmp/BACKUP-1/BACKUP-1.1.ctl'
readDataFileHeader: Error reading header
Failed to read /tmp/BACKUP-1/BACKUP-1.1.ctl


NDBT_ProgramExit: 1 - Failed
```

Restricting write access to a MySQL Cluster with single-user mode

Most MySQL Clusters will have more than one SQL node (mysqld process) as well as the option for other API nodes such as ndb_restore to connect to the cluster. Occasionally, it is essential for only one API node to access the cluster. MySQL Cluster has a single-user mode which, allows you to temporarily specify only a single API node that may execute the queries against the cluster.

In this recipe, we will use an example cluster with two SQL nodes, nodeIDs 13 and 14, execute a query against both the nodes, enter single-user mode, repeat the experiment, and finish by verifying that once the single user mode is exited, the query works as it did at the beginning of the exercise.

Within a single SQL node, the standard MySQL LOCK TABLES queries will work as expected, if no other nodes are changing the data in NDBCLUSTER tables. The only way to be sure of this is to use a single-user mode.

How to do it...

A single-user mode is controlled with the following two management client commands:

```
ndb_mgm> ENTER SINGLE USER NODE X
ndb_mgm> EXIT SINGLE USER MODE
```

For this recipe, the sample cluster initial state is as follows (It is important to notice the number of storage nodes, and the storage node IDs that are in each nodegroup, as we will require this information when restoring using ndb_restore while in the single user mode. For a reminder on how nodegroups work, see *Chapter 1*.):

```
ndb_mgm> SHOW
Cluster Configuration
---------------------
[ndbd(NDB)]  4 node(s)
id=3  @10.0.0.1  (mysql-5.1.34 ndb-7.0.6, Nodegroup: 0)
id=4  @10.0.0.2  (mysql-5.1.34 ndb-7.0.6, Nodegroup: 0, Master)
id=5  @10.0.0.3  (mysql-5.1.34 ndb-7.0.6, Nodegroup: 1)
id=6  @10.0.0.4  (mysql-5.1.34 ndb-7.0.6, Nodegroup: 1)


[ndb_mgmd(MGM)]  2 node(s)
id=1  @10.0.0.5  (mysql-5.1.34 ndb-7.0.6)
id=2  @10.0.0.6  (mysql-5.1.34 ndb-7.0.6)


[mysqld(API)]  4 node(s)
id=11 @10.0.0.1  (mysql-5.1.34 ndb-7.0.6)
id=12 @10.0.0.2  (mysql-5.1.34 ndb-7.0.6)
id=13 (not connected, accepting connect from any host)
id=14 (not connected, accepting connect from any host)
```

SQL node 1:

```
mysql> SELECT * from City WHERE 1 ORDER BY ID LIMIT 0,1;
+----+-------+-------------+----------+------------+
| ID | Name  | CountryCode | District | Population |
+----+-------+-------------+----------+------------+
|  1 | Kabul | AFG         | Kabol    |    1780000 |
+----+-------+-------------+----------+------------+
1 row in set (0.04 sec)
```

SQL node 2:

```
mysql> SELECT * from City WHERE 1 ORDER BY ID LIMIT 0,1;
+----+-------+-------------+----------+------------+
| ID | Name  | CountryCode | District | Population |
+----+-------+-------------+----------+------------+
|  1 | Kabul | AFG         | Kabol    |    1780000 |
+----+-------+-------------+----------+------------+
1 row in set (0.05 sec)
```

We now enter single-user mode, allowing only node 11 (the first SQL node, as shown by the output from SHOW command):

Management client:

```
ndb_mgm> ENTER SINGLE USER NODE 11;
Single user mode entered
Access is granted for API node 11 only.
```

SQL node 1 still continues to work (as it has node ID of 11):

```
mysql> SELECT * from City WHERE 1 ORDER BY ID LIMIT 0,1;
+----+-------+-------------+----------+------------+
| ID | Name  | CountryCode | District | Population |
+----+-------+-------------+----------+------------+
|  1 | Kabul | AFG         | Kabol    |    1780000 |
+----+-------+-------------+----------+------------+
1 row in set (0.04 sec)
```

SQL node 2, however, will not execute any query (including SELECT queries):

```
mysql> SELECT * from City WHERE 1 ORDER BY ID LIMIT 0,1;
ERROR 1296 (HY000): Got error 299 'Operation not allowed or aborted due
to single user mode' from NDBCLUSTER
```

At this point, we can execute any queries on SQL node 1 and we also know that nothing else is changing the cluster (tables that are not in the cluster are unaffected). However, note that SQL node 1 can still run more than one query so we should ensure that we only do one thing at a time, and use appropriate locks when we do not want other processes to affect our work. During single-user mode, the management client shows storage (not SQL / API) nodes as being in single-user mode:

```
ndb_mgm> SHOW
Cluster Configuration
---------------------
[ndbd(NDB)]  4 node(s)
id=3 @10.0.0.1   (mysql-5.1.34 ndb-7.0.6, single user mode, Nodegroup: 0)
id=4 @10.0.0.2   (mysql-5.1.34 ndb-7.0.6, single user mode, Nodegroup: 0,
Master)
id=5 @10.0.0.3   (mysql-5.1.34 ndb-7.0.6, single user mode, Nodegroup: 1)
id=6 @10.0.0.4   (mysql-5.1.34 ndb-7.0.6, single user mode, Nodegroup: 1)
```

Once we have finished the tasks that were required for this mode, we can exit from the single-user mode.

On the management client, use the following command to exit single-user mode:

```
ndb_mgm> EXIT SINGLE USER MODE;
Exiting single user mode in progress.
Use ALL STATUS or SHOW to see when single user mode has been exited.
ndb_mgm> ALL STATUS
Node 3: started (mysql-5.1.34 ndb-7.0.6)
Node 4: started (mysql-5.1.34 ndb-7.0.6)
Node 5: started (mysql-5.1.34 ndb-7.0.6)
Node 6: started (mysql-5.1.34 ndb-7.0.6)
```

Verify that the SQL commands executed on SQL node 1 are again working as follows:

```
mysql> SELECT * from City WHERE 1 ORDER BY ID LIMIT 0,1;
+----+-------+-------------+----------+------------+
| ID | Name  | CountryCode | District | Population |
+----+-------+-------------+----------+------------+
|  1 | Kabul | AFG         | Kabol    |    1780000 |
+----+-------+-------------+----------+------------+
1 row in set (0.04 sec)
```

Finally, verify that the SQL commands executed on SQL node 2 are also working:

```
mysql> SELECT * from City WHERE 1 ORDER BY ID LIMIT 0,1;
+----+-------+-------------+----------+------------+
| ID | Name  | CountryCode | District | Population |
+----+-------+-------------+----------+------------+
|  1 | Kabul | AFG         | Kabol    |    1780000 |
+----+-------+-------------+----------+------------+
1 row in set (0.05 sec)
```

There's more...

To be 100 percent sure that `ndb_restore` will be the only thing connecting to a cluster, it is possible to pass `--ndb-nodeid=x` to `ndb_restore` to ensure that `ndb_restore` picks up the node to which you have granted the single-user mode. This can be useful when SQL nodes in a cluster also serve up non-clustered databases and therefore just because a cluster is down, it is not acceptable to take down the SQL nodes to restore the cluster data. Unfortunately, using `ndb_restore` with single-user mode (by definition) requires you to run each `ndb_restore` one after the other, which will be significantly slower, particularly, in larger clusters.

For example, if you are running `ndb_restore`, on a node `10.0.0.10` you can add a dedicated `ndb_restore` API node to `config.ini` file:

```
[mysqld]
id=20
HostName=10.0.0.10
```

Restart the cluster to add this new node and enter single-user mode on node `20`:

```
ndb_mgm> ENTER SINGLE USER NODE 20;
Single user mode entered
Access is granted for API node 20 only.
```

Run `ndb_restore` ensuring that it connects as node `20` (and therefore is not blocked out by single-user mode):

```
[root@node1 mysql-cluster]# ndb_restore --ndb-nodeid=20 -m -b 1 -n 3 -r
/tmp/BACKUP-1/
```

In the case of running `ndb_restore`, it is often easier to pre-allocate one API node per storage node in the `config.ini` file. In addition, it's easy if you are running a SQL node on storage nodes for testing to shut down the `mysqld` processes prior to attempting a cluster restart, and finally, to run `ndb_restore` in parallel once in every storage node.

Taking an offline backup with MySQL Cluster

The MySQL client RPM includes the binary `mysqldump`, which produces SQL statements from a MySQL database. In this recipe, we will explore the usage of this tool with MySQL Clusters.

Taking a backup with `mysqldump` for MySQL Cluster (NDB) tables is identical to other table engines and has all of the same disadvantages—most importantly that it requires significant locking to take a consistent backup. However, it is simple, easy to verify, and trivial to restore from and also provides a way to restore the backup from a MySQL Cluster into a standalone server (for example, by using InnoDB) in the case that a cluster is not available for recovery.

How to do it...

To run `mysqldump` in the simplest way possible is to execute the following command:

```
mysqldump [options] db_name [tables]
```

It is often desirable to backup more than one or all databases. In that case, `mysqldump` must run with the `--all-databases` option. It is also often desirable to compress backups on-the-fly, and pipe the output to a file with a timestamp in its name, which we will do in the first example. To get a point in time (consistent) backup of an entire MySQL Cluster with `mysqldump`, you must ensure two things as follows:

- Only the SQL node to which `mysqldump` is connected is able to change the data in the cluster
- On that SQL node, the only query running is the `mysqldump`. This can be achieved with the `--lock-all-tables` option which will take a global read lock for the duration of the backup

These two requirements effectively take your cluster down for the duration of the backup, which may not be acceptable. If you require availability at all times then MySQL Cluster *Hot Backups* are more appropriate. However, if you do need point in time backups using `mysqldump`, the process is covered in detail in the following *There's more...* section.

If you are using disk-based tables with MySQL Cluster, mysqldump can run with the --all-tablespaces option to include tablespace creation commands which are required for importing disk-based tables to an entirely new cluster.

Once created with mysqldump, a SQL file can be imported using the recipe *Importing SQL files to a MySQL Server and converting to MySQL Cluster*, although if compressed with gzip, it should be uncompressed first. Additionally, the steps in this recipe to ALTER the imported tables or to replace MyISAM with NDB are unnecessary, as mysqldump will include ENGINE=NDBCLUSTER in the SQL dump, which it produces for clustered tables.

To create a non-consistent backup of the world database, execute the mysqldump command on a SQL node as follows (the following command also compresses the output and saves it to a file in /tmp/):

```
[root@node1 ~]# mysqldump world | gzip -9 > /tmp/backup-world-$(date
'+%F_%T').sql.gz
```

Replace the database name with the --all-databases flag to backup all databases on the node.

To import this backup in a new clustered database, world_new, first create the new database:

```
[root@node1 ~]# mysql
Welcome to the MySQL monitor.  Commands end with ; or \g.
Your MySQL connection id is 13
Server version: 5.1.34-ndb-7.0.6-cluster-gpl MySQL Cluster Server (GPL)


Type 'help;' or '\h' for help. Type '\c' to clear the current input
statement.


mysql> CREATE DATABASE world_new;
Query OK, 1 row affected (0.22 sec)
```

To uncompress the backup, use the following command:

```
[root@node1 ~]# gunzip /tmp/backup-world-2009-07-28_00\:14\:56.sql.gz
```

Import the backup as follows:

```
[root@node1 ~]# mysql world_new < /tmp/backup-world-2009-07-28_
00\:14\:56.sql
```

Now, check that it has imported correctly:

```
[root@node1 ~]# mysql
Welcome to the MySQL monitor.  Commands end with ; or \g.
Your MySQL connection id is 15
Server version: 5.1.34-ndb-7.0.6-cluster-gpl MySQL Cluster Server (GPL)


Type 'help;' or '\h' for help. Type '\c' to clear the current input
statement.


mysql> USE world_new
Reading table information for completion of table and column names
You can turn off this feature to get a quicker startup with -A


Database changed
mysql> SHOW TABLES;
+---------------------+
| Tables_in_world_new |
+---------------------+
| City                |
| Country             |
| CountryLanguage     |
+---------------------+
3 rows in set (0.00 sec)
```

We can see that there is still a full count of rows in the City table:

```
mysql> SELECT COUNT(id) FROM City WHERE 1;
+-----------+
| count(id) |
+-----------+
|      2084 |
+-----------+
1 row in set (0.00 sec)
```

There's more...

There are a couple of tricks that can make `mysqldump` more useful, which are covered briefly in the following section.

Importing a cluster SQL file to an unclustered MySQL Server

To import a `mysqldump` produced `SQL` file from a NDB cluster as another (non-clustered) engine, we can use a simple `sed` substitution. This could be useful in a disaster recovery situation where a cluster is physically destroyed and there are not enough machines available for an immediate rebuild of the cluster, but it is desirable to have some access to the data.

This example creates a new database, `world_innodb` and imports the NDB backup created earlier as an InnoDB table. This process is similar to the process described in the *Importing SQL files to a MySQL server and converting them to MySQL Cluster* recipe earlier in this section, so, for a line-by-line guide, refer to that recipe.

The first key difference is that you must create the new database:

```
mysql> CREATE DATABASE world_innodb;

Query OK, 1 row affected (0.15 sec)

mysql> exit
```

This time the regular expression changes `NDBCLUSTER` to `InnoDB`:

```
[root@node1 tmp]# cat /tmp/backup-world-2009-07-28_00\:14\:56.sql | sed
-e 's/ENGINE=ndbcluster/ENGINE=innodb/g' | mysql world_innodb;
```

Note that the same caveat discussed earlier on `sed` applies—if your data includes the string `NDBCLUSTER`, it could be replaced.

Running mysqldump for a consistent backup

To take a consistent, point in time, backup with `mysqldump`, we must:

- Enter the single-user mode to ensure that only one SQL node (`mysqld` process) can make queries against the cluster
- Lock the tables on that node to ensure that only our `dump` query is running during the backup

To do this, we start by identifying the node on which we will run `mysqldump` command.

```
[root@node5 ~]# ndb_mgm

-- NDB Cluster -- Management Client --

ndb_mgm> SHOW

Connected to Management Server at: 10.0.0.5:1186
```

```
Cluster Configuration
--------------------

[ndbd(NDB)]   2 node(s)
id=3   @10.0.0.1   (mysql-5.1.34 ndb-7.0.6, Nodegroup: 0, Master)
id=4   @10.0.0.2   (mysql-5.1.34 ndb-7.0.6, Nodegroup: 0)


[ndb_mgmd(MGM)]   1 node(s)
id=1   @10.0.0.5   (mysql-5.1.34 ndb-7.0.6)


[mysqld(API)]   4 node(s)
id=11  @10.0.0.1   (mysql-5.1.34 ndb-7.0.6)
id=12  @10.0.0.2   (mysql-5.1.34 ndb-7.0.6)
id=13  @10.0.0.3   (mysql-5.1.34 ndb-7.0.6)
id=14  @10.0.0.4   (mysql-5.1.34 ndb-7.0.6)
```

In this example, we will use the SQL node on node ID 12; it makes no difference which node you choose, but it may be best to select a relatively high-performance SQL node (specifically, one with good disks) for lower backup times.

If there is any confusion as to which SQL node is which, there is a command that quickly identifies the connection details for a SQL node:

```
mysql> SHOW ENGINE NDBCLUSTER STATUS;
```

This shows, among its output, the node ID of the SQL node in the format cluster_node_id=12.

When we enter single-user mode, it locks the cluster down to only allow this node to access; see the previous recipe for more details:

```
ndb_mgm> ENTER SINGLE USER MODE 12
Single user mode entered
Access is granted for API node 12 only.
```

Now, we can run mysqldump on that node:

```
[root@node2 ~]# mysqldump --lock-all-tables --all-tablespaces world > /
tmp/backup.sql
```

As soon as this completes, we exit single-user mode and the cluster returns quickly to normal:

```
ndb_mgm> EXIT SINGLE USER MODE;
Exiting single user mode in progress.
Use ALL STATUS or SHOW to see when single user mode has been exited.
ndb_mgm> SHOW
Cluster Configuration
---------------------
[ndbd(NDB)]   2 node(s)
id=3   @10.0.0.1   (mysql-5.1.34 ndb-7.0.6, Nodegroup: 0, Master)
id=4   @10.0.0.2   (mysql-5.1.34 ndb-7.0.6, Nodegroup: 0)

[ndb_mgmd(MGM)]   1 node(s)
id=1   @10.0.0.5   (mysql-5.1.34 ndb-7.0.6)

[mysqld(API)] 4 node(s)
id=11   @10.0.0.1   (mysql-5.1.34 ndb-7.0.6)
id=12   @10.0.0.2   (mysql-5.1.34 ndb-7.0.6)
id=13   @10.0.0.3   (mysql-5.1.34 ndb-7.0.6)
id=14   @10.0.0.4   (mysql-5.1.34 ndb-7.0.6)
```

The backup should now be compressed with `gzip`:

```
[root@node2 ~]# gzip -9 /tmp/backup.sql
```

A checksum may be recorded for verification:

```
[root@node2 ~]# md5sum /tmp/backup.sql
d8e8fca2dc0f896fd7cb4cb0031ba249   /tmp/backup.sql
```

And sent to an offsite location, for example with `scp`:

```
[root@node2 ~]# scp /tmp/backup-sql user@remote.host:/mnt/backups/
/tmp/backup.sql
```

You may find it useful, before doing any of this, to move it to a more descriptive name, for example:

```
[root@node2 ~]#  mv /tmp/backup.sql /tmp/$(hostname -s)_backup_world_
$(date +"%F_%H").sql
```

Which produces the following more useful filename:

```
[root@node2 ~]# ls /tmp/ | grep sql
Node2_backup_world_2009-12-10_23.sql
```

These files can be more useful to archive.

3
MySQL Cluster Management

In this chapter, we will cover:

- ▸ Configuring multiple management nodes
- ▸ Obtaining usage information
- ▸ Adding storage nodes online
- ▸ Replication between MySQL Clusters
- ▸ Replication between MySQL Clusters with a backup channel
- ▸ User-defined partitioning
- ▸ Disk-based tables
- ▸ Calculating `DataMemory` and `IndexMemory`

Introduction

This chapter contains recipes that cover common management tasks for a MySQL Cluster. This includes tasks that are carried out on almost every production cluster such as adding multiple management nodes for redundancy and monitoring the usage information of a cluster to ensure that a cluster does not run out of memory. Additionally, it covers the tasks that are useful for specific situations such as setting up replication between clusters (useful for protection against entire site failures) and using disk-based tables (useful when a cluster is required, but it's not cost-effective to store all the data in memory).

Configuring multiple management nodes

Every MySQL Cluster must have a management node to start and also to carry out critical tasks such as allowing other nodes to restart, running online backups, and monitoring the status of the cluster. The previous chapter demonstrated how to build a MySQL Cluster with just one management node for simplicity. However, it is strongly recommended for a production cluster to ensure that a management node is always available, and this requires more than one management node. In this recipe, we will discuss the minor complications that more than one management node will bring before showing the configuration of a new cluster with two management nodes. Finally, the modification of an existing cluster to add a second management node will be shown.

Getting ready

In a single management node cluster, everything is simple. Nodes connect to the management node, get a node ID, and join the cluster. When the management node starts, it reads the `config.ini` file, starts and prepares to give the cluster information contained within the `config.ini` file out to the cluster nodes as and when they join.

This process can become slightly more complicated when there are multiple management nodes, and it is important that each management node takes a different ID. Therefore, the first additional complication is that it is an extremely good idea to specify node IDs and ensure that the `HostName` parameter is set for each management node in the `config.ini` file.

It is technically possible to start two management nodes with different cluster configuration files in a cluster with multiple management nodes. It is not difficult to see that this can cause all sorts of bizarre behavior including a likely cluster shutdown in the case of the primary management node failing. Ensure that every time the `config.ini` file is changed, the change is correctly replicated to all management nodes. You should also ensure that all management nodes are always using the same version of the `config.ini` file.

It is possible to hold the `config.ini` file on a shared location such as a NFS share, although to avoid introducing complexity and a single point of failure, the best practice would be to store the configuration file in a configuration management system such as Puppet (`http://www.puppetlabs.com/`) or Cfengine (`http://www.cfengine.org/`).

How to do it...

The following process should be followed to configure a cluster for multiple management nodes. In this recipe, we focus on the differences from the recipes in *Chapter 1, High Availability with MySQL Cluster.* Initially, this recipe will cover the procedure to be followed in order to configure a new cluster with two management nodes. Thereafter, the procedure for adding a second management node to an already running single management node cluster will be covered.

The first step is to define two management nodes in the global configuration file `config.ini` on both management nodes.

In this example, we are using IP addresses `10.0.0.5` and `10.0.0.6` for the two management nodes that require the following two entries of `[ndb_mgmd]` in the `config.ini` file:

```
[ndb_mgmd]
Id=1
HostName=10.0.0.5
DataDir=/var/lib/mysql-cluster

[ndb_mgmd]
Id=2
HostName=10.0.0.6
DataDir=/var/lib/mysql-cluster
```

Update the `[mysql_cluster]` section of each storage node's `/etc/my.cnf` to point the node to the IP address of both management nodes:

```
[mysql_cluster]
ndb-connectstring=10.0.0.5,10.0.0.6
```

Update the `[mysqld]` section of each SQL node's `/etc/my.cnf` to point to both management nodes:

```
[mysqld]
ndb-connectstring=10.0.0.5,10.0.0.6
```

Now, prepare to start both the management nodes. Install the management node on both nodes, if it does not already exist (Refer to the recipe *Installing a management node* in *Chapter 1*).

 Before proceeding, ensure that you have copied the updated `config.ini` file to both management nodes.

Start the first management node by changing to the correct directory and running the management node binary (ndb_mgmd) with the following flags:

- `--initial`: Deletes the local cache of the `config.ini` file and updates it (you must do this every time the `config.ini` file is changed).

- `--ndb-nodeid=X`: Tells the node to connect as this `nodeid`, as we specified in the `config.ini` file. This is technically unnecessary if there is no ambiguity as to which `nodeid` this particular node may connect to (in this case, both nodes have a `HostName` defined). However, defining it reduces the possibility of confusion.

- ▸ `--config-file=config.ini`: This is used to specify the configuration file. In theory, passing a value of the `config.ini` file in the local directory is unnecessary because it is the default value. But in certain situations, it seems that passing this in any case avoids issues, and again this reduces the possibility of confusion.

```
[root@node6 mysql-cluster]# cd /usr/local/mysql-cluster
[root@node6 mysql-cluster]# ndb_mgmd --config-file=config.ini --initial
--ndb-nodeid=2
2009-08-15 20:49:21 [MgmSrvr] INFO      -- NDB Cluster Management Server.
mysql-5.1.34 ndb-7.0.6
2009-08-15 20:49:21 [MgmSrvr] INFO      -- Reading cluster configuration
from 'config.ini'
```

Repeat this command on the other node using the correct node ID:

```
[root@node5 mysql-cluster]# cd /usr/local/mysql-cluster
[root@node5 mysql-cluster]# ndb_mgmd --config-file=config.ini --initial
--ndb-nodeid=1
```

Now, start each storage node in turn, as shown in the previous chapter. Use the storage management client's `show` command to show that both management nodes are connected and that all storage nodes have been reconnected:

```
ndb_mgm> show
Connected to Management Server at: 10.0.0.5:1186
Cluster Configuration
---------------------
[ndbd(NDB)]     4 node(s)
id=3    @10.0.0.1   (mysql-5.1.34 ndb-7.0.6, Nodegroup: 0, Master)
id=4    @10.0.0.2   (mysql-5.1.34 ndb-7.0.6, Nodegroup: 0)
id=5    @10.0.0.3   (mysql-5.1.34 ndb-7.0.6, Nodegroup: 1)
id=6    @10.0.0.4   (mysql-5.1.34 ndb-7.0.6, Nodegroup: 1)

[ndb_mgmd(MGM)]     2 node(s)
id=1    @10.0.0.5   (mysql-5.1.34 ndb-7.0.6)
id=2    @10.0.0.6   (mysql-5.1.34 ndb-7.0.6)

[mysqld(API)]     4 node(s)
id=11   @10.0.0.1   (mysql-5.1.34 ndb-7.0.6)
id=12   @10.0.0.2   (mysql-5.1.34 ndb-7.0.6)
id=13   @10.0.0.3   (mysql-5.1.34 ndb-7.0.6)
id=14   @10.0.0.4   (mysql-5.1.34 ndb-7.0.6)
```

Finally, restart all SQL nodes (`mysqld` processes). On RedHat-based systems, this can be achieved using the `service` command:

```
[root@node1 ~]# service mysqld restart
```

Congratulations! Your cluster is now configured with multiple management nodes. Test that failover works by killing a management node, in turn, the remaining management nodes should continue to work.

There's more...

It is sometimes necessary to add a management node to an existing cluster if for example, due to a lack of hardware or time, an initial cluster only has a single management node.

Adding a management node is simple. Firstly, install the management client on the new node (refer to the recipe in *Chapter 1*). Secondly, modify the `config.ini` file, as shown earlier in this recipe for adding the new management node, and copy this new `config.ini` file to both management nodes. Finally, stop the existing management node and start the new one using the following commands:

For the existing management node, type:

```
[root@node6 mysql-cluster]# killall ndb_mgmd [root@node6 mysql-cluster]#
ndb_mgmd --config-file=config.ini --initial --ndb-nodeid=2

2009-08-15 21:29:53 [MgmSrvr] INFO      -- NDB Cluster Management Server.
mysql-5.1.34 ndb-7.0.6

2009-08-15 21:29:53 [MgmSrvr] INFO      -- Reading cluster configuration
from 'config.ini'
```

Then type the following command for the new management node:

```
[root@node5 mysql-cluster]# ndb_mgmd --config-file=config.ini --initial
--ndb-nodeid=1

2009-08-15 21:29:53 [MgmSrvr] INFO      -- NDB Cluster Management Server.
mysql-5.1.34 ndb-7.0.6

2009-08-15 21:29:53 [MgmSrvr] INFO      -- Reading cluster configuration
from 'config.ini'
```

Now, restart each storage node one at a time. Ensure that you only stop one node per nodegroup at a time and wait for it to fully restart before taking another node in the nodegroup, when offline, in order to avoid any downtime.

See also

Look at the section for the online addition of storage nodes (discussed later in this chapter) for further details on restarting storage nodes one at a time. Also look at *Chapter 1* for detailed instructions on how to build a MySQL Cluster (with one management node).

Obtaining usage information

This recipe explains how to monitor the usage of a MySQL Cluster, looking at the memory, CPU, IO, and network utilization on storage nodes.

Getting ready

MySQL Cluster is extremely memory-intensive. When a MySQL Cluster starts, the storage nodes will start using the entire `DataMemory` and `IndexMemory` allocated to them. In a production cluster with a large amount of RAM, it is likely that this will include a large proportion of the physical memory on the server.

How to do it...

An essential part of managing a MySQL Cluster is looking into what is happening inside each storage node. In this section, we will cover the vital commands used to monitor a cluster.

To monitor the memory (RAM) usage of the nodes within the cluster, execute the `<nodeid> REPORT MemoryUsage` command within the management client as follows:

```
ndb_mgm> 3 REPORT MemoryUsage
Node 3: Data usage is 0%(21 32K pages of total 98304)
Node 3: Index usage is 0%(13 8K pages of total 131104)
```

This command can be executed for all storage nodes rather than just one by using `ALL nodeid`:

```
ndb_mgm> ALL REPORT MemoryUsage

Node 3: Data usage is 0%(21 32K pages of total 98304)
Node 3: Index usage is 0%(13 8K pages of total 131104)
Node 4: Data usage is 0%(21 32K pages of total 98304)
Node 4: Index usage is 0%(13 8K pages of total 131104)
Node 5: Data usage is 0%(21 32K pages of total 98304)
Node 5: Index usage is 0%(13 8K pages of total 131104)
Node 6: Data usage is 0%(21 32K pages of total 98304)
Node 6: Index usage is 0%(13 8K pages of total 131104)
```

This information shows that these nodes are actually using `0%` of their `DataMemory` and `IndexMemory`.

> Memory allocation is important and unfortunately a little more complicated than a percentage used on each node. There is more detail about this in the *How it works...* section of this recipe, but the vital points to remember are:
>
> ▸ It is a good idea never to go over 80 percent of memory usage (particularly not for `DataMemory`)
>
> ▸ In the case of a cluster with a very high memory usage, it is possible that a cluster will not restart correctly

MySQL Cluster storage nodes make extensive use of disk storage unless specifically configured not to, regardless of whether a cluster is using disk-based tables. It is important to ensure the following:

▸ There is sufficient storage available

▸ There is sufficient IO bandwidth for the storage node and the latency is not too high

To confirm the disk usage on Linux, use the command `df -h` as follows:

```
[root@node1 mysql-cluster]# df -h
Filesystem              Size  Used Avail Use% Mounted on
/dev/mapper/system-root
                        7.6G  2.0G  5.3G  28% /
/dev/xvda1               99M   21M   74M  22% /boot
tmpfs                   2.0G     0  2.0G   0% /dev/shm
/dev/mapper/system-ndb_data
                        2.0G   83M  1.8G   5% /var/lib/mysql-cluster
/dev/mapper/system-ndb_backups
                        2.0G   68M  1.9G   4% /var/lib/mysql-cluster/
BACKUPS
```

In this example, the cluster data directory and backup directory are on different logical volumes. This provides the following benefits:

▸ It is easy to see their usage (`5%` for data and `4%` for backups)

▸ Each volume is isolated from other partitions or logical volumes—it means that they are protected from, let's say, a logfile growing in the `logs` directory

To confirm the rate at which the kernel is writing to and reading from the disk, use the `vmstat` command:

```
[root@node1 ~]# vmstat 1
procs -----------memory---------- ---swap-- -----io---- --system-- --
---cpu------
 r  b   swpd   free   buff   cache   si   so   bi    bo    in   cs us
sy id wa st
 0  0      0 2978804 324784 353856    0    0    1   121    39   15  0
 0 100  0  0
 3  0      0 2978804 324784 353856    0    0    0     0   497  620  0
 0  99  0  1
 0  0      0 2978804 324784 353856    0    0    0   172   529  665  0
 0 100  0  0
```

The `bi` and `bo` columns represent the blocks read from a disk and blocks written to a disk, respectively. The first line can be ignored (it's the average since boot), and the number passed to the command, in this case, the refresh rate in seconds. By using a tool such as `bonnie` (refer to the *See also* section at the end of this recipe) to establish the potential of each block device, you can then check to see the maximum proportion of each block device currently being used.

At times of high stress, like during a hot backup, if the disk utilization is too high it is potentially possible that the storage node will start spending a lot of time in the `iowait` state—this will reduce performance and should be avoided. One way to avoid this is by using a separate block device (that is, disk or raid controller) for the `backups` mount point.

How it works...

Data within the MySQL Cluster is stored in two parts. In broader terms, the fixed part of a row (fields with a fixed width, such as `INT`, `CHAR`, and so on) is stored separately from variable length fields (for example, `VARCHAR`).

As data is stored in 32 KB pages, it is possible for variable-length data to become quite fragmented in cases where a cluster only has free space in existing pages that are available because data has been deleted.

Fragmentation is clearly bad. To reduce it, run the SQL command `optimize table` as follows:

```
mysql> optimize table City;
+-----------+----------+----------+----------+
| Table     | Op       | Msg_type | Msg_text |
```

```
+-------------+----------+----------+----------+
| world.City  | optimize | status   | OK       |
+-------------+----------+----------+----------+
```

1 row in set (0.02 sec)

To know more about fragmentation, check out the GPL tool `chkfrag` at
`http://www.severalnines.com/chkfrag/index.php`.

There's more...

It is also essential to monitor network utilization because latency will dramatically increase
as utilization gets close to 100 percent of either an individual network card or a network
device like a switch. If network latency increases by a very small amount, then its effect on
performance will be significant. This book will not discuss the many techniques for monitoring
the overall network health. However, we will see a tool called `iptraf` that is very useful inside
clusters for working out which node is interacting with which node and what proportion of
network resources it is using.

A command such as `iptraf -i eth0` will show the network utilization broken down by
connection, which can be extremely useful when trying to identify connections on a node
that are causing problems. The screenshot for the `iptraf` command is as follows:

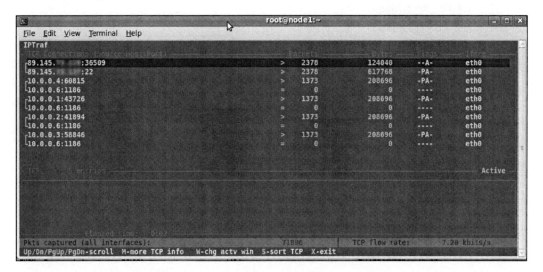

The previous screenshot shows the connections on the second interface (dedicated to cluster
traffic) for the first node in a four-storage node cluster. The connection that each node makes
with the others (10.0.0.2, 10.0.0.3, and 10.0.0.4 are other storage nodes) is obvious as well
as the not entirely obvious ports selected for each connection. There is also a connection to
the management node. The **Bytes** column gives a clear indication of which connections are
most utilized.

See also

Bonnie—disk reporting and benchmarking tool at:
`http://www.garloff.de/kurt/linux/bonnie/`

Adding storage nodes online

The ability to add a new node without any downtime is a relatively new feature of MySQL Cluster which dramatically improves long-term uptime in cases where the regular addition of nodes is required, for example, where data volume or query load is continually increasing.

Getting ready

In this recipe, we will show an example of how to add two nodes to an existing two-node cluster (while maintaining `NoOfReplicas=2` or two copies of each fragment of data).

The start point for this recipe is a cluster with two storage nodes and one management node running successfully with some data imported (such as the `world` database as covered in *Chapter 1*). Ensure that the `world` database has been imported as an `NDB` table.

How to do it...

Firstly, ensure that your cluster is fully running (that is, all management and storage nodes are running). The command to do this is as follows:

```
[root@node5 mysql-cluster]# ndb_mgm
ndb_mgm> show
Cluster Configuration
---------------------
[ndbd(NDB)]     2 node(s)
id=2    @10.0.0.1   (mysql-5.1.34 ndb-7.0.6, Nodegroup: 0, Master)
id=3    @10.0.0.2   (mysql-5.1.34 ndb-7.0.6, Nodegroup: 0)

[ndb_mgmd(MGM)]     1 node(s)
id=1    @10.0.0.5   (mysql-5.1.34 ndb-7.0.6)

[mysqld(API)]   4 node(s)
id=4    @10.0.0.1   (mysql-5.1.34 ndb-7.0.6)
id=5    @10.0.0.2   (mysql-5.1.34 ndb-7.0.6)
id=6 (not connected, accepting connect from any host)
id=7 (not connected, accepting connect from any host)
```

Edit the global cluster configuration file on the management node (`/usr/local/mysql-cluster/config.ini`) with your favorite text editor to add the new nodes as follows:

```
[ndb_mgmd]
Id=1
HostName=10.0.0.5
DataDir=/var/lib/mysql-cluster

[ndbd default]
DataDir=/var/lib/mysql-cluster

MaxNoOfConcurrentOperations = 150000
MaxNoOfAttributes = 10000
MaxNoOfOrderedIndexes=512
DataMemory=3G
IndexMemory=1G
NoOfReplicas=2

[ndbd]
HostName=10.0.0.1

[ndbd]
HostName=10.0.0.2

[ndbd]
HostName=10.0.0.3

[ndbd]
HostName=10.0.0.4

[mysqld]
HostName=10.0.0.1
[mysqld]
HostName=10.0.0.2
```

Now, perform a rolling cluster management node restart by copying the new `config.ini` file to all management nodes and executing the following commands on all management nodes as follows:

```
[root@node5 mysql-cluster]#  killall ndb_mgmd
[root@node5 mysql-cluster]# ndb_mgmd --initial --config-file=/usr/local/
mysql-cluster/config.ini
```

At this point, you should see the storage node status as follows:

```
[root@node5 mysql-cluster]# ndb_mgm
-- NDB Cluster -- Management Client --
ndb_mgm> show
Connected to Management Server at: 10.0.0.5:1186
Cluster Configuration
---------------------
[ndbd(NDB)]     4 node(s)
id=2    @10.0.0.1   (mysql-5.1.34 ndb-7.0.6, Nodegroup: 0, Master)
id=3    @10.0.0.2   (mysql-5.1.34 ndb-7.0.6, Nodegroup: 0)
id=4 (not connected, accepting connect from 10.0.0.3)
id=5 (not connected, accepting connect from 10.0.0.4)
```

Now, restart the active current nodes—in this case, the nodes with id 2 and 3 (10.0.0.1 and 10.0.0.2). This can be done with the management client command <nodeid> RESTART or by killing the ndbd process and restarting (there is no need for --initial):

```
ndb_mgm> 3 restart;
Node 3: Node shutdown initiated
Node 3: Node shutdown completed, restarting, no start.
Node 3 is being restarted
Node 3: Start initiated (version 7.0.6)
Node 3: Data usage decreased to 0%(0 32K pages of total 98304)
Node 3: Started (version 7.0.6)
ndb_mgm> 2 restart;
Node 2: Node shutdown initiated
Node 2: Node shutdown completed, restarting, no start.
Node 2 is being restarted
Node 2: Start initiated (version 7.0.6)
Node 2: Data usage decreased to 0%(0 32K pages of total 98304)
Node 2: Started (version 7.0.6)
```

At this point, the new nodes have still not joined the cluster. Now, run ndbd --initial on both these nodes (10.0.0.3 and 10.0.0.4) as follows:

```
[root@node1 ~]# ndbd
2009-08-18 20:39:32 [ndbd] INFO     -- Configuration fetched from
'10.0.0.5:1186', generation: 1
```

If you check the status of the `show` command in the management client, shortly after starting the new storage nodes, you will notice that the newly-started storage nodes move to a *started* state very rapidly (when compared to other nodes in the cluster). However, they are shown as belonging to "`no nodegroup`" as shown in the following output:

```
ndb_mgm> show
Cluster Configuration
--------------------
[ndbd(NDB)]     4 node(s)
id=2     @10.0.0.1   (mysql-5.1.34 ndb-7.0.6, Nodegroup: 0)
id=3     @10.0.0.2   (mysql-5.1.34 ndb-7.0.6, Nodegroup: 0, Master)
id=4     @10.0.0.3   (mysql-5.1.34 ndb-7.0.6, no nodegroup)
id=5     @10.0.0.4   (mysql-5.1.34 ndb-7.0.6, no nodegroup)
```

Now, we need to create a new `nodegroup` for these nodes. We have set `NoOfReplicas=2` in the `config.ini` file, so each `nodegroup` must contain two nodes. We use the `CREATE NODEGROUP <nodeID>,<nodeID>` command to add a nodegroup.

 If we had `NoOfReplicas=4`, we would pass four comma-separated `nodeID`s to this command.

Issue the following command to the management client, as follows:

```
ndb_mgm> CREATE NODEGROUP 4,5
Nodegroup 1 created
```

`Nodegroup 1` now exists. To see the information, use the `show` command as follows:

```
ndb_mgm> show
Cluster Configuration
--------------------
[ndbd(NDB)]     4 node(s)
id=2     @10.0.0.1   (mysql-5.1.34 ndb-7.0.6, Nodegroup: 0)
id=3     @10.0.0.2   (mysql-5.1.34 ndb-7.0.6, Nodegroup: 0, Master)
id=4     @10.0.0.3   (mysql-5.1.34 ndb-7.0.6, Nodegroup: 1)
id=5     @10.0.0.4   (mysql-5.1.34 ndb-7.0.6, Nodegroup: 1)
```

Congratulations! You have now added two new nodes to your cluster, which will be used by the cluster for new fragments of data. Look at the *There's more...* section of this recipe to see how you can get these nodes used right away and the *How it works...* section for a brief explanation of what is going on behind the scenes.

How it works...

After you have added the new nodes, it is possible to take a look at how a table is being stored within the cluster. If you used the `world` sample database imported in *Chapter 1*, then you will have a `City` table inside the `world` database. Running the `ndb_desc` binary as follows on a storage or management node shows you where the data is stored.

 The first parameter, after `-d`, is the database name and the second is the table name. If a `[mysql_cluster]` section is not defined in `/etc/my.cnf`, the management node IP address may be passed with `-c`.

```
[root@node1 ~]# ndb_desc -d world City -p
-- City --
Version: 1
Fragment type: 9
K Value: 6
Min load factor: 78
Max load factor: 80
Temporary table: no
Number of attributes: 5
Number of primary keys: 1
Length of frm data: 324
Row Checksum: 1
Row GCI: 1
SingleUserMode: 0
ForceVarPart: 1
FragmentCount: 2
TableStatus: Retrieved
-- Attributes --
ID Int PRIMARY KEY DISTRIBUTION KEY AT=FIXED ST=MEMORY AUTO_INCR
Name Char(35;latin1_swedish_ci) NOT NULL AT=FIXED ST=MEMORY
CountryCode Char(3;latin1_swedish_ci) NOT NULL AT=FIXED ST=MEMORY
District Char(20;latin1_swedish_ci) NOT NULL AT=FIXED ST=MEMORY
Population Int NOT NULL AT=FIXED ST=MEMORY
```

```
-- Indexes --
PRIMARY KEY(ID)  -  UniqueHashIndex
PRIMARY(ID)  -  OrderedIndex
```

```
-- Per partition info --
```

Partition memory	Row count	Commit count	Frag fixed memory	Frag varsized memory
0	2084	2084	196608	0
1	1995	1995	196608	0

```
NDBT_ProgramExit: 0 - OK
```

There are two partitions—one is active on one of the initial nodes, and the other is active on the second of the initial nodes. The new node is not being used at all.

If you import exactly the same table with the new cluster into a new database (four nodes), then you will notice that there are four partitions, and they are as follows:

```
-- Per partition info --
```

Partition memory	Row count	Commit count	Frag fixed memory	Frag varsized memory
0	1058	1058	98304	0
2	1026	1026	98304	0
1	1018	1018	98304	0
3	977	977	98304	0

Therefore, when we add a new `nodegroup`, it is important to reorganize the data in the existing nodes to ensure that it is spread out across the whole cluster and this does not happen automatically. New data, however, is automatically spread out across the whole cluster.

The process to reorganize data in the cluster to use all storage nodes is outlined in the next section.

There's more...

To reorganize the data within a cluster to use all new storage nodes, run the ALTER TABLE x REORGANIZE PARTITION query in a SQL node, substituting x for a table name. This command must be run once per table in the cluster.

 In NDB 7.0, the redistribution does not include unique indexes (only ordered indexes are redistributed) or BLOB table data. This is a limitation that is likely to be removed in later releases. If you have a large amount of these two forms of data, then it is likely to that you will notice unequal loadings on your new nodes even after this process. Newly inserted data will, however, be distributed across all nodes correctly.

This query can be executed on any storage node and should not affect the execution of other queries—although it will, of course, increase the load on the storage nodes involved:

```
[root@node1 ~]# mysql
Welcome to the MySQL monitor.  Commands end with ; or \g.
Your MySQL connection id is 5
Server version: 5.1.34-ndb-7.0.6-cluster-gpl MySQL Cluster Server (GPL)


Type 'help;' or '\h' for help. Type '\c' to clear the current input
statement.
mysql> use world;
Reading table information for completion of table and column names
You can turn off this feature to get a quicker startup with -A
Database changed
mysql> ALTER ONLINE TABLE City REORGANIZE PARTITION;
Query OK, 0 rows affected (9.04 sec)
Records: 0  Duplicates: 0  Warnings: 0
```

After this, run an OPTIMIZE TABLE query to reduce fragmentation significantly, as follows:

```
mysql> OPTIMIZE TABLE City;
+------------+----------+----------+----------+
| Table      | Op       | Msg_type | Msg_text |
+------------+----------+----------+----------+
| world.City | optimize | status   | OK       |
+------------+----------+----------+----------+
1 row in set (0.03 sec)
```

Now, use the `ndb_desc` command as follows—it shows four partitions and our data spread across all the new storage nodes:

```
[root@node1 ~]# ndb_desc -d world City -p
```

```
-- Per partition info --
```

Partition memory	Row count	Commit count	Frag fixed memory	Frag varsized memory
0	1058	4136	196608	0
3	977	977	98304	0
1	1018	3949	196608	0
2	1026	1026	98304	0

Replicating between MySQL Clusters

Replication is commonly used for single MySQL servers. In this recipe, we will explain how to use this technique with MySQL Cluster—replicating from one MySQL Cluster to another and replicating from a MySQL Cluster to a standalone server.

Getting ready

Replication is often used to provide a Disaster Recovery site, some distance away from a primary location, which is asynchronous (in contrast with the synchronous nature of the information flows within a MySQL Cluster). The asynchronous nature of replication means that the main cluster does not experience any performance degradation at the expense of a potential loss of a small amount of data in the event of the *master cluster* failing.

Replication involving a MySQL Cluster introduces the concept of **replication channels**. A **replication channel** is made up of two replication nodes. One of these nodes is in the source machine or cluster, and the other in the destination machine or cluster. It is good practice to have more than one replication channel for redundancy but only one channel may be active at a time.

The following diagram illustrates the replication channel:

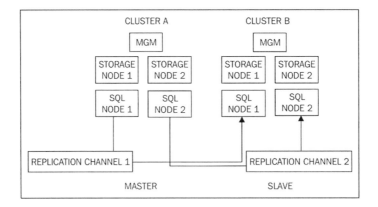

 Note that this diagram shows two replication channels. Currently, with Cluster Replication, only one channel can be active at any one time. It is good practice to have another channel set up almost ready to go, so that in the event one of the nodes involved in the primary channel fails, it is very quick to bring up a new channel.

In general, all replication nodes should be of the same, or very similar, MySQL version.

How to do it...

Firstly, prepare the two parts of the replication channel. In this example, we will replicate from one cluster to another. The source end of the channel is referred to as the master and the destination as the slave.

All `mysqld` processes (SQL nodes or standalone MySQL servers) involved as a replication agent (either as master or slave) must be configured to have a unique server-ID. Additionally, the master must also have some additional configuration in the `[mysqld]` section of `/etc/my.cnf`. Start by adding this to the master SQL node's `/etc/my.cnf` file as follows:

```
# Enable cluster replication
log-bin
binlog-format=ROW
server-id=3
```

Add the `server-id` parameter only to all MySQL servers that are acting as slave nodes, and restart all SQL nodes that have had `my.cnf` modified:

```
[root@node4 ~]# service mysql restart
Shutting down MySQL...                                    [  OK  ]
Starting MySQL.                                           [  OK  ]
```

On the master node, add an account for the slave node as follows:

```
[root@node1 ~]# mysql
Welcome to the MySQL monitor.  Commands end with ; or \g.
Your MySQL connection id is 2
Server version: 5.1.34-ndb-7.0.6-cluster-gpl-log MySQL Cluster Server
(GPL)


Type 'help;' or '\h' for help. Type '\c' to clear the current input
statement.


mysql> GRANT REPLICATION SLAVE ON *.* TO 'slave'@'10.0.0.3' IDENTIFIED BY
'password';
Query OK, 0 rows affected (0.00 sec)


mysql> FLUSH PRIVILEGES;
Query OK, 0 rows affected (0.00 sec)
```

On the master, run the command SHOW MASTER STATUS to establish the current logfile name and position as follows:

```
mysql> SHOW MASTER STATUS;
+-------------------+----------+---------------+------------------+
| File              | Position | Binlog_Do_DB  | Binlog_Ignore_DB |
+-------------------+----------+---------------+------------------+
| node1-bin.000001  |    318   |               |                  |
+-------------------+----------+---------------+------------------+
1 row in set (0.00 sec)
```

On the slave, issue a CHANGE MASTER TO command as follows to tell the slave where the master is, what user and password to use to log in, what logfile it is currently at, and what logfile position to start from:

```
mysql> CHANGE MASTER TO MASTER_HOST='10.0.0.1', MASTER_USER='slave',
MASTER_PASSWORD='password', MASTER_LOG_FILE='node1-bin.000001', MASTER_
LOG_POS=318
Query OK, 0 rows affected (0.00 sec)


mysql> start slave;
Query OK, 0 rows affected (0.00 sec)
```

Now, check the status, as follows, to ensure that the node has connected correctly:

```
mysql> SHOW SLAVE STATUS\G;
*************************** 1. row ***************************
               Slave_IO_State: Waiting for master to send event
                  Master_Host: 10.0.0.1
                  Master_User: slave
                  Master_Port: 3306
                Connect_Retry: 60
              Master_Log_File: node1-bin.000001
          Read_Master_Log_Pos: 318
               Relay_Log_File: node3-relay-bin.000002
                Relay_Log_Pos: 253
        Relay_Master_Log_File: node1-bin.000001
             Slave_IO_Running: Yes
            Slave_SQL_Running: Yes
              Replicate_Do_DB:
          Replicate_Ignore_DB:
           Replicate_Do_Table:
       Replicate_Ignore_Table:
      Replicate_Wild_Do_Table:
  Replicate_Wild_Ignore_Table:
                   Last_Errno: 0
                   Last_Error:
                 Skip_Counter: 0
          Exec_Master_Log_Pos: 318
              Relay_Log_Space: 409
              Until_Condition: None
               Until_Log_File:
                Until_Log_Pos: 0
            Master_SSL_Allowed: No
            Master_SSL_CA_File:
            Master_SSL_CA_Path:
               Master_SSL_Cert:
```

```
                Master_SSL_Cipher:
                   Master_SSL_Key:
            Seconds_Behind_Master: 0
Master_SSL_Verify_Server_Cert: No
                    Last_IO_Errno: 0
                    Last_IO_Error:
                   Last_SQL_Errno: 0
                   Last_SQL_Error:
                      Master_Bind:
1 row in set (0.00 sec)


ERROR:
No query specified
```

Replication is now working. To be sure, connect to the master node and run some SQL queries. In this example, we will create a database as follows:

```
[master node] mysql> CREATE DATABASE test1;
Query OK, 1 row affected (0.26 sec)
```

Ensure that this database is created on the slave node:

```
[slave node] mysql> SHOW DATABASES;
+--------------------+
| Database           |
+--------------------+
| information_schema |
| mysql              |
| test1              |
+--------------------+
8 rows in set (0.00 sec)
```

Now, from another node in the same cluster as the master, create another database as follows:

```
[node in master cluster] mysql> CREATE DATABASE test2;
Query OK, 1 row affected (0.26 sec)
```

And ensure that it appears on the slave node:

```
[slave_node] mysql> SHOW DATABASES;
+--------------------+
| Database           |
+--------------------+
| information_schema |
| mysql              |
| test1              |
| test2              |
+--------------------+
8 rows in set (0.00 sec)
```

If your slave node is also a member of a (different) cluster, then check that this new database has appeared on all nodes in that cluster too:

```
[node in slave cluster] mysql> SHOW DATABASES;
+--------------------+
| Database           |
+--------------------+
| information_schema |
| mysql              |
| test1              |
| test2              |
+--------------------+
8 rows in set (0.00 sec)
```

You can see that the new database has been correctly replicated to the slave cluster. It is good practice to test this replication channel with some real data, perhaps by importing the world dataset into the new database on the master cluster.

How it works...

MySQL Cluster replication is implemented by a dedicated thread—the *NDB binlog injector thread* that runs on each SQL node and produces a standard binary log (binlog), which a slave can connect to normally. This binlog injector thread ensures that all changes within the cluster that the SQL node is a member of are inserted into the binary log and not just the queries that were executed on that specific SQL node. This thread additionally ensures that these transactions are inserted in the correct serialization order. Therefore, the vast majority of the process is identical to the standard MySQL Replication.

If you only had a single SQL node in a cluster, then there would be no need for this thread, and standard MySQL Replication would work perfectly. Unfortunately, there is very little use in a MySQL Cluster with one SQL node.

There's more...

Cluster replication is an extremely powerful tool. In the following section, we will cover a couple of the most useful and more advanced techniques of cluster replication.

Replication between clusters with a backup channel

The previous recipe showed how to connect a MySQL Cluster to another MySQL server or another MySQL Cluster using a single replication channel. Obviously, this means that this replication channel has a single point of failure (if either of the two replication agents {machines} fail, the channel goes down).

If you are designing your disaster recovery plan to rely on MySQL Cluster replication, then you are likely to want more reliability than that. One simple thing that we can do is run multiple replication channels between two clusters. With this setup, in the event of a replication channel failing, a single command can be executed on one of the backup channel slaves to continue the channel.

 It is not currently possible to automate this process (at least, not without scripting it yourself). The idea is that with a second channel ready and good monitoring of the primary channel, you can quickly bring up the replication channel in the case of failure, which means significantly less time spent with the replication channel down.

How to do it...

Setting up this process is not vastly different, however, it is vital to ensure that both channels are not running at any one time, or the data at the slave site will become a mess and the replication will stop. To guarantee this, the first step is to add the following to the `mysqld` section of `/etc/my.cnf` on all slave MySQL Servers (of which there are likely to be two):

```
skip-slave-start
```

Once added, restart `mysqld`. This `my.cnf` parameter prevents the MySQL Server from automatically starting the slave process. You should start one of the channels (normally, whichever channel you decide will be your master) normally, while following the steps in the previous recipe.

To configure the second slave, follow the instructions in the previous recipe, but stop just prior to the CHANGE MASTER TO step on the second (backup) slave.

If you configure two replication channels simultaneously (that is, forget to stop the existing replication channel when testing the backup), you will end up with a broken setup. Do not proceed to run CHANGE MASTER TO on the backup slave unless the primary channel is not operating.

As soon as the primary communication channel fails, you should execute the following command on any one of the SQL nodes in your slave (destination) cluster and record the result:

```
[slave] mysql> SELECT MAX(epoch) FROM mysql.ndb_apply_status;
+----------------+
| MAX(epoch)     |
+----------------+
| 5952824672272  |
+----------------+
1 row in set (0.00 sec)
```

The previous highlighted number is the ID of the most recent global checkpoint, which is run every couple of seconds on all storage nodes in the master cluster and as a result, all the REDO logs are synced to disk. Checking this number on a SQL node in the slave cluster tells you what the last global checkpoint that made it to the slave cluster was.

You can run a similar command SELECT MAX(epoch) FROM mysql. ndb_binlog_index on any SQL node in the master (source) cluster to find out what the most recent global checkpoint on the master cluster is. Clearly, if your replication channel goes down, then these two numbers will diverge quickly.

Use this number (5952824672272 in our example) to find the correct logfile and position that you should connect to. You can do this by executing the following command on any SQL node in the master (source) cluster that you plan to make the new master, ensuring that you substitute the output of the previous command with the correct number as an epoch field as follows:

```
mysql> SELECT
    -> File,
    -> Position
    -> FROM mysql.ndb_binlog_index
    -> WHERE epoch > 5952824672272
    -> ORDER BY epoch ASC LIMIT 1;
```

```
+----------------------+----------+
| File                 | Position |
+----------------------+----------+
| ./node2-bin.000003   |   200998 |
+----------------------+----------+
1 row in set (0.00 sec)
```

If this returns NULL, firstly, ensure that there is some activity in your cluster since the failure (if you are using batched updates, then there should be 32 KB of updates or more) and secondly, ensure that there is no active replication channel between the nodes (that is, ensure the primary channel has really failed).

Using the filename and position mentioned previously, run the following command on the backup slave:

> It is critical that you run these commands on the correct node. The previous command, from which you get the filename and position, must be run on the new master (this is in the "source" cluster). The following command, which tells the new slave which master to connect to and its relevant position and filename, must be executed on the new slave (this is the "destination" cluster).
>
> While it is technically possible to connect the old slave to a new master or vice versa, this configuration is not recommended by MySQL and should not be used.

If all is okay, then the highlighted rows in the preceding output will show that the slave thread is running and waiting for the master to send an event.

```
[NEW slave] mysql> CHANGE MASTER TO MASTER_HOST='10.0.0.2', MASTER_
USER='slave', MASTER_PASSWORD='password', MASTER_LOG_FILE='node2-
bin.000003', MASTER_LOG_POS=200998;
Query OK, 0 rows affected (0.01 sec)


mysql> START SLAVE;
Query OK, 0 rows affected (0.00 sec)


mysql> show slave status\G;
*************************** 1. row ***************************
               Slave_IO_State: Waiting for master to send event
                  Master_Host: 10.0.0.2
                  Master_User: slave
                  Master_Port: 3306
```

```
[snip]
        Relay_Master_Log_File: node2-bin.000003
            Slave_IO_Running: Yes
           Slave_SQL_Running: Yes
             Replicate_Do_DB:
         Replicate_Ignore_DB:
          Replicate_Do_Table:
      Replicate_Ignore_Table:
[snip]
       Seconds_Behind_Master: 233
```

After a while, the `Seconds_Behind_Master` value should return to `0` (if the primary replication channel has been down for some time or if the master cluster has a very high write rate, then this may take some time).

There's more...

It is possible to increase the performance of MySQL Cluster replication by enabling batched updates. This can be accomplished by starting slave `mysqld` processes with the `slave-allow-batching` option (or add the `slave-allow-batching` option line to the `[mysqld]` section in `my.cnf`). This has the effect of applying updates in 32 KB batches rather than as soon as they are received, which generally results in lower CPU usage and higher throughput (particularly when the mean update size is low).

See also

To know more about *Replication Compatibility Between MySQL Versions* visit:
`http://dev.mysql.com/doc/refman/5.1/en/replication-compatibility.html`

User-defined partitioning

MySQL Cluster vertically partitions data, based on the primary key, unless you configure it otherwise. The main aim of user-defined partitioning is to increase performance by grouping data likely to be involved in common queries onto a single node, thus reducing network traffic between nodes while satisfying queries. In this recipe, we will show how to define our own partitioning functions.

If the NoOfReplicas in the global cluster configuration file (discussed in *Chapter 1*) is equal to the number of storage nodes, then each storage node contains a complete copy of the cluster data and there is no partitioning involved. Partitioning is only involved when there are more storage nodes than replicas.

Getting ready

Look at the City table in the world dataset; there are two integer fields (ID and Population). MySQL Cluster will choose ID as the default partitioning scheme as follows:

```
mysql> desc City;
+--------------+----------+------+-----+---------+----------------+
| Field        | Type     | Null | Key | Default | Extra          |
+--------------+----------+------+-----+---------+----------------+
| ID           | int(11)  | NO   | PRI | NULL    | auto_increment |
| Name         | char(35) | NO   |     |         |                |
| CountryCode  | char(3)  | NO   |     |         |                |
| District     | char(20) | NO   |     |         |                |
| Population   | int(11)  | NO   |     | 0       |                |
+--------------+----------+------+-----+---------+----------------+
5 rows in set (0.00 sec)
```

Therefore, a query that searches for a specific ID will use only one partition. In the following example, partition p3 is used:

```
mysql> explain partitions select * from City where ID=1;
+----+-------------+-------+------------+-------+---------------+---------
-+---------+-------+------+-------+
| id | select_type | table | partitions | type  | possible_keys | key |
key_len | ref   | rows | Extra |
+----+-------------+-------+------------+-------+---------------+---------
-+---------+-------+------+-------+
|  1 | SIMPLE      | City  | p3         | const | PRIMARY       | PRIMARY
| 4       | const |   1  |       |
+----+-------------+-------+------------+-------+---------------+---------
-+---------+-------+------+-------+
1 row in set (0.00 sec)
```

However, searching for a `Population` involves searching all partitions as follows:

```
mysql> explain partitions select * from City where Population=42;
+----+-------------+-------+-------------+------+---------------+------+---------+------+------+---------------------------------+
| id | select_type | table | partitions  | type | possible_keys | key  | key_len | ref  | rows | Extra                           |
+----+-------------+-------+-------------+------+---------------+------+---------+------+------+---------------------------------+
|  1 | SIMPLE      | City  | p0,p1,p2,p3 | ALL  | NULL          | NULL | NULL    | NULL | 4079 | Using where with pushed condition |
+----+-------------+-------+-------------+------+---------------+------+---------+------+------+---------------------------------+
1 row in set (0.01 sec)
```

The first thing to do when considering user-defined partitioning is to decide if you can improve on the default partitioning scheme. In this case, if your application makes a lot of queries against this table specifying the `City ID`, it is unlikely that you can improve performance with user-defined partitioning. However, in case it makes a lot of queries by the `Population` and `ID` fields, it is likely that you can improve performance by switching the partitioning function from a hash of the primary key to a hash of the primary key and the `Population` field.

How to do it...

In this example, we are going to add the field `Population` to the partitioning function used by MySQL Cluster.

 We will add this field to the primary key rather than solely using this field. This is because the `City` table has an auto-increment field on the `ID` field, and in MySQL Cluster, an auto-increment field must be part of the primary key.

Firstly, modify the primary key in the table to add the field that we will use to partition the table by:

```
mysql> ALTER TABLE City DROP PRIMARY KEY, ADD PRIMARY KEY(ID,
Population);
Query OK, 4079 rows affected (2.61 sec)
Records: 4079  Duplicates: 0  Warnings: 0
```

Now, tell MySQL Cluster to use the `Population` field as a partitioning function as follows:

```
mysql> ALTER TABLE City partition by key (Population);
Query OK, 4079 rows affected (2.84 sec)
Records: 4079  Duplicates: 0  Warnings: 0
```

Now, verify that queries executed against this table only use one partition as follows:

```
mysql> explain partitions select * from City where Population=42;
+----+-------------+-------+------------+------+---------------+------+--
-------+------+------+------------------------------------+
| id | select_type | table | partitions | type | possible_keys | key |
key_len | ref  | rows | Extra                              |
+----+-------------+-------+------------+------+---------------+------+--
-------+------+------+------------------------------------+
|  1 | SIMPLE      | City  | p3         | ALL  | NULL          | NULL |
NULL    | NULL | 4079 | Using where with pushed condition  |
+----+-------------+-------+------------+------+---------------+------+--
-------+------+------+------------------------------------+
1 row in set (0.01 sec)
```

Now, notice that queries against the old partitioning function, `ID`, use all partitions as follows:

```
mysql> explain partitions select * from City where ID=1;
+----+-------------+-------+-------------+------+---------------+--------
-+---------+-------+------+-------+
| id | select_type | table | partitions  | type | possible_keys | key
| key_len | ref   | rows | Extra |
+----+-------------+-------+-------------+------+---------------+--------
-+---------+-------+------+-------+
|  1 | SIMPLE      | City  | p0,p1,p2,p3 | ref  | PRIMARY       | PRIMARY
| 4       | const |   10 |       |
+----+-------------+-------+-------------+------+---------------+--------
-+---------+-------+------+-------+
1 row in set (0.00 sec)
```

Congratulations! You have now set up user-defined partitioning. Now, benchmark your application to see if you have gained an increase in performance.

There's more...

User-defined partitioning can be particularly useful where you have multiple tables and a join. For example, if you had a table of Areas within Cities consisting of an ID field (primary key, auto increment, and default partitioning field) and then a City ID, you would likely find an enormous number of queries that select all of the locations within a certain city and also select the relevant city row. It would therefore make sense to keep:

▸ all of the rows with the same City value inside the Areas table together on one node

▸ each of these groups of City values inside the Areas table on the same node as the relevant City row in the City table

This can be achieved by configuring both tables to use the City field as a partitioning function, as described earlier in the Population field.

Disk-based tables

It is possible to configure the data nodes in a MySQL Cluster to store most of their data on disk rather than in RAM. This can be useful where the amount of data to be stored is impossible to store in RAM (for example, due to financial constraints). However, disk-based tables clearly have significantly reduced performance as compared to memory tables.

 Disk-based tables still store columns with indexes in RAM. Only columns without indexes are stored on disk. This can result in a large RAM requirement even for disk-based tables.

Getting ready

To configure disk-based tables, data nodes should have spare space on a high performance block device.

To configure disk-based tables, we must configure each data node with a set of two files as follows:

▸ TABLESPACES—disk-based tables store their data in TABLESPACES, which are made up of one or more data files

▸ Logfile groups—disk-based tables store their ndb data in a logfile group made up of one or more undo logfiles

Disk-based tables do not support variable length fields—these fields are stored as fixed-width fields (for example, VARCHAR(100) is stored as CHAR(100). This means that a disk-based NDB table that uses lots of variable-width fields will take up significantly more space than it would as compared to either an NDB in-memory table or a non-clustered storage engine format.

How to do it...

Firstly, check that you have sufficient storage on your storage nodes using a command such as df as follows:

```
[root@node1 ~]# df -h  | grep mysql-cluster
                   2.0G  165M  1.8G   9% /var/lib/mysql-cluster
                   2.0G   68M  1.9G   4% /var/lib/mysql-cluster/
BACKUPS
```

In this example, there is 1.8G space available in the Data Directory. For this example, using a small amount of test data, this is sufficient.

Create a log file and undo file:

```
mysql> CREATE LOGFILE GROUP world_log ADD UNDOFILE 'world_undo.dat'
INITIAL_SIZE=200M ENGINE=NDBCLUSTER;
Query OK, 0 rows affected (4.99 sec)
```

These files are created, by default, in the subfolder ndb_nodeid_fs in DataDir on each storage node. However, it is possible to pass an absolute path to force the undo file (previous one) and data file (next step) to be created on another filesystem or use symbolic links. You can also specify an UNDO log size. See the *There's more... section* for an example.

Now, create a TABLESPACE using the CREATE TABLESPACE SQL command (you can execute this on any SQL node in the cluster):

```
mysql>  CREATE TABLESPACE world_ts ADD DATAFILE 'world_data.dat' USE
LOGFILE GROUP world_log INITIAL_SIZE=500M ENGINE=NDBCLUSTER;
Query OK, 0 rows affected (8.80 sec)
```

Now, you can create disk-based tables as follows:

```
mysql> CREATE TABLE `City` (
    ->    `ID` int(11) NOT NULL auto_increment,
    ->    `Name` char(35) NOT NULL default '',
    ->    `CountryCode` char(3) NOT NULL default '',
    ->    `District` char(20) NOT NULL default '',
    ->    `Population` int(11) NOT NULL default '0',
    ->    PRIMARY KEY  (`ID`)
    -> )
    -> TABLESPACE world_ts STORAGE DISK
    -> ENGINE NDBCLUSTER;
Query OK, 0 rows affected (2.06 sec)
```

Note that in this example, the ID field will still be stored in memory (due to the primary key).

How it works...

Disk-based tables are stored in fixed-width fields with 4-byte aligned. You can view the files (both the `tablespace` and `logfile` group): If you want to view the logfiles, then the following query shows the active logfiles and their parameters:

```
mysql> SELECT LOGFILE_GROUP_NAME, LOGFILE_GROUP_NUMBER, EXTRA FROM
INFORMATION_SCHEMA.FILES;
+--------------------+----------------------+-----------------------------------------+
| LOGFILE_GROUP_NAME | LOGFILE_GROUP_NUMBER | EXTRA                                   |
+--------------------+----------------------+-----------------------------------------+
| world_log          |                   25 | CLUSTER_NODE=2;UNDO_BUFFER_SIZE=8388608 |
| world_log          |                   25 | CLUSTER_NODE=3;UNDO_BUFFER_SIZE=8388608 |
| world_log          |                   25 | UNDO_BUFFER_SIZE=8388608                |
+--------------------+----------------------+-----------------------------------------+
3 rows in set (0.00 sec)
```

If you want to view the data files, then execute the following query that shows you each data file, its size, and its free capacity:

```
mysql> SELECT
    -> FILE_NAME,
    -> (TOTAL_EXTENTS * EXTENT_SIZE)/(1024*1024) AS 'Total MB',
    -> (FREE_EXTENTS * EXTENT_SIZE)/(1024*1024) AS 'Free MB',
    -> EXTRA
    -> FROM
    -> INFORMATION_SCHEMA.FILES;
+-----------------+----------+----------+-----------------------------------
--------+
| FILE_NAME       | Total MB | Free MB  | EXTRA
|
+-----------------+----------+----------+-----------------------------------
--------+
| world_undo.dat  | 200.0000 |     NULL | CLUSTER_NODE=2;UNDO_BUFFER_
SIZE=8388608  |
| world_undo.dat  | 200.0000 |     NULL | CLUSTER_NODE=3;UNDO_BUFFER_
SIZE=8388608  |
| NULL            |     NULL | 199.8711 | UNDO_BUFFER_SIZE=8388608
|
+-----------------+----------+----------+-----------------------------------
--------+
3 rows in set (0.00 sec)
```

This shows that 199.87 MB is unused in this data file, and the file exists on two storage nodes. Note that all data on disk is stored in fixed-width columns, 4-byte aligned. This can result in significantly larger data files than you may expect. You can estimate the disk storage required using the methods in the *Calculating DataMemory and IndexMemory* recipe later in this chapter.

There's more...

The CREATE LOGFILE GROUP command can have a custom UNDO buffer size passed to it. A larger UNDO_BUFFER_SIZE will result in higher performance, but the parameter is limited by the amount of system memory available (that is free).

To use this command, add the UNDO_BUFFER_SIZE parameter to the command:

```
mysql> CREATE LOGFILE GROUP world_log UNDO_BUFFER_SIZE 200M ADD UNDOFILE
'world_undo.dat' INITIAL_SIZE=200M ENGINE=NDBCLUSTER;
Query OK, 0 rows affected (4.99 sec)
```

An existing data file may be removed by executing an ALTER TABLESPACE DROP DATAFILE command as follows:

```
mysql> ALTER TABLESPACE world_ts DROP DATAFILE 'world_data.dat'
ENGINE=NDBCLUSTER;

Query OK, 0 rows affected (0.47 sec)
```

To delete a `tablespace`, use the DROP TABLESPACE statement:

```
mysql> DROP TABLESPACE world_ts ENGINE=NDBCLUSTER;

Query OK, 0 rows affected (0.51 sec)
```

In the event that the `tablespace` is still used, you will get a slightly cryptic error. Before dropping a `tablespace`, you must remove any data files associated with it.

```
mysql> DROP TABLESPACE world_ts ENGINE=NDBCLUSTER;

ERROR 1529 (HY000): Failed to drop TABLESPACE

mysql> SHOW WARNINGS;

+-------+------+-----------------------------------------------------
--------+
| Level | Code | Message
|
+-------+------+-----------------------------------------------------
--------+
| Error | 1296 | Got error 768 'Cant drop filegroup, filegroup is used'
from NDB |
| Error | 1529 | Failed to drop TABLESPACE
|
+-------+------+-----------------------------------------------------
--------+

2 rows in set (0.00 sec)
```

The performance of a MySQL Cluster that uses disk data storage can be improved significantly by placing the `tablespace` and `logfile` group on separate block devices. One way to do this is to pass absolute paths to the commands that create these files, while another is symbolic links in the data directory.

Using symbolic links create the following two symbolic links on each storage node, assuming that you have `disk2` and `disk3` mounted in `/mnt/`, substituting `<NODEID>` for the correct value as follows:

```
[root@node1 mysql-cluster]# ln -s /mnt/disk1 /var/lib/mysql-cluster/ndb_
<NODEID>_fs/logs

[root@node1 mysql-cluster]# ln -s /mnt/disk2 /var/lib/mysql-cluster/ndb_
<NODEID>_fs/data
```

Now, create the `logfile` group and `tablespace` inside these directories as follows:

```
mysql> CREATE LOGFILE GROUP world_log ADD UNDOFILE 'logs/world_undo.dat'
INITIAL_SIZE=200M ENGINE=NDBCLUSTER;

Query OK, 0 rows affected (4.99 sec)

mysql> CREATE TABLESPACE world_ts ADD DATAFILE 'data/world_data.dat' USE
LOGFILE GROUP world_log INITIAL_SIZE=500M ENGINE=NDBCLUSTER;

Query OK, 0 rows affected (8.80 sec)
```

You should note that performance is significantly improved as data files I/O operations will be on a different block device to the logs. If given the choice of different specification block devices, it is generally wiser to give the highest performance to the device hosting the UNDO log.

Calculating DataMemory and IndexMemory

Before a migration to a MySQL Cluster, it is likely that you will want to be sure that the resources available are sufficient to handle the proposed cluster. Generally, MySQL Clusters are more memory intensive than anything else, and this recipe explains how you can estimate your memory usage in advance.

The script that is used in this recipe, `ndb_size.pl`, is provided by MySQL Cluster in a cluster binary. In the _See also_ section, an alternative and more accurate tool is mentioned. `ndb_size.pl` is excellent for estimates, but it is worth remembering that it is only an estimate based on, sometimes inaccurate, assumptions.

Getting ready

This recipe demonstrates how to estimate, from a table scheme or an existing non-clustered table, the memory-usage of that table in the NDB (MySQL Cluster) storage engine. We will use a script, `ndb_size.pl`, provided in the `MySQL-Cluster-gpl-tools` package that is installed as part of the storage node installation in the recipe in _Chapter 1_.

To use this script, you will require the following:

- A working installation of Perl.
- The Perl `DBI` module (this can be installed with `yum install perl-DBI`, if the EPEL yum repository is installed, see _Appendix A, Base Installation_).
- The Perl `DBD::MySQL` module. This does exist in the EPEL repository, but will not install if you have installed the cluster specific `mysql` RPM. See _There's more..._ for instructions on how to install this on a clean install of RHEL5 with the storage node RPMs installed, as described in _Chapter 1_.

▶ The `perl-Class-MethodMaker` package (`yum install perl-Class-MethodMaker`).

▶ The tables that you wish to examine that are imported into a MySQL server to which you have access (this can be done using any storage engine).

▶ A running MySQL server. The server instance does not require to provide support for MySQL Cluster as we are running this script on `MyISAM` and `InnoDB` tables before they have been converted.

How to do it...

In this example, we will run `ndb_size.pl` against the `world` database and go through the `global` output and the output for the `City` table.

Firstly, run the script with a username and password as follows:

```
[root@node1 ~]# ndb_size.pl world --user=root --password=secret --format=text
```

The script then confirms that it is running for the `world` database on the local host and includes information for MySQL Cluster 4.1, 5, and 5.1.

MySQL Cluster differs enormously between versions in the amount of `DataMemory` and `IndexMemory` used (in general, getting significantly more efficient with each release). In this recipe, we will only look at the output for version 5.1. It is the closest to MySQL Cluster version 7, which is the current version.

```
ndb_size.pl report for database: 'world' (3 tables)
----------------------------------------------------
Connected to: DBI:mysql:host=localhost

Including information for versions: 4.1, 5.0, 5.1
```

There is now some output for some other tables (if you imported the whole `world` dataset), which is skipped as it is identical to the output for the `City` table.

The first part of the output of the `City` table shows the `DataMemory` required for each column (showing the number of bytes per row), ending with a summary of the memory requirement for both fixed-and variable-width columns (there are no variable-width columns in this table):

```
world.City
----------

DataMemory for Columns (* means varsized DataMemory):
              Column Name                    Type    Varsized    Key
4.1         5.0         5.1
                        ID               int(11)                 PRI
```

4	4	4		
			District	char(20)
20	20	20		
			Name	char(35)
36	36	36		
			CountryCode	char(3)
4	4	4		
			Population	int(11)
4	4	4		
--	--	--		
Fixed Size Columns DM/Row				
68	**68**	**68**		
	Varsize Columns DM/Row			
0	0	0		

So, this table has approximately **68** bytes `DataMemory` requirement per row. The next part of the output shows how much `DataMemory` is required for indexes. In this case, there is none because the only index is a primary key (which is stored in `IndexMemory`) as follows:

```
DataMemory for Indexes:
                Index Name                   Type        4.1         5.0
5.1
                   PRIMARY                  BTREE        N/A         N/
A           N/A

-                   --
            Total Index DM/Row                            0           0
0
```

The next part of the output shows the `IndexMemory` requirement per index as follows:

```
IndexMemory for Indexes:
                Index Name      4.1         5.0         5.1
                   PRIMARY       29          16          16
                                --          --          --
            Indexes IM/Row       29          16          16
```

Therefore, we can see that we require **16** bytes of `IndexMemory` per row.

The per-table output of `ndb_size.pl` concludes with a summary of total memory usage, and we can see the overall `IndexMemory` and `DataMemory` requirement for this table under MySQL Cluster 5.1:

```
Summary (for THIS table):
                                4.1         5.0         5.1
            Fixed Overhead DM/Row        12          12          16
                 NULL Bytes/Row           0           0           0
```

```
           DataMemory/Row          80          80          84   (Includes
overhead, bitmap and indexes)

   Varsize Overhead DM/Row          0           0           8
   Varsize NULL Bytes/Row           0           0           0
      Avg Varside DM/Row            0           0           0

                No. Rows         4079        4079        4079

        Rows/32kb DM Page          408         408         388
 Fixedsize DataMemory (KB)         320         320         352

Rows/32kb Varsize DM Page           0           0           0
    Varsize DataMemory (KB)         0           0           0

        Rows/8kb IM Page          282         512         512
          IndexMemory (KB)        120          64          64
```

The final part of the output aggregates all of the tables examined by the scripts and produces configuration parameter recommendations:

```
Parameter Minimum Requirements
------------------------------
* indicates greater than default

              Parameter        Default            4.1
5.0             5.1
           DataMemory (KB)        81920            480
480             512
        NoOfOrderedIndexes         128              3
3               3
             NoOfTables            128              3
3               3
           IndexMemory (KB)      18432            192
88              88
     NoOfUniqueHashIndexes         64              0
0               0
           NoOfAttributes        1000             24
24              24
             NoOfTriggers         768             15
15              15
```

Remember that:

> ▶ These parameters are only estimates
>
> ▶ It is a very bad idea to run a cluster close to its limits on any of these parameters
>
> ▶ This output does not include any temporary tables that may be created
>
> ▶ However, at the same time, this output is useful to get a low end estimate of usage

There's more...

In this section, we explain in greater detail how to install the DBD::mysql Perl module and a couple of other options that can be passed to ndb_size.pl. The easiest way to install DBD::mysql is from MCPAN with these commands:

1. Firstly, install a compiler as follows:

   ```
   [root@node1 ~]# yum install gcc
   ```

2. Now, download the MySQL Cluster devel package as follows:

   ```
   [root@node1 ~]# wget http://dev.mysql.com/get/Downloads/MySQL-
   Cluster-7.0/MySQL-Cluster-gpl-devel-7.0.6-0.rhel5.x86_64.rpm/from/
   http://mirrors.dedipower.com/www.mysql.com/
   ```

3. Install the RPM as follows:

   ```
   [root@node1 ~]# rpm -ivh MySQL-Cluster-gpl-devel-7.0.6-0.rhel5.
   x86_64.rpm
   ```

4. Create a database and add a user for the DBD::mysql module to use to test as follows:

   ```
   mysql> create database test;
   Query OK, 1 row affected (0.21 sec)
   mysql> grant all privileges on test.* to 'root'@'localhost'
   identified by 's3kr1t';
   Query OK, 0 rows affected (0.00 sec)
   ```

5. Now, install the DBD::mysql Perl module from CPAN as follows:

   ```
   [root@node1 ~]# perl -MCPAN -e 'install DBD::mysql'
   ```

   If this is the first time you have run this command, then you will have to first answer some questions (defaults are fine) and select your location to choose a mirror.

The following additional options can be passed to `ndb_size.pl`:

Option	Explanation
`--database=<db name>`	`ALL` may be specified to examine all databases
`--hostname=<host>:<port>`	Designate a specific host and port (defaults to `localhost` on port `3306`)
`--format={html,text}`	Create either text or HTML output
`--excludetables=`	Comma-separated list of table names to skip
`--excludedbs=`	Comma-separated list of database names to skip

See also

`sizer—http://www.severalnines.com/sizer/`. `sizer` is more accurate than `ndb_size.pl` because `sizer` calculates:

- ▸ Correct record overheads
- ▸ Cost for unique indexes
- ▸ Averages storage costs for VAR* columns (user specified by either estimation (loadfactor) or actual data)
- ▸ Cost for BLOB / TEXT

`sizer` is marginally more complicated to use and involves a couple of steps, but can sometimes be useful if accuracy is vital.

4

MySQL Cluster Troubleshooting

In this chapter, we will cover:

- Single storage node failure
- Multiple storage node failures
- Storage node partitioning and arbitration
- Debugging MySQL Clusters
- Seeking help
- NIC teaming with MySQL Cluster

Introduction

In this chapter, we will discuss some of the troubleshooting aspects of MySQL Cluster. The first recipe *Single storage node failure* explains how MySQL Clusters manage to survive the failure of individual nodes without any significant interruption to the overall operation of the cluster and without any risk of data becoming inconsistent across the cluster. The second recipe *Multiple storage node failures* covers what happens in a MySQL Cluster if multiple storage nodes are to fail, which can result in either no downtime or a total shutdown depending on the event and the configuration. The third recipe *Storage node partitioning and arbitration* explores what is going on inside the cluster to maintain high availability and consistency. The fourth recipe provides some steps to carry out when something isn't working perfectly in your cluster—both to help find the problem and to document the problem. *Seeking help* provides advice on what to do when you are unable to fix a problem. The final recipe *NIC teaming with MySQL Cluster* illustrates a practical example of a best-practice setup for MySQL Cluster, providing redundancy at the network level (that is, removing a single switch as a single point of failure).

Single storage node failure

MySQL Clusters can survive the failure of any single storage node as long as `NoOfReplicas` is greater than 1 (and there is almost no point in a cluster if it is not). In this recipe, we will demonstrate how a MySQL Cluster detects and handles the failure of a single storage node (where all other nodes are working). In the next recipe, we will cover how a cluster copes with multiple storage node failures.

Getting ready

MySQL Cluster has an algorithm for high availability with two, slightly competing, aims:

  ▸ Prevent database inconsistencies in the event of a *split-brain*

  ▸ Keep the database up and running (that is, to keep the database users happy)

In every MySQL Cluster, there are many copies of each fragment of data (using `NoOfReplicas`). If we consider the common case where `NoOfReplicas` equals to 2, then each fragment of data is stored on two nodes, and therefore, each nodegroup consists of two nodes with identical data.

In the next section, we will demonstrate the failure of a single node with a practical exercise. This lab consists of a cluster of four storage nodes and a management node. For testing, we are running a SQL node on all four storage nodes. In our recipe (and the configuration examples within), nodes 1 to 5 have private IP addresses of 10.0.0.x, where x is their node number between 1 and 5.

How to do it...

To demonstrate the failure of a single node in a lab, we start with our simple four storage node cluster fully running, as shown with the following output from `ndb_mgm -e SHOW`:

```
[root@node5 mysql-cluster]# ndb_mgm -e show
Connected to Management Server at: 10.0.0.5:1186
Cluster Configuration
---------------------
[ndbd(NDB)]     4 node(s)
id=1    @10.0.0.1  (mysql-5.1.39 ndb-7.0.9, Nodegroup: 0, Master)
id=2    @10.0.0.2  (mysql-5.1.39 ndb-7.0.9, Nodegroup: 0)
id=3    @10.0.0.3  (mysql-5.1.39 ndb-7.0.9, Nodegroup: 1)
id=4    @10.0.0.4  (mysql-5.1.39 ndb-7.0.9, Nodegroup: 1)
```

```
[ndb_mgmd(MGM)]       1 node(s)
id=10     @10.0.0.5   (mysql-5.1.39 ndb-7.0.9)


[mysqld(API)]     4 node(s)
id=11     @10.0.0.1   (mysql-5.1.39 ndb-7.0.9)
id=12     @10.0.0.2   (mysql-5.1.39 ndb-7.0.9)
id=13     @10.0.0.3   (mysql-5.1.39 ndb-7.0.9)
id=14     @10.0.0.4   (mysql-5.1.39 ndb-7.0.9)
```

To simulate a single node failing, while keeping access to the logs for that node, we will use the iptables command to block all traffic over the private network. You could also unplug network cables, disable the interface (ifdown eth1), or kill the power to the nodes—use whichever method is the easiest. We use iptables because it is the easiest to reverse, if you can still connect via SSH to the public interface, and thus most convenient for a lab environment.

Open a SSH connection to the public IP address on the node that you are going to kill. Clear any existing iptables rules, and check that there are no rules enabled:

```
[root@node3 ~]# iptables -F
[root@node3 ~]# iptables -L
```

Now, open a SSH or terminal session to another node in the same nodegroup, another node in a different nodegroup, and the management node.

For the three storage nodes that you now have sessions open to, tail the ndb_x_out.log file in the MySQL Cluster DataDir (likely /var/lib/mysql-cluster). Use the -f flag to update the output in your terminal window. On the management node, tail the ndb_x_cluster.log in the management node DataDir. For example, the following is the correct command to run on the management node in our example:

```
[root@node5 mysql-cluster]# tail -f /var/lib/mysql-cluster/ndb_10_
cluster.log
```

Now, assuming that eth1 is the dedicated private network used for cluster traffic (and cluster traffic only), block out all inbound and outbound traffic for the interface on the node that you wish to simulate killing:

```
[root@node3 ~]# iptables -A INPUT -i eth1 -j DROP
[root@node3 ~]# iptables -A OUTPUT -o eth1 -j DROP
```

This will only work if you have followed the strong recommendation to have a private network dedicated to cluster traffic, and are able to connect to the nodes in some other way—for example, using SSH with a different interface. If this is really impossible, use some sort of remote management card or virtual machine console. If you only have a single interface in your test nodes, then you can run an iptables command that blocks all traffic except for your SSH traffic.

You will notice that the following occurs:

On the node that you have isolated from the network, logs such as these will appear in the local log (for example /var/lib/mysql-cluster/ndb_3_out.log on node3):

```
2010-02-01 20:53:22 [ndbd] INFO      -- findNeighbours from: 4419 old
(left: 1 right: 2) new (2 2)

2010-02-01 20:53:29 [ndbd] INFO      -- Arbitrator decided to shutdown
this node
2010-02-01 20:53:29 [ndbd] INFO      -- QMGR (Line: 5532) 0x0000000e
2010-02-01 20:53:29 [ndbd] INFO      -- Error handler shutting down
system
2010-02-01 20:53:29 [ndbd] INFO      -- Error handler shutdown
completed - exiting
2010-02-01 20:53:29 [ndbd] ALERT     -- Node 3: Forced node shutdown
completed. Caused by error 2305: 'Node lost connection to other nodes
and cannot form a unpartitioned cluster, please investigate if there
are error(s) on other node(s)(Arbitration error). Temporary error,
restart node'.
```

This tells you that the node is unable to see its neighbors, and that after seven seconds the arbitrator decided to shut down the node. In fact, what happened is that this node could not contact the arbitrator (the management node) or any of its neighbors. In this case, the decision of the arbitrator is simple—it will always decide to shut down the node.

When we look at the local log on other nodes in the same nodegroup (for example /var/lib/mysql-cluster/ndb_4_out.log on node4), we see that the node detects the failure and makes the buckets (holding fragments of data which it was holding as backups in case node3 fails) active as follows:

```
2010-02-01 20:53:10 [ndbd] INFO      -- findNeighbours from: 4419 old
(left: 1 right: 3) new (1 2)
start_resend(0, empty bucket (747/15 747/14) -> active
```

By looking at the `local` log on another node in a different nodegroup (for example /var/lib/mysql-cluster/ndb_2_out.log on node2), we see that the node notices that the nodes have failed, but it takes no action on its own:

```
2010-02-01 20:53:02 [ndbd] INFO     -- findNeighbours from: 4419 old
(left: 3 right: 1) new (4 1)
```

Finally, look at the most important log—the `cluster` log (for example /var/lib/mysql-cluster/ndb_10_cluster.log on node5). This log shows that nodes 3 and 13 miss heartbeats. Remember that there is a SQL node on each storage node; in our example, the SQL node ID is 13 and the storage node ID is 3. Notice that each warning is printed three times—this is because the management node is interested in the availability of node3 not only from its own perspective, but also from the view of the other nodes that remain alive. The log is shown as follows:

```
2010-02-01 20:53:02 [MgmtSrvr] WARNING  -- Node 2: Node 3 missed
heartbeat 2
2010-02-01 20:53:03 [MgmtSrvr] WARNING  -- Node 1: Node 3 missed
heartbeat 2
2010-02-01 20:53:03 [MgmtSrvr] WARNING  -- Node 4: Node 3 missed
heartbeat 2
```

This output repeats for `node3` and for heartbeats 3 and 4. After four missed heartbeats, the following output appears:

```
2010-02-01 20:53:06 [MgmtSrvr] WARNING  -- Node 2: Node 3 missed
heartbeat 4
2010-02-01 20:53:06 [MgmtSrvr] ALERT    -- Node 2: Node 3 declared
dead due to missed heartbeat
2010-02-01 20:53:06 [MgmtSrvr] INFO     -- Node 2: Communication to
Node 3 closed
2010-02-01 20:53:06 [MgmtSrvr] INFO     -- Node 4: Communication to
Node 3 closed
2010-02-01 20:53:06 [MgmtSrvr] INFO     -- Node 1: Communication to
Node 3 closed
```

At this point, you can see that each of the surviving nodes in turn declares the failed node dead and ends communication.

As you can see, the failure of one node is simple—the other nodes realize that the node has failed as it missed heartbeats and declare it dead and break off communication with it. The other nodes in the same nodegroup promote the backup fragments that they have to activate, thus ensuring that the cluster remains up. If the `ndbd` process is still running on the storage node that has failed (because someone has blocked network traffic rather than because the server has exploded), then it will shut itself down.

How it works...

To establish which nodes have failed, each storage and management node maintains a local record of the status of every other node by making periodical heartbeat requests to all other nodes in a cluster. The heartbeat interval is specified by the `config.ini` file's parameter `HeartbeatIntervalDbDb` (for storage nodes heart beating other storage nodes), and `HeartbeatIntervalDbApi` (for storage nodes heart beating SQL nodes). These parameters should be identical on all nodes, and are set to a default value of 1500 milliseconds (1.5 seconds). They set both how often a node sends a heartbeat to other nodes as well as how often a node expects to receive a heartbeat from the other nodes in the cluster.

 If a node conducts a successful operation with another node, for example in the case of a storage node sends part of a query to another storage node to satisfy a query and receives an answer, then this takes the place of the next heartbeat.

The principle of arbitration in MySQL Cluster is simple. Each node sends heartbeats as often as configured to and expects to receive a heartbeat packet from all nodes in the cluster. If any node does not receive three consecutive heartbeat packets from any other node in the cluster, it considers that node dead and kicks it out. It communicates this new status to other nodes, reporting that this node is now dead (thus the management node not only knows the state of each node from its own point of view, but also from the point of view of every other node).

There's more...

If the storage node does not actually fail, but is simply isolated from the other storage nodes (perhaps due to a network failure), then it is obviously possible that a SQL node, which was stuck in the same partition, would continue to modify the data on the storage node. This would be extremely bad, as the cluster data would *fork* and be impossible to reconcile.

This process is covered in the recipe *Storage node partitioning and arbitration*. For the purpose of this recipe, be aware that if this did happen, the storage node that was isolated would shut itself down to prevent the data forking.

Multiple storage node failures

MySQL Clusters are designed to survive node failures, regardless of exactly how they occur. In the case of multiple node failures, working out what can happen can be a little more complicated. There are several options for multiple node failures as follows:

- One node can fail in multiple nodegroups, but one node remains per nodegroup (cluster will remain working).

- All the nodes in a single nodegroup can fail (in such a case, the cluster will be shut down).

- One node per nodegroup can split into one group. Another node can split into another group, which are then partitioned from each other. This occurs most often when some nodes are connected to one network switch, the others are connected to a different switch, and the connections between the switches fail. This can cause a *split-brain* problem, requiring an arbitrator to shut down some nodes to ensure only one group is left alive.

Getting ready

In this recipe, we will cover how MySQL Cluster handles the failure of nodes and how it ensures that a split-brain never occurs. We are using the same lab environment as in the previous recipe for examples.

How to do it...

In this section, we will cover what will happen in each of the three cases discussed in this recipe.

1. **Multiple node failure, but one node remains per nodegroup**

    In this case, the result is exactly the same as in the previous recipe—the remaining nodes still have access to all cluster data and the cluster will remain *up*.

    You can use the process in the previous recipe to demonstrate this, but instead of running `iptables` only on a single node, run it on two nodes—taking care to run it on two nodes in different nodegroups.

    If `NoOfReplicas` is greater than 2, for example 3, then the cluster could survive more failures (if `NoOfReplicas` is 3, there are three copies of each chunk of data, and each nodegroup could lose two of them without any problem).

2. **Total failure of a nodegroup**

    In this case, the result is that the cluster will shut down. The process that prevents this will be as follows:

    - Surviving nodes notice that all nodes in a nodegroup are down and notify arbitrator (management node by default)
    - Arbitrator realizes that there is no combination of nodes that can contact at least one storage node in each nodegroup
    - Arbitrator sends a message to all surviving storage nodes to shut down
    - Cluster is shut down

To demonstrate this practically, jump back to the example cluster shown in the previous recipe. Run the two `iptables` commands to block traffic on the relevant interface (in our example `eth1`) on both nodes with hostname `node1` and `node2` (that is both the nodes in a nodegroup), while ensuring that you have the `tail -f` command running on the `cluster` log. You will notice output like the following on the `cluster` log (the log on the management node):

```
2010-02-01 22:02:12 [MgmtSrvr] WARNING  -- Node 3: Node 2 missed
heartbeat 3
2010-02-01 22:02:13 [MgmtSrvr] ALERT    -- Node 10: Node 2
Disconnected
2010-02-01 22:02:16 [MgmtSrvr] WARNING  -- Node 4: Node 1 missed
heartbeat 2
2010-02-01 22:02:19 [MgmtSrvr] ALERT    -- Node 10: Node 1
Disconnected
```

As expected, firstly the other nodes notice that the two nodes are down and disconnect them (remember that if you have an SQL node on the storage node, there will be two errors per missed heartbeat—one for the storage node and one for the SQL node). In the previous example, some output is truncated, but it is all the same—every remaining node notices that the nodes have gone down.

The second part of the process is that after the dead nodes have missed three heartbeats, the arbitrator will force the other two nodes (nodes 3 and 4) to shut down as follows, in order to ensure that they do not carry on changing the data that they have:

```
2010-02-01 22:02:19 [MgmtSrvr] ALERT    -- Node 4: Forced node
shutdown completed. Caused by error 2305: 'Node lost connection
to other nodes and cannot form a unpartitioned cluster, please
investigate if there are error(s) on other node(s)(Arbitration
error). Temporary error, restart node'.
2010-02-01 22:02:20 [MgmtSrvr] ALERT    -- Node 3: Forced node
shutdown completed. Caused by error 2305: 'Node lost connection
to other nodes and cannot form a unpartitioned cluster, please
investigate if there are error(s) on other node(s)(Arbitration
error). Temporary error, restart node'.
2010-02-01 22:02:20 [MgmtSrvr] ALERT    -- Node 10: Node 4
Disconnected
2010-02-01 22:02:20 [MgmtSrvr] ALERT    -- Node 10: Node 3
Disconnected
```

At this point, as you would expect, your cluster shuts down even though half of the nodes and the management node did not fail.

3. **Nodes are isolated in more than one viable cluster**

   In this case, the arbitration procedure that is demonstrated in the next recipe kicks in.

Storage node partitioning and arbitration

In this recipe, we explore what happens when a MySQL Cluster has its storage nodes split into two groups that cannot communicate, but each of which has a full set of cluster data. We will look at this with a practical example, with the explanation of the process in the *There's more...* section.

Getting ready

In our example lab, nodes 1 and 2 make up nodegroup 0 and nodes 3 and 4 make up nodegroup 1 (look at the output in the recipe *Single storage node failure* from the SHOW command inside ndb_mgm to see this). In earlier recipes, we have covered what happens if we shut down any combination of nodes, but not what occurs if one node in each nodegroup is isolated from the rest of the cluster.

How to do it...

In our example, we physically isolate node 1 and node 3 from nodes 2, 4, and 5. This means that in effect we are isolating one storage node per nodegroup (with a SQL node running on each) from the other storage nodes (each with a SQL node) and the management node. If we looked at it superficially, these two could keep going separately—both halves have a full set of cluster data and two SQL nodes. Fortunately, as we will see, this is not what happens.

Firstly, ensure that your cluster is running and tail the four storage node cluster logs and the cluster log on the management node. Then partition your node. The easiest way to do this is by connecting the two nodes you wish to isolate through a different switch and unplug the cable that connects the second switch to the rest of your cluster (this is what we are doing in this example).

Once you have unplugged this cable, you should immediately notice in the cluster log that the management node detects that the two isolated nodes have missed heartbeats from the unisolated nodes as follows:

```
2010-02-07 21:32:45 [MgmtSrvr] WARNING  -- Node 2: Node 1 missed
heartbeat 1
2010-02-07 21:32:46 [MgmtSrvr] WARNING  -- Node 2: Node 3 missed
heartbeat 1
```

The management node continues to record this information in the cluster log until both nodes have missed four heartbeats. At this point, the two nodes are declared dead not only from the point of view of the management node but also from the point of view of the surviving two storage nodes—nodes 2 and 3, as shown in the following cluster log output:

```
2010-02-07 21:32:46 [MgmtSrvr] ALERT    -- Node 2: Node 1 declared
dead due to missed heartbeat
2010-02-07 21:32:46 [MgmtSrvr] ALERT    -- Node 2: Node 3 declared
dead due to missed heartbeat
```

Now, the cluster management node is smart enough to realize that we have a problem—what if the other two nodes have gone away and set up a cluster all on their own? (We will come to what they have done in a moment.). It declares that `arbitration required`—in other words, we now have two viable different clusters that cannot talk to each other, and it is essential that only one of them survives:

```
2010-02-07 21:32:46 [MgmtSrvr] ALERT    -- Node 2: Network
partitioning - arbitration required
```

The result of the arbitration is simple, the management node instructs the currently alive half to stay alive (node 10 is the management node):

```
2010-02-07 21:32:46 [MgmtSrvr] ALERT    -- Node 2: Arbitration won -
positive reply from node 10
```

There is then some information as the surviving nodes take over as primary for the fragments that are now missing.

Now, let's look at what happened on the two isolated machines. In their `local` log, we can see that the first problem shown is with `findNeighbours` (that is we can no longer see the other node in our nodegroup). After a short while, each node realizes that they can no longer talk to their management node. As they cannot contact the arbitrator, they shut down with the following slightly confusing message:

```
2010-02-07 21:33:04 [ndbd] INFO    -- Arbitrator decided to shutdown
this node
```

What this actually means is that the node knows that the arbitrator would shut the node down, as it cannot actually talk to the arbitrator (which is the management node, the other side of the unplugged network cable).

Finally, the nodes shut themselves down:

```
2010-02-07 21:33:04 [ndbd] INFO    -- Error handler shutting down
system
2010-02-07 21:33:04 [ndbd] INFO    -- Error handler shutdown
completed - exiting
```

And then they attempt to report this to the management node (but sadly, they are not able to connect to the management node):

```
2010-02-07 21:33:21 [ndbd] WARNING  -- Unable to report shutdown
reason to 10.0.0.5:1186: Could not connect to socket : Unable to
connect with connect string: nodeid=0,10.0.0.5:1186
```

Look at the cluster status from the other side of the partition (that is the side still working) and you can see that the expected status exists as follows:

```
ndb_mgm> show
Cluster Configuration
---------------------
[ndbd(NDB)]     4 node(s)
id=1 (not connected, accepting connect from 10.0.0.1)
id=2    @10.0.0.2   (mysql-5.1.39 ndb-7.0.9, Nodegroup: 0, Master)
id=3 (not connected, accepting connect from 10.0.0.3)
id=4    @10.0.0.4   (mysql-5.1.39 ndb-7.0.9, Nodegroup: 1)


[ndb_mgmd(MGM)]     1 node(s)
id=10    @10.0.0.5   (mysql-5.1.39 ndb-7.0.9)


[mysqld(API)] 4 node(s)
id=11 (not connected, accepting connect from 10.0.0.1)
id=12    @10.0.0.2   (mysql-5.1.39 ndb-7.0.9)
id=13 (not connected, accepting connect from 10.0.0.3)
id=14    @10.0.0.4   (mysql-5.1.39 ndb-7.0.9)
```

How it works...

In the case of storage nodes becoming partitioned from each other, the MySQL Cluster arbitration process kicks in. In effect, when a node becomes inaccessible from another node, the cluster Arbitrator is consulted on what action to take. Arbitrators can be management or SQL nodes, and each arbitrator has a priority, ArbitrationRank, that specifies in which order these nodes become arbitrator. It has the following options:

- 0—the node will never be used as an arbitrator (the default for SQL nodes)
- 1—the node has high priority, that is, it will be preferred as an arbitrator over low-priority nodes (the default for management nodes)
- 2—indicates a low-priority node that will be used as an arbitrator only if a node with a higher priority is not available for that purpose.

As you can see, the default for a management node is to be the Arbitrator (and we have assumed this in the examples so far).

In the event where it is not obvious what to do when nodes cannot contact each other (that is, if a group of nodes that potentially could make a valid cluster can no longer communicate with another group of nodes that could also potentially make a valid cluster), the overall decision making looks like this:

1. If all the nodes in any single nodegroup are down, then shut the cluster down (because the cluster no longer has access to all fragments of data).

2. If the storage nodes that are talking to the management node consist, as a group, of one node per nodegroup and represent at least 50 percent of the storage nodes plus one, then the arbitrator instructs the nodes to take over as primary for all of their fragments.

3. If the storage nodes that are talking to the management node, however, consist of exactly 50 percent of the storage nodes in the cluster, then it is possible that there is a second group of storage nodes that consist of the other 50 percent of nodes. The arbitrator then makes a decision.

4. If the arbitrator can only see one of these groups, it then instructs them to continue as primary. The other group will automatically shut down, as they do not have more than 50 percent of storage nodes and cannot see the arbitrator.

5. If the arbitrator can see two groups each with 50 percent of storage nodes, but within each group unable to talk to the other storage nodes, it will select one of the groups and instruct it to die, and instruct the other to become primary for all fragments. This is unlikely unless you have an extremely bizarre network layout.

Debugging MySQL Clusters

In this recipe, we will cover some of the common things to check in the case of a problem with a MySQL Cluster.

Getting ready

Prior to attempting to debug a problem, it is advisable to take some time to write down exactly what is wrong. In particular,

- What is supposed to happen (if anything)
- What is happening
- What has changed recently

With this information, it is likely that you will be able to find the solution with a methodical approach rather than to look for the problem directly.

How to do it...

Often, the problem is an error message. So the first step is to check the following places for error logs:

- ▶ `stdout`—when you start management or storage nodes (this is printed to the console)
- ▶ Node error logs—`/var/lib/mysql-cluster/ndb_<nodeid>_out.log` on storage and management nodes
- ▶ `cluster` logs—`/var/lib/mysql-cluster/ndb_<nodeid>_cluster.log` on management nodes
- ▶ SQL node logs—The location of these logs depends on the `log_error` variable, which you can discover with the following command at the SQL node:

```
mysql> SHOW VARIABLES LIKE 'log_error';
+---------------+---------------------+
| Variable_name | Value               |
+---------------+---------------------+
| log_error     | /var/log/mysqld.log |
+---------------+---------------------+
1 row in set (0.00 sec)
```

Check all of these logs to spot anything unusual or any errors.

 Even if there is one immediate and obvious problem, be sure to check all of these sources, as an obvious root cause may become visible!

Often, you will get a NDB error number, which you can translate to an English description with the POSIX error command, `perror`:

```
[root@node1 mysql-cluster]# perror --ndb 830
NDB error code 830: Out of add fragment operation records: Temporary
error: Temporary Resource error
```

This can be extremely useful for finding out what is going on, as error logs on nodes often cannot be particularly clear.

There are a couple of extremely common things to check in the event of any problem. They are covered in the next section.

There's more...

The following three problems—firewalls blocking traffic between nodes, hostnames used in configuration files and slightly intermittent DNS resolution, and nodes running out of RAM—account for the vast majority of problems reported with MySQL Clusters. In this section, we will look at each of these in turn.

Firewalls

Check thoroughly that there is no firewall between nodes. It is extremely common for firewalls to cause extremely bizarre problems between nodes. You can use the nmap package (available in the yum repository of RedHat or CentOS) to check that the same ports are visible locally as on a remote host. Note that different storage nodes will listen on different ports and may listen on different ports after a restart as follows:

```
[root@node1 mysql-cluster]# nmap localhost

Starting Nmap 4.11 ( http://www.insecure.org/nmap/ ) at 2009-09-09 21:52
BST
Interesting ports on node1 (127.0.0.1):
Not shown: 1674 closed ports
PORT     STATE SERVICE
22/tcp   open  ssh
25/tcp   open  smtp
111/tcp  open  rpcbind
631/tcp  open  ipp
773/tcp  open  submit
3306/tcp open  mysql

Nmap finished: 1 IP address (1 host up) scanned in 0.086 seconds
```

Now, from a different node, check that the same ports are open:

```
[root@node2 mysql-cluster]# nmap node1

Starting Nmap 4.11 ( http://www.insecure.org/nmap/ ) at 2009-09-09 21:52
BST
Interesting ports on node1 (127.0.0.1):
Not shown: 1674 closed ports
PORT     STATE SERVICE
22/tcp   open  ssh
25/tcp   open  smtp
111/tcp  open  rpcbind
631/tcp  open  ipp
```

```
773/tcp   open   submit
3306/tcp open   mysql
```

```
Nmap finished: 1 IP address (1 host up) scanned in 0.089 seconds
```

Host resolution

If you are not using IP addresses in the `config.ini` file (strongly recommended), ensure that you have all of the hosts involved in the cluster in a `/etc/hosts` file to ensure that a simple DNS outages does not take down the entire cluster. For example, your `/etc/hosts` may look as follows:

```
[root@node1 mysql-cluster]# cat /etc/hosts
# Do not remove the following line, or various programs
# that require network functionality will fail.
127.0.0.1    node1.xxx.com node1 localhost.localdomain localhost
::1     localhost6.localdomain6 localhost6
10.0.0.1 node1.xxx.com node1
10.0.0.2 node2.xxx.com node2
10.0.0.3 node3.xxx.com node3
10.0.0.4 node4.xxx.com node4
10.0.0.5 node5.xxx.com node5
```

Memory

It is extremely common for `IndexMemory` and `DataMemory` to use more memory than the system's free memory.

> This is commonly caused by running another process on the same server as a storage node, such as a standard MySQL server (which may use a large amount of RAM while executing a specific query). It is recommended that storage nodes only run the storage node processes.

In the case that this becomes a regular problem, it is possible to tune the Linux kernel *out of memory (OOM) killer* (this is the piece of code which decides which process to kill in the case of running out of physical memory) to kill another process and not the `ndbd` process. There is a value, `/proc/<pid>/oom-adj`, which ranges from -16 to +15 (-17 means *never kill this process*). The following bash snippet can be used to run after a storage node has started to significantly reduce the change of the OOM killer, killing `ndbd`:

```
[root@node1 mysql-cluster]# for pid in $(pidof ndbd); do echo "-10" > /proc/$pid/oom_adj; done;
[root@node1 mysql-cluster]#
```

However, it is still recommended not to come near to running out of physical memory on a storage node!

Seeking help

In this recipe, we will cover what to do when help is required and where the tips in the *Debugging a MySQL Cluster* recipe have not helped.

Getting ready

Before considering *Seeking help*, it is important to ensure that you have attempted everything yourself.

 If you are experiencing a critical problem with a production system, then it is likely a good idea to engage professional support immediately (available from MySQL and other firms).

Community support is excellent for MySQL Cluster and comes in several forms. To use any support, however, it is important to know exactly what you are asking. In this recipe, we will first cover confirming exactly what the problem is (and how to describe it), then discuss how to look for help, and finally briefly cover the process of submitting a bug to MySQL (if this is what you have found).

How to do it...

Firstly, ensure that you have carried out all the steps in the previous debugging recipe.

It is also a good idea to see if you can reproduce your issue, either on the same cluster or on a different development cluster. If you can, then write down a clear test case that someone else could use to recreate your problem for themselves. If you can do this, then the chances of your problem or bug being resolved increase enormously.

Having established exactly what is wrong and attempted to reproduce it, search the MySQL online manual at `http://dev.mysql.com/doc/`. Also search the `bugs` database at `http://bugs.mysql.com/` to see whether the bug has been reported and fixed. Finally, search the MySQL mailing list archives at `http://lists.mysql.com/`. You can also use `http://www.mysql.com/search/` to search all the web pages (this search includes the manual, mailing list, and forums).

 During the searching process, keep a record of URLs that seem to be related to your problem. Even if they do not help you immediately, including them when you directly ask the community for help saves someone else a search and may help others help you.

It is an extremely good idea to ensure that you are running the latest version of MySQL in your cluster if you are experiencing problems. People are naturally reluctant to help users fix problems when running versions of MySQL more than a couple of minor releases behind current, as this is, in effect, known buggy software and many bugs are fixed in each release. If upgrading is impossible, then be sure to check the changelists of later versions to ensure that whatever issue you have experienced has not been reported and fixed.

If nothing has helped you, then it is now time to ask the community directly for help. The MySQL Cluster mailing list, which you can subscribe to at `http://lists.mysql.com/cluster`, contains a large number of developers and active members of the community.

When posting a bug, ensure that you include the following details:

- Your setup, number of nodes, architecture, kernel version, operating system, and network connections. Everything—you really cannot give too much detail
- Your `config.ini` file
- What you did to cause the problem (if anything)
- What was supposed to happen
- What actually happened
- If possible, a test case (for example, the SQL query that caused the problem)
- What you have already attempted to fix the problem (include links to URLs that you have looked at that appear relevant)

It is likely that someone will quickly give feedback and help you narrow down your issue.

There's more...

In the event that you are sure that you have found a problem with MySQL or MySQL Cluster, you may well be asked to submit a bug report. Good bug reports follow the template given for a mailing list posted previously.

Bugs are reported at `http://bugs.mysql.com/`.

NIC teaming with MySQL Cluster

In this recipe, we will briefly discuss the specific requirements that a MySQL Cluster will bring to your network and show an example configuration with additional redundancy provided by a network. While this is not directly a troubleshooting step, it is an extremely common technique, and we cover the troubleshooting points during the recipe.

Getting ready

The strongly recommended best practice is to ensure that all nodes involved in your cluster have dedicated NICs connected to different switches.

It is also strongly recommended to ensure that a switch does not become a single point of failure and that the MySQL Cluster nodes are connected at least to two dedicated switches for redundancy.

The public network may also require one or two switches, depending on how the application connects to the cluster. However, it is critical for truly high availability that no single network device can take out the link to the fully-redundant cluster.

The following diagram shows a design consisting of two storage nodes, two SQL nodes, and two management nodes all connected to two dedicated cluster switches (using the first two NICs bonded) and also connected to two public (that is not dedicated to internal cluster traffic) switches. The diagram shows two application servers connected to each of the public switches.

Note that this recipe requires a special configuration on the Linux servers to allow the use of multiple network connections; this is called bonding and is covered shortly. Additionally, this diagram demonstrates switches connected using multiple cables - without proprietary technology and special configuration on the switches. It is likely that only one of these links would ever be active and delays of up to 50 seconds may occur on failure before the backup link activates. This time may be enough to cause your cluster to shut down, so ensure that your network is set up properly for fast failover as this book does not cover such configuration.

There is really no need for the cluster storage and management nodes to be connected to the public network except for management. It would be, for example, perfectly possible to connect to the SQL nodes on their public network. From there, connect to storage and management nodes via the private network. There is certainly no need for bonded interfaces on the public network for the storage and management nodes, but these are shown here as a best practice, which allows any single switch to fail without **any** effect on cluster availability.

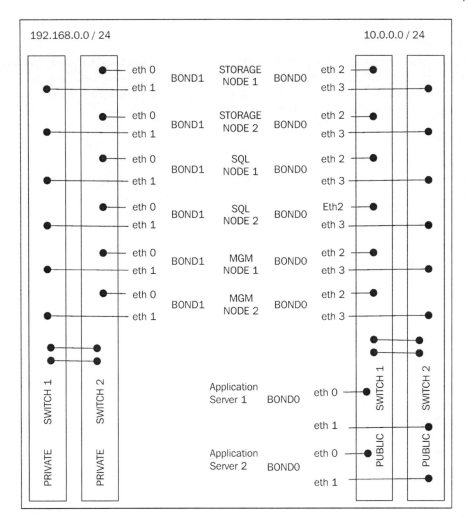

The two private switches must be connected together, ideally using a high-bandwidth and redundant connection (such as a EtherChannel on Cisco devices).

Fortunately, the Linux kernel includes an excellent support for bonding network links together, and in this recipe, we will show how to configure, test, and troubleshoot bonded interfaces.

How to do it...

The first step is to configure each pair of bonded interfaces. We will show the configuration for the first bond, bond0, which is made up of eth0 and eth1. In these files, remove settings such as whether to use DHCP or an IP address and netmask, and configure the interfaces as slaves with the following configuration files:

/etc/sysconfig/network-scripts/ifcfg-eth0:

```
DEVICE=eth0
# Ensure that the MAC address is connected to the same switch
# For each of the eth0's (e.g. private switch 2)
HWADDR=00:16:3E:xx:xx:xx
BOOTPROTO=none
ONBOOT=yes
MASTER=bond0
SLAVE=yes
USERCTL=no
```

/etc/sysconfig/network-scripts/ifcfg-eth1:

```
DEVICE=eth1
# Ensure that the MAC address is connected to the same switch
# For each of the eth1's (e.g. private switch 1)
HWADDR=00:16:3E:xx:xx:xx
BOOTPROTO=none
ONBOOT=yes
MASTER=bond0
SLAVE=yes
USERCTL=no
```

For the second pair, bond1, modify the ifcfg-eth2 and ifcfg-eth3 files in the same directory, repeat changing MASTER=bond0 to MASTER=bond1.

The bonding configuration file /etc/sysconfig/network-scripts/ifcfg-bond0 (and ifcfg-bond1) defines the logical interface that sits *above* the raw interfaces, and this file should contain the following for the public interface bond0:

```
DEVICE=bond0
# Change fourth octet to correct IP for server
IPADDR=10.0.0.1
NETMASK=255.255.255.0
USERCTL=no
BOOTPROTO=none
ONBOOT=yes
BONDING_OPTS="mode=1 miimon=100"
```

mode=1 means active / passive. Other modes are available but may require you to configure the link port aggregation on the switches. Review the `networking/bonding.txt` file in the kernel documentation for more information (`yum install kernel-doc` and look at the `/usr/share/doc/kernel-doc*` directory).

Now add the following for the private interface `bond1`:

```
DEVICE=bond1
# Change fourth octet to correct IP for server
IPADDR=10.2.0.2
NETMASK=255.255.255.0
USERCTL=no
BOOTPROTO=none
ONBOOT=yes
BONDING_OPTS="mode=1 miimon=100"
```

In CentOS and RHEL 5, it is necessary to manually configure a second bonding interface (there is only one allowed by default) by adding the following to `/etc/modprobe.conf`:

```
alias bond0 bonding
alias bond1 bonding
```

If everything goes well, you will now be able to bring up your new network interfaces with a standard network restart. Do this from the console of the server, if possible, as follows:

```
[root@node1 ~]# service network restart
Shutting down interface bond0:                           [  OK  ]
Shutting down interface eth0:                            [  OK  ]
...
Bringing up interface bond0:                             [  OK  ]
Bringing up interface eth0:                              [  OK  ]
```

Check that you can `ping` across your new bonded interface as follows:

```
[root@node1 network-scripts]# ping 10.0.0.2
PING 10.0.0.2 (10.0.0.2) 56(84) bytes of data.
64 bytes from 10.0.0.2: icmp_seq=1 ttl=64 time=0.178 ms
64 bytes from 10.0.0.2: icmp_seq=2 ttl=64 time=0.122 ms
```

If this works, reboot, and confirm that the bond remains. If it does not, then check the upcoming *There's more...* section discussion.

The next step is to double-check that failover works. Set up a terminal window to continually ping across one of the bonded interfaces, and prepare to unplug a cable. In a console window, run `tail -f` on `/var/log/messages`.

You should notice that at the moment you unplug a cable, a very small number of pings drop (with `miimon` set to `100`, probably about two) and a message like the following appears in the `syslog`:

```
Feb  2 00:53:35 node1 kernel: eth1: link down
Feb  2 00:53:37 node1 kernel: bonding: bond0: link status definitely
down for interface eth1, disabling it
Feb  2 00:53:37 node1 kernel: bonding: bond0: making interface eth2
the new active one.
```

When the cable is reconnected, the following message should appear:

```
Feb  2 00:55:28 node1 kernel: eth1: link up
Feb  2 00:55:28 node1 kernel: bonding: bond0: link status definitely
up for interface eth1.
```

At this point, you will notice that the kernel has not failed back to using the previously active link—it will generally not do this to reduce the number of times that it fails over:

```
[root@node1 ~]# cat /proc/net/bonding/bond0  | grep Currently
Currently Active Slave: eth2
```

If this works, congratulations! You have eliminated your network switches and cards as a single point of failure.

There's more...

If you notice that lots of duplicate packets appear when pinging across your bonded interface, like in the following example, you may have configured the mode wrongly:

```
[root@node1 ~]# ping 10.0.0.2
PING 10.0.0.2 (10.0.0.2) 56(84) bytes of data.
64 bytes from 10.0.0.2: icmp_seq=1 ttl=64 time=0.146 ms
64 bytes from 10.0.0.2: icmp_seq=1 ttl=64 time=0.168 ms (DUP!)
64 bytes from 10.0.0.2: icmp_seq=2 ttl=64 time=0.110 ms
64 bytes from 10.0.0.2: icmp_seq=2 ttl=64 time=0.139 ms (DUP!)
```

To verify the mode, as well as some other useful settings, read the live settings from the virtual filesystem `/proc` provided by the kernel:

```
[root@node1 ~]# cat /proc/net/bonding/bond0
Ethernet Channel Bonding Driver: v3.4.0 (October 7, 2008)
```

```
Bonding Mode: load balancing (round-robin)
MII Status: up
MII Polling Interval (ms): 0
Up Delay (ms): 0
Down Delay (ms): 0
```

This clearly shows that the mode is not mode 1 (which is active / backup), but is in fact round robin. Round Robin is no use unless the switches that the servers are connected to are able to and configured for such operation, the detail of which is outside the scope for this book. If they are not, ensure that you are using active / backup. Check the BONDING_OPTS setting in ifcfg-bondx, and restart the bonded interface.

In the correct mode, this file should show the following:

```
[root@node1 ~]# cat /proc/net/bonding/bond0
Ethernet Channel Bonding Driver: v3.4.0 (October 7, 2008)

Bonding Mode: fault-tolerance (active-backup)
Primary Slave: None
Currently Active Slave: eth1
MII Status: up
MII Polling Interval (ms): 100
Up Delay (ms): 0
Down Delay (ms): 0

Slave Interface: eth1
MII Status: up
Link Failure Count: 0
Permanent HW addr: 00:0c:29:e7:a7:2e

Slave Interface: eth2
MII Status: up
Link Failure Count: 0
Permanent HW addr: 00:50:56:ae:70:04
```

 The status of the individual network interfaces can be seen at the bottom of the previous output page. This can be useful to confirm the status of individual interfaces within the bond.

5
High Availability with MySQL Replication

In this chapter, we will cover:

- ▶ Designing a replication setup
- ▶ Configuring a replication master
- ▶ Configuring a replication slave without synchronizing data
- ▶ Configuring a replication slave and migrating data with a simple SQL dump
- ▶ Using LVM to reduce downtime on master when bringing a slave online
- ▶ Replication safety tricks
- ▶ Multi Master Replication Manager (MMM)
    - ❏ Initial installation
    - ❏ Installing the MySQL nodes
    - ❏ Installing the monitoring node
- ▶ Managing and using Multi Master Replication Manager (MMM)

Introduction

MySQL Replication is a feature of the MySQL server that allows you to *replicate* data from one MySQL database server (called the **master**) to one or more MySQL database servers (**slaves**). Replication is asynchronous, that is, the process of replication is not immediate and there is no guarantee that slaves have the same contents as the master (this is in contrast to MySQL Cluster, which was covered earlier in this book).

MySQL Replication has been supported in MySQL for a very long time and is an extremely flexible and powerful technology. Depending on the configuration, you can replicate all databases, selected databases, or even selected tables within a database.

Designing a replication setup

There are many ways to architect a MySQL Replication setup, with the number of options increasing enormously with the number of machines. In this recipe, we will look at the most common topologies and discuss the advantages and disadvantages of each, in order to show you how to select the appropriate design for each individual setup.

Getting ready

MySQL replication is simple. A server involved in a replication setup has one of following two roles:

- **Master**: Master MySQL servers write all transactions that change data to a binary log

- **Slave**: Slave MySQL servers connect to a master (on start) and download the transactions from the master's binary log, thereby applying them to the local server

 Slaves can themselves act as masters; the transactions that they apply from their master can be added in turn to their log as if they were made directly against the slave.

Binary logs are binary files that contain details of every transaction that the MySQL server has executed. Running the server with the binary log enabled makes performance about 1 percent slower.

The MySQL master creates binary logs in the forms name.000001, name.000002, and so on. Once a binary log reaches a defined size, it starts a new one. After a certain period of time, MySQL removes old logs.

The exact steps for setting up both slaves and masters are covered in later recipes, but for the rest of this recipe it is important to understand that slaves contact masters to retrieve newer bits of the binary log, and to apply these changes to their local database.

How to do it...

There are several common architectures that MySQL replication can be used with. We will briefly mention and discuss benefits and problems with the most common designs, although we will explore in detail only designs that achieve **high availability** (as is the focus of this book).

Master and slave

A single master with one or more slaves is the simplest possible setup. A master with one slave connected from the local network, and one slave connected via a VPN over the Internet, is shown in the following diagram:

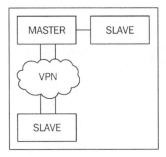

A setup such as this—with vastly different network connections from the different slaves to the master—will result in the two slaves having slightly different data. It is likely that the locally attached slave may be more up to date, because the latency involved in data transfers over the Internet (and any possible restriction on bandwidth) may slow down the replication process.

This Master-Slave setup has the following common uses and advantages:

- ▶ A local slave for backups, ensuring that there is no massive increase in load during a backup period.

- ▶ A remote location—due to the asynchronous nature of MySQL replication, there is no great problem if the link between the master and the slave goes down (the slave will catch up when reconnected), and there is no significant performance hit at the master because of the slave.

- ▶ It is possible to run slightly different structures (such as different indexes) and focus a small number of extremely expensive queries at a dedicated slave in order to avoid slowing down the master.

- ▶ This is an extremely simple setup to configure and manage.

A Master-Slave setup unfortunately has the following disadvantages:

- ▶ No automatic redundancy. It is common in setups such as this to use lower specification hardware for the slaves, which means that it may be impossible to "promote" a slave to a master in the case of an master failure.

- ▶ Write queries cannot be committed on the slave node. This means write transactions will have to be sent over the VPN to the master (with associated latency, bandwidth, and availability problems).

- ▶ Replication is equivalent to a RAID 1 setup, which is not an enormously efficient use of disk space (In the previous example diagram, each piece of data is written three times.).

- ▶ Each slave does put a slight load on the master as it downloads its binary log. The number of slaves thus can't increase infinitely.

Multi-master (active / active)

Multi-master replication involves two MySQL servers, both configured as replication masters and slaves. This means that a transaction executed on one is picked up by the other, and vice versa, as shown in the following diagram:

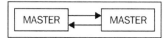

A SQL client connecting to the master on the left will execute a query, which will end up in that master's binary log. The master on the right will pick this query up and execute it. The same process, in reverse, occurs when a query is executed on the master on the right. While this looks like a fantastic solution, there are problems with this design:

▶ It is very easy for the data on the servers to become inconsistent due to the non-deterministic nature of some queries and "race conditions" where conflicting queries are executed at the same time on each node

 Recent versions of MySQL include various tricks to minimize the likelihood of these problems, but they are still almost inevitable in most real-world setups.

▶ It is extremely difficult to discover if this inconsistency exists, until it gets so bad that the replication breaks (because a replicated query can't be executed on the other node)

This design is only mentioned here for completeness; it is often strongly recommended not to use it. Either use the next design, or if more than one "active" node is required, use one of the other high-availability techniques covered in this book.

Active / passive master

Active / passive master replication involves two MySQL servers configured as per active / active master replication, but with some form of "write barrier" around a "passive" node in order to ensure that only one node is able to execute queries that change the data at any one point of time. This design is demonstrated in the following diagram:

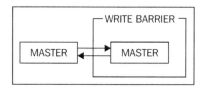

In the preceding diagram, the master on the left is the active master and the master on the right is passive. By running the example we discussed in active / active replication, if a SQL query is executed on the master on the left, it is injected into the binary log. This query is then picked up and executed by the master on the right. If a SQL query is executed on the node on the right, the "write barrier" prevents the query from being executed.

This barrier could consist of one of the following with various degrees of enforcement:

- A virtual IP address shared between the nodes (with one node having its ownership at any point of time)
- Permissions set on the "passive" node to prevent all connections except those for the replication user
- An application configured only to connect to the active node and no untrustworthy user
- In many ways, the simplest and easiest, by configuring all slave nodes as "read-only" on startup with the following `my.cnf` entry on the slave:

```
[mysqld]
read_only
```

When set as read-only, the node will reject all `UPDATE` and `DELETE` queries, and thus can't allow a standard database user (such as an application or mistaken user) to change data although changes that are received by the master are executed as normal.

To promote a slave node to a master node, either remove the `read_only` parameter from `my.cnf` or to set the parameter for the currently running MySQL Server only, execute the following query:

```
mysql> FLUSH TABLES WITH READ LOCK;
mysql> SET GLOBAL read_only = ON;
```

The server will now respond to all queries normally. This trick is covered in more detail later in this chapter in the *Replication safety tricks* recipe.

The effect is that there is one node that is asynchronously up to date with the other node (this node may or may not be used for read-only queries). In the event of the failure of the master, the passive node can be quickly "promoted" to the active master using the following procedure:

1. Install a write barrier around the previously active node to prevent all new `MODIFY` queries.
2. Wait for the passive node to catch up with any queries left in the master's binary log.
3. Remove the write barrier around the passive (which now becomes the active) node.

Clearly, if the active node has failed, step 2 may not be possible (and, depending on the type of write barrier, step 1 may be difficult). In this case, the passive node is promoted to master node and some transactions are lost. If this is not acceptable, you need a synchronous high-availability technique—several of these techniques are covered in this book (such as shared storage and MySQL Cluster).

How it works...

In this section, we will cover how MySQL replication works in slightly more detail. MySQL supports two forms of replication: statement-based and row-based replication. There is also a hybrid mode ("mixed") that is used by default.

Mixed-mode replication

Mixed-mode replication (the default) will use statement-based replication for almost everything, but it will switch to row-based replication for certain events. Full documentation on every event that will cause this can be found at `http://dev.mysql.com/doc/refman/5.1/en/binary-log-mixed.html`, but the most common events that cause row-based replication to be used are as follows:

- When a query updates a MySQL Cluster table
- When a query includes the `UUID()` function
- When two or more tables with `AUTO_INCREMENT` columns are modified
- When any `INSERT DELAYED` query is executed

There is no need to configure anything to get mixed-mode replication to work, because it is enabled as soon as you turn on binary logging (by adding the `log-bin` parameter to the `[mysqld]` section in `my.cnf`, which we shall cover in the later recipes in this chapter).

Statement-based replication

Statement-based replication quite literally keeps a record of every statement executed on the master that the slaves then executed. With this form of replication, which has been around from MySQL 3.1 version, binary logs can be converted to text for inspection with the `mysqlbinlog` command.

The following command runs the output of `mysqlbinlog` (which is verbose, and includes many comments and details on the environment) using `grep` command to look for a SQL query executed on the node:

```
[root@node1 mysql]# mysqlbinlog /var/lib/mysql/node1.000001
| grep -in "create database"
23:create database world
```

Unfortunately, statement-based replication has problems with queries that can cause different results when executed at the same time on the same dataset, such as `DELETE` or `UPDATE` with a `LIMIT` and no `ORDER BY` clause. Go to `http://dev.mysql.com/doc/refman/5.4/en/replication-sbr-rbr.html` for a complete list of limitations.

To force MySQL to use statement-based replication, modify the `binlog-format my.cnf` parameter and restart MySQL:

```
[mysqld]
binlog-format=mixed
```

Row-based replication

As a consequence of the limitations inherent to a statement-based replication system, row-based replication was added in MySQL 5.1.5.

If you enable MySQL Cluster on a SQL node (you'll see how later in this book), row-based replication will be used by default. MySQL Cluster is not compatible with statement-based replication.

Row-based replication literally replicates the actual changes ("events") to data in a database. Rather than a slave executing an entire single transaction, it simply executes the required queries to achieve the same results (this can, in some cases, increase performance). For example, if a `DELETE` query includes a delete subquery, the log would only contain details of the events—that is, the rows actually deleted.

Even with row-based replication, some queries (such as `OPTIMIZE TABLE`, `ALTER TABLE`, and `ANALYZE TABLE`) must be stored as queries and executed on the slaves as queries.

While it is not possible to inspect the actual queries within the binary log, it is possible to run `mysqlbinlog` with the `--base64-output=DECODE-ROWS` and `--verbose` parameters in order to see which rows are being updated.

There are some unresolved issues with row-based replication and concurrent large bulk `INSERT` and `SELECT` queries. However, with other uses of a database, it is likely that row-based replication is more deterministic and less likely to cause problems.

Row-based replication is required for replication involving MySQL Clusters, as covered in the *Master and slave* section. To configure row-based replication explicitly, modify the `binlog-format` parameter in `my.cnf` and restart MySQL:

```
[mysqld]
binlog-format=row
```

To check which replication mode a MySQL server is running in, SELECT the value of the `binlog_format` system variable:

```
mysql> SHOW VARIABLES LIKE 'binlog_format';
+---------------+-------+
| Variable_name | Value |
+---------------+-------+
| binlog_format | MIXED |
+---------------+-------+
1 row in set (0.00 sec)
```

Configuring a replication master

In this recipe, we will configure a master. Once configured, a replication master can have as many slaves as required connecting to it and retrieving its binary log.

Getting ready

The process of setting up a master is as follows:

▶ Configure a replication user account, with restricted permissions, for slaves to use when they log in

▶ Configure the master to start recording information into a binary log (using row-based, statement-based or hybrid-based replication modes)

How to do it...

We will firstly cover the parameters that must be set in the [mysqld] section in /etc/my.cnf on the master node.

1. **Configuring a node ID**

    Every server involved in a replication agreement with any other server must have a unique ID, set in my.cnf with the server-id parameter:

    ```
    server-id = 1
    ```

2. **Configuring a binary log**

The master must be told to store a binary log. The parameter `log-bin` will do this, but it is a good idea to pass a name for this logfile.

 If you fail to do so, it can cause confusion—particularly if machine hostnames change.

For a machine with a hostname, the following will place logfiles in the form `<MySQL datadir> node1-bin.xxxxxx`. For example, `/var/lib/mysql/node1-bin.000001`:

```
log-bin=node1
```

It is possible to pass a full path to this logfile. This is extremely desirable if you have a dedicated block device to store the binary logs, as on IO intensive systems this may reduce the overhead of binary logging:

```
log-bin=/mnt/disk2/node1
```

 In addition to the log files, a file `prefix.index` (for example `node1.index`) is created in the same directory that tells you which is the most recent binary log file.

You must restart the `mysql` server after changing this setting:

```
[root@node1 tmp]# service mysql restart
Shutting down MySQL.                                    [  OK  ]
Starting MySQL.                                         [  OK  ]
```

3. **Configuring a replication user account**

Each slave that connects to a master in a replication setup (for the purposes of reading the binary log on the master) must have an account to log in. This account must be granted the dedicated permission `REPLICATION SLAVE`. It is common practice to also grant this account `REPLICATION CLIENT`, which allows monitoring of the replication setup.

If possible, grant this permission only to a specific host—in this example, node 1 (`10.0.0.1`):

```
mysql> GRANT REPLICATION SLAVE, REPLICATION CLIENT ON *.* TO
'replication'@'10.0.0.1' IDENTIFIED BY 'password';
Query OK, 0 rows affected (0.00 sec)
```

To update the permissions table, flush the privileges:

```
mysql> FLUSH PRIVILEGES;
Query OK, 0 rows affected (0.01 sec)
```

How it works...

The process of replication is a little more complicated than we earlier alluded to. In this section, we will explain the details behind MySQL replication in slightly more detail.

When a transaction is sent to a MySQL server running with binary logging enabled, the transaction is executed normally, and just prior to completing the transaction the server records the change serially in the binary log. Once this is done, it tells the storage engine that the transaction is ready to be committed.

> Even if statements are concurrent during execution, they are recorded serially in the binary log.

The slave runs two threads to handle its role as a slave.

Firstly, the slave runs a I/O thread that opens a standard client connection to the master (using the replication user account) and starts a non-SQL BINARYLOG DUMP command, which causes the master to start a "Binlog dump thread" and allows the slave to read log entries from the master's binary log. The slave compares each entry with the latest entry that it already has on the disk. If it fails to find new entries, it sleeps and waits for the master to send a new entry signal. If there are new entries, it records these in the "relay log" on the slave.

A second thread, the "SQL slave thread", reads from the relay log and replays the queries, which completes the process that started with a query being sent to the master and ends with the query being committed to the slave server database.

When the slave thread executes a query, it does not, by default, record the query in its own binary log—this can be changed with the my.cnf parameter log-slave-updates.

There's more...

The following is a checklist of things to consider when setting up a master:

Disk space

Binary logs take up disk space, and if you have them stored in the same partition as the MySQL data because you are running out of space, it will prevent changes to your database.

There are a couple of ways to approach this problem, outlined here.

Only logging some databases

You may well have some databases that you do not wish to replicate. Unless you are using binary logs for some other purpose (such as, for backups), you can stop the MySQL server from logging these queries with the my.cnf parameter binlog-ignore-db.

When using row-based replication, this works as expected (all queries made against this database are ignored and not logged). When using statement-based replication, things are a little more complicated—the effect of this parameter is to not log any statement where the default database (that is, the one selected by `USE`) is db_name:

```
binlog-ignore-db = mysql
```

 To specify more than one database you wish to ignore, use this option multiple times. Do not use commas.

If you only want to replicate a specific database, you can use the inverse parameter `binlog-do-db`.

Limiting individual binary log size

Binary logs can become unmanageable, and the default maximum size for a binary log is 1G. This is tunable with the `my.cnf` parameter `max_binlog_size`:

```
max_binlog_size=200M
```

Rotating binary logs

It is good practice to automatically delete old binary logs. You can rotate binary logs older than two days with the `my.cnf` parameter `expire_log_days`.

The default value for this parameter is 0, which means "no automatic removal".

```
expire_logs_days = 2
```

 Removals occur when the MySQL server is started and when the logs are flushed (note that the logs are flushed when the current logfile reaches `max_binlog_size`, providing a further reason to set this parameter to a relatively small value).

Performance

In addition to the recommendation of storing your binary log on a block device separate from your MySQL data directory, there are some additional tricks you can use to increase performance while logging:

Binary log caching

The `my.cnf` parameter named `binlog_cache_size` sets the size of the cache that is used to hold SQL statements before they are inserted into the binary log during a transaction. Big, multi-statement transactions can benefit from an increased value (the default is 32M):

```
binlog_cache_size = 64M
```

This buffer is allocated per connection on the first `UPDATE` or `INSERT` query.

Configuring a replication slave without syncing data

In this recipe, we will see how to configure a replication slave and initiate the replication process. This recipe assumes that a master server is already configured, with a replication user account configured for the slave.

How to do it...

In this recipe, we show how to configure a slave server without showing how to sync data, which is shown in the next recipe. This recipe would be perfect if you have two freshly installed MySQL servers for example, or if you have a slave, which is a clone of a master that is not being updated, using virtualization.

The first step is to verify that the two servers have different server ID parameters in `my.cnf` by executing the following command in the `mysql` client on both servers:

```
mysql> SHOW VARIABLES LIKE "server_id";
+---------------+-------+
| Variable_name | Value |
+---------------+-------+
| server_id     | 5     |
+---------------+-------+
1 row in set (0.00 sec)
```

 If two servers in a replication agreement have the same server ID, replication will fail.

If the two servers do have the same server ID, modify the `server-id` parameter in `my.cnf` in order to ensure that both nodes have a server ID explicitly set, and that the two IDs are different.

The second step is to verify the master status on the master. In the MySQL Client, execute the following SQL query:

```
mysql> SHOW MASTER STATUS;
+--------------+----------+--------------+------------------+
| File         | Position | Binlog_Do_DB | Binlog_Ignore_DB |
+--------------+----------+--------------+------------------+
| node1.000003 |      107 |              |                  |
+--------------+----------+--------------+------------------+
1 row in set (0.00 sec)
```

Take note of the filename (node1.000003) and position (107). On the master, we have already configured a replication user account (replication) and the corresponding password.

The next step is to tell the slave where the master is, what user account to use in order to log in, what logfile to start reading from, and what position to jump to. This is all encased in a CHANGE MASTER TO query. Jump onto the slave, enter the MySQL Client, and execute the following query:

```
mysql> CHANGE MASTER TO master_host = '10.0.0.1', master_
user='replication', master_password='password', master_log_
file='node1.000003', master_log_pos=107;
Query OK, 0 rows affected (0.01 sec)
```

Now start the slave threads on the new slave:

```
mysql> START SLAVE;

Query OK, 0 rows affected (0.00 sec)
```

And check that the slave has come up using:

```
mysql> SHOW SLAVE STATUS\G;
*************************** 1. row ***************************
              Slave_IO_State: Waiting for master to send event
                 Master_Host: 10.0.0.1
                 Master_User: replication
...

            Slave_IO_Running: Yes
           Slave_SQL_Running: Yes
...

       Seconds_Behind_Master: 0
1 row in set (0.00 sec)
```

Congratulations! Your replication agreement is now working.

At this point, do something on the master (such as creating a table, inserting a row, and so on) and ensure that it appears in the slave. If it does not, review the output of SHOW SLAVE STATUS and ensure that the slave thread is running, and that there is no error displayed.

Configuring a replication slave, migrating data with a simple SQL dump

In this recipe, we will show how to configure a replication slave while coping with a master that both has data on it and potentially has that data changing, while minimizing the time for which the master must be "locked" from updates.

In the common case of adding a slave to a master that already has data in it, the simplest technique is to use the `mysqldump` binary provided by MySQL to inject the data from master to slave, and to reset the slave at the same time.

For this one-line command on the master to work, the following requirements must be met:

> ▸ Any existing slave process must be stopped on the slave (`STOP SLAVE`)
>
> ▸ A user account must exist that is able to create databases and tables, and insert rows when connecting to the slave from the master
>
> ▸ It must be acceptable to lock the tables on the master for the duration of the operation

This technique copies all data from the master to the slave, including all of the `mysql` database—with the exclusion of the `users` table. It is likely that all of the other tables are identical if the software versions are the same.

Ensure you have `replicate-ignore-db = mysql` in `/etc/my.cnf` on the slave, if you don't wish to replicate the `mysql` database, or remove the `--ignore-table` parameter using the next command (recommended).

How to do it...

The command to execute on the master, in full, is as follows:

```
[root@node1 mysql]# mysqldump --delete-master-logs --ignore-table=mysql.
user --master-data --lock-all-tables --all-databases -u root
--password='' --hex-blob | mysql -h 10.0.0.2 -u root --password=''
```

We can explain this command in chunks as follows:

> ▸ `mysqldump`: Binary for producing SQL statements from a MySQL database. This means, "take my database and produce a file that contains SQL statements, which would build an identical database if executed".
>
> ▸ `--delete-master-logs`: Deletes all logs on the master from the moment you start the backup (these are not needed; the slave only requires logs after this point).
>
> ▸ `--master-data`: Includes a `CHANGE MASTER TO` command within the dump.

- ▶ `--lock-all-tables`: Locks all tables on the master during the period of the backup, in order to ensure that every transaction before the time of the backup is logged, and every transaction after the backup is in the binary log. If you have a lot of data, this may involve a very long lock on all tables. Look at the next recipe for a solution.

- ▶ `--all-databases`: Backs up all databases on the master.

- ▶ `--hex-blob`: If you have BLOBs (binary objects) in your database, this option ensures they are stored in a way that allows them to be imported correctly (that is, stored as hexadecimal characters).

- ▶ The pipe command (|): Takes output from the command on the left and passes it to the command on the right.

- ▶ `mysql -h 10.0.0.2`: Connects to the slave.

- ▶ `-u root --password='x'`: Uses these details.

Once this command has finished execution, run `START SLAVE` as shown in the preceding section to start your slave up.

How it works...

The `CHANGE MASTER TO` command is only one of several ways to point a slave at a master (it is the most recommended way). Internally, this command creates a file `master.info` in the MySQL data directory (`/var/lib/mysql` by default), which keeps the details. This file is updated every time this `CHANGE MASTER TO` query is executed, and it is this file that the server uses when it begins to see the latest logfile that the slave was reading from, and at what position, when the server shuts down.

Using LVM to reduce downtime on a master when bringing a slave online

It is possible to use the **Logical Volume Manager** (**LVM**) which comes with most Linux distributions, including Redhat / CentOS, to take a read-only snapshot of the block device that the MySQL Data directory is residing on, and use this to synchronize a slave with only a very short period of table locks on the master.

In many cases of 24x7 use of a database, this is essential and it can be useful when you do not want to wait for a scheduled outage interval every time a slave needs re-synchronizing.

Getting ready

For the purpose of this recipe, we will require that you already have the MySQL data directory residing on a volume group with enough free space to hold the data that will change during the time the backup is running (perhaps, 10-20% for a very busy server).

In order to check if you have space in a volume group, use the `vgs` command:

```
[root@node2 mysql]# vgs
  VG      #PV #LV #SN Attr    VSize  VFree
  system   1   2   0 wz--n- 14.62G  4.88G
```

In this case, the volume group `system` has free space of 4.88G. If you do not have any or enough space, refer to Operating System documentation to find out how to modify volume groups, or the manual pages for `pvcreate` and `vgextend`.

Once the MySQL data directory is on a filesystem residing on a logical volume and there is sufficient space in the volume group, the following process must be carried out:

- ▶ Lock the tables in the master
- ▶ Take a snapshot (very quick)
- ▶ Record the binary log name and position on the master
- ▶ Unlock the tables
- ▶ Synchronize the data directory on the master with the slave
- ▶ Update the slave to point at the correct log name and position
- ▶ Start the slave
- ▶ Remove the snapshot on the master

We will now do this in an example with a master on `node1` (`10.0.0.1`) and slave on `node2` (`10.0.0.2`). The master has a logical volume `mysql` in volume group `system`. We assume that SSH is possible between the nodes, and in this example we set it to use a key.

How to do it...

Firstly, open two sessions to the master (when a LOCK TABLES query is run in a MySQL Client, it is ended if the client connection is closed). Secondly, prepare the `lvcreate` command in a second window to minimize downtime. Then, in quick succession, run the following four commands:

Lock all tables in window 1:

```
mysql> FLUSH TABLES WITH READ LOCK;
Query OK, 0 rows affected (0.01 sec)
```

In a busy server, this may take some time. Wait for the command to complete before moving on.

Create a snapshot volume in window 2, passing a new name (mysql_snap), and pass the size that will be devoted to keeping the data that changes during the course of the backup, and the path to the logical volume that the MySQL data directory resides on:

```
[root@node1 lib]# lvcreate --name=mysql_snap --snapshot --size=200M \
/dev/system/mysql
  Rounding up size to full physical extent 224.00 MB
  Logical volume "mysql_snap" created
```

Return to window 1, and check the master log position:

```
mysql> SHOW MASTER STATUS;
+---------------+----------+--------------+------------------+
| File          | Position | Binlog_Do_DB | Binlog_Ignore_DB |
+---------------+----------+--------------+------------------+
| node1.000012  |     997  |              |                  |
+---------------+----------+--------------+------------------+
1 row in set (0.00 sec)
```

Only after the lvcreate command in window 2 gets completed, unlock the tables:

```
mysql> UNLOCK TABLES;
Query OK, 0 rows affected (0.00 sec)
```

The next step is to move the data on this snapshot to the slave. On the master, mount the snapshot:

```
[root@node1 lib]# mkdir /mnt/mysql-snap
[root@node1 lib]# mount /dev/system/mysql_snap /mnt/mysql-snap/
```

On the slave, stop the running MySQL server and rsync the data over:

```
[root@node2 mysql]# rsync -e ssh -avz node1:/mnt/mysql-snap /var/lib/
mysql/
root@node1's password:
receiving file list ... done
mysql-snap/
mysql-snap/ib_logfile0
mysql-snap/ib_logfile1
```

```
mysql-snap/ibdata1

...

mysql-snap/world/db.opt


sent 1794 bytes  received 382879 bytes  85482.89 bytes/sec

total size is 22699298  speedup is 59.01
```

Ensure the permissions are set correctly on the new data, and start the MySQL slave server:

```
[root@node2 mysql]# chown -R mysql:mysql /var/lib/mysql

[root@node2 mysql]# service mysql start

Starting MySQL.                                    [  OK  ]
```

Now carry out the CHANGE MASTER TO command in the *Setting up slave with master having same data* section of this recipe to tell the slave where the master is, by using the position and logfile name recorded in the output from window 1 (that is, log name node1.000012 and Position 997).

Replication safety tricks

MySQL replication in anything but an extremely simple setup with one master handling every single "write". A guarantee of no writes being made to other nodes is highly prone to a couple of failures. In this recipe, we look at the most common causes of replication failure that can be prevented with some useful tricks.

This section shows how to solve auto increment problems in multi-master setups, and also how to prevent the data on MySQL servers, which you wish should remain read-only, from being changed (a common cause of a broken replication link). Auto-increment is the single largest cause of problems.

It is not difficult to see that it is not possible to have more than one server handling asynchronous writes when auto-increments are involved (if there are two servers, both will give out the next free auto-increment value, and then they will die when the slave thread attempts to insert a second row with the same value).

Getting ready

This recipe assumes that you already have replication working, using the recipes discussed earlier in this chapter.

How to do it...

In a master-master replication agreement, the servers may insert a row at almost the same time and give out the same auto-increment value. This is often a primary key, thus causing the replication agreement to break, because it is impossible to insert two different rows with the same primary key. To fix this problem, there are two extremely useful `my.cnf` values:

1. `auto_increment_increment` that controls the difference between successive `AUTO_INCREMENT` values.

2. `auto_increment_offset` that determines the first `AUTO_INCREMENT` value given out for a new auto-increment column.

By selecting a unique `auto_increment_offset` value and an `auto_increment_increment` value greater than the maximum number of nodes you ever want in order to handle a write query, you can eliminate this problem. For example, in the case of a three-node cluster, set:

- Node1 to have `auto_increment_increment` of 3 and `auto_increment_offset` of 1

- Node2 to have `auto_increment_increment` of 3 and `auto_increment_offset` of 2

- Node3 to have `auto_increment_increment` of 3 and `auto_increment_offset` of 3

Node1 will use value 1 initially, and then values 4, 7, and 10. Node2 will give out value 2, then values 5, 8, and 11. Node3 will give out value 3, then 6, 9, and 12. In this way, the nodes are able to successfully insert nodes asynchronously and without conflict.

These `mysqld` parameters' values can be set in the `[mysqld]` section of `my.cnf`, or within the server without restart:

```
[node A] mysql> set auto_increment_increment = 10;
[node A] mysql> set auto_increment_offset = 1;
```

There's more...

A MySQL server can be started or set to read-only mode using a `my.cnf` parameter or a `SET` command. This can be extremely useful to ensure that a helpful user does not come along and accidentally inserts or updates a row on a slave, which can (and often does) break replication when a query that comes from the master can't be executed successfully due to the slightly different state on the slave. This can be damaging in terms of time to correct (generally, the slave must be re-synchronized).

When in read-only mode, all queries that modify data on the server are ignored unless they meet one of the following two conditions:

1. They are executed by a user with SUPER privileges (including the default root user).

2. They are executed by the a replication slave thread.

To put the server in the read-only mode, simply add the following line to the [mysqld] section in /etc/my.cnf:

```
read-only
```

This variable can also be modified at runtime within a mysql client:

```
mysql> show variables like "read_only";
+---------------+-------+
| Variable_name | Value |
+---------------+-------+
| read_only     | OFF   |
+---------------+-------+
1 row in set (0.00 sec)


mysql> SET GLOBAL read_only=1;
Query OK, 0 rows affected (0.00 sec)


mysql> show variables like "read_only";
+---------------+-------+
| Variable_name | Value |
+---------------+-------+
| read_only     | ON    |
+---------------+-------+
1 row in set (0.00 sec)
```

Multi Master Replication Manager (MMM): initial installation

Multi Master Replication Manager for MySQL ("MMM") is a set of open source Perl scripts designed to automate the process of creating and automatically managing the "Active / Passive Master" high availability replication setup discussed earlier in this chapter in the *MySQL Replication design* recipe, which uses two MySQL servers configured as masters with only one of the masters accepting write queries at any point in time. This provides redundancy without any significant performance cost.

This setup is asynchronous, and a small number of transactions can be lost in the event of the failure of the master. If this is not acceptable, any asynchronous replication-based high availability technique is not suitable.

Over the next few recipes, we shall configure a two-node cluster with MMM.

 It is possible to configure additional slaves and more complicated topologies. As the focus of this book is high availability, and in order to keep this recipe concise, we shall not mention these techniques (although, they all are documented in the manual available at `http://mysql-mmm.org/`).

MMM consists of several separate Perl scripts, with two main ones:

1. `mmmd_mon`: Runs on one node, monitors all nodes, and takes decisions.
2. `mmmd_agent`: Runs on each node, monitors the node, and receives instructions from `mmm_mon`.

In a group of MMM-managed machines, each node has a node IP, which is the normal server IP address. In addition, each node has a "read" IP and a "write" IP. Read and write IPs are moved around depending on the status of each node as detected and decided by `mmmd_mon`, which migrates these IP address around to ensure that the write IP address is always on an active and working master, and that all read IPs are connected to another master that is in sync (which does not have out-of-date data).

 `mmmd_mon` should not run on the same server as any of the databases to ensure good availability. Thus, the best practice would be to keep a minimum number of three nodes.

In the examples of this chapter, we will configure two MySQL servers, `node 5` and `node 6` (`10.0.0.5` and 6) with a virtual writable IP of `10.0.0.10` and two read-only IPs of `10.0.0.11` and `10.0.0.12`, using a monitoring node `node 4` (`10.0.0.4`). We will use RedHat / CentOS provided software where possible.

 If you are using the same nodes to try out any of the other recipes discussed in this book, be sure to remove MySQL Cluster RPMs and `/etc/my.cnf` before attempting to follow this recipe.

There are several phases to set up MMM. Firstly, the MySQL and monitoring nodes must have MMM installed, and each node must be configured to join the cluster. Secondly, the MySQL server nodes must have MySQL installed and must be configured in a master-master replication agreement. Thirdly, a monitoring node (which will monitor the cluster and take actions based on what it sees) must be configured. Finally, the MMM monitoring node must be allowed to take control of the cluster.

In this chapter, each of the previous four steps is a recipe in this book. The first recipe covers the initial installation of MMM on the nodes.

How to do it...

The MMM documentation provides a list of required Perl modules. With one exception, all Perl modules currently required for both monitoring agents and server nodes can be found in either the base CentOS / RHEL repositories, or the EPEL library (see the Appendices for instructions on configuration of this repository), and will be installed with the following yum command:

```
[root@node6 ~]# yum -y install perl-Algorithm-Diff  perl-Class-Singleton
perl-DBD-MySQL perl-Log-Log4perl perl-Log-Dispatch perl-Proc-Daemon perl-
MailTools
```

Not all of the package names are obvious for each module; fortunately, the actual perl module name is stored in the Other field in the RPM spec file, which can be searched using this syntax:

```
[root@node5 mysql-mmm-2.0.9]# yum whatprovides "*File::
stat*"

Loaded plugins: fastestmirror

...

4:perl-5.8.8-18.el5.x86_64 : The Perl programming language

Matched from:

Other        : perl(File::stat) = 1.00

Filename     : /usr/share/man/man3/File::stat.3pm.gz

...
```

This shows that the Perl File::stat module is included in the base perl package (this command will dump once per relevant file; in this case, the first file that matches is in fact the manual page).

The first step is to download the MMM source code onto all nodes:

```
[root@node4 ~]# mkdir mmm
[root@node4 ~]# cd mmm
[root@node4 mmm]# wget http://mysql-mmm.org/_media/:mmm2:mysql-mmm-
2.0.9.tar.gz
--13:44:45--  http://mysql-mmm.org/_media/:mmm2:mysql-mmm-2.0.9.tar.gz
...
13:44:45 (383 KB/s) - `mysql-mmm-2.0.9.tar.gz' saved [50104/50104]
```

Then we extract it using the `tar` command:

```
[root@node4 mmm]# tar zxvf mysql-mmm-2.0.9.tar.gz
mysql-mmm-2.0.9/
mysql-mmm-2.0.9/lib/
...
mysql-mmm-2.0.9/VERSION
mysql-mmm-2.0.9/LICENSE
[root@node4 mmm]# cd mysql-mmm-2.0.9
```

Now, we need to install the software, which is simply done with the `make` file provided:

```
[root@node4 mysql-mmm-2.0.9]# make install
mkdir -p  /usr/lib/perl5/vendor_perl/5.8.8/MMM /usr/bin/mysql-mmm /usr/
sbin /var/log/mysql-mmm /etc /etc/mysql-mmm /usr/bin/mysql-mmm/agent/ /
usr/bin/mysql-mmm/monitor/
...
[ -f /etc/mysql-mmm/mmm_tools.conf  ] || cp etc/mysql-mmm/mmm_tools.conf
/etc/mysql-mmm/
```

Ensure that the exit code is `0` and that there are no errors:

```
[root@node4 mysql-mmm-2.0.9]# echo $?
```
0

> Any errors are likely caused as a result of dependencies—ensure that you have a working `yum` configuration (refer to *Appendices*) and have run the correct `yum install` command.

Multi Master Replication Manager (MMM): installing the MySQL nodes

In this recipe, we will install the MySQL nodes that will become part of the MMM cluster. These will be configured in a multi-master replication setup, with all nodes initially set to read-only.

How to do it...

First of all, install a MySQL server:

```
[root@node5 ~]# yum -y install mysql-server
Loaded plugins: fastestmirror

...


Installed: mysql-server.x86_64 0:5.0.77-3.el5
Complete!
```

Now configure the mysqld section /etc/my.cnf on both nodes with the following steps:

1. Prevent the server from modifying its data until told to do so by MMM. Note that this does not apply to users with SUPER privilege (that is, probably you at the command line!):

    ```
    read-only
    ```

2. Prevent the server from modifying its mysql database as a result of a replicated query it receives as a slave:

    ```
    replicate-ignore-db = mysql
    ```

3. Prevent this server from logging changes to its mysql database:

    ```
    binlog-ignore-db = mysql
    ```

4. Now, on the first node (in our example node5 with IP 10.0.0.5), add the following to the [mysqld] section in /etc/my.cnf:

    ```
    log-bin=node5-binary
    relay-log=node5-relay
    server-id=5
    ```

5. And on the second node (in our example node6 with IP 10.0.0.6), repeat with the correct hostname:

    ```
    log-bin=node6-binary
    relay-log=node6-relay
    server-id=6
    ```

Ensure that these are correctly set. Identical node IDs or logfile names will cause all sorts of problems later.

On both servers, start the MySQL server (the `mysql_install_db` script will be run automatically for you to build the initial MySQL database):

```
[root@node5 mysql]# service mysqld start
...
Starting MySQL:                                        [  OK  ]
```

The next step is to enter the `mysql` client and add the users required for replication and the MMM agent. Firstly, add a user for the other node (you could specify the exact IP of the peer node if you want):

```
mysql> grant replication slave on *.* to 'mmm_replication'@'10.0.0.%'
identified by 'changeme';
Query OK, 0 rows affected (0.00 sec)
```

Secondly, add a user for the monitoring node to log in and check the status (specify the IP address of the monitoring host):

```
mysql> grant super, replication client on *.* to 'mmm_agent'@'10.0.0.4'
identified by 'changeme';
Query OK, 0 rows affected (0.00 sec)
```

Finally, flush the privileges (or restart the MySQL server):

```
mysql> flush privileges;
Query OK, 0 rows affected (0.00 sec)
```

Repeat these three commands on the second node.

With the users set up on each node, now we need to set up the Multi Master Replication link.

At this point, we have started everything from scratch, including installing MySQL and running it in read-only mode. Therefore, creating a replication agreement is trivial as there is no need to sync the data. If you already have data on one node that you wish to sync to the other, or both nodes are not in a consistent state, refer to the previous recipe for several techniques to achieve this.

First, ensure that the two nodes are indeed consistent. Run the command SHOW MASTER STATUS in the MySQL Client:

```
[root@node5 mysql]# mysql
Welcome to the MySQL monitor.  Commands end with ; or \g.
Your MySQL connection id is 2
Server version: 5.0.77-log Source distribution


Type 'help;' or '\h' for help. Type '\c' to clear the buffer.


mysql> show master status;
+---------------------+----------+--------------+-------------------+
| File                | Position | Binlog_Do_DB | Binlog_Ignore_DB  |
+---------------------+----------+--------------+-------------------+
| node5-binary.000003 |       98 |              | mysql             |
+---------------------+----------+--------------+-------------------+
1 row in set (0.00 sec)
```

Ensure that the logfile name is correct (it should be a different name on each node) and ensure that the position is identical.

If this is correct, execute a CHANGE MASTER TO command on both nodes:

In our example, on node5 (10.0.0.5), configure it to use node6 (10.0.0.6) as a master:

```
mysql> change master to master_host = '10.0.0.6', master_user='mmm_
replication', master_password='changeme', master_log_file='node6-
binary.000003', master_log_pos=98;
Query OK, 0 rows affected (0.00 sec)
```

Configure node6 (10.0.0.6) to use node5 (10.0.0.5) as a master:

```
mysql> change master to master_host = '10.0.0.6', master_user='mmm_
replication', master_password='changeme', master_log_file='node6-
binary.000003', master_log_pos=98;
Query OK, 0 rows affected (0.00 sec)
```

On both nodes, start the slave threads by running:

```
mysql> start slave;
Query OK, 0 rows affected (0.00 sec)
```

And check that the slave has come up:

```
mysql> show slave status\G;
*************************** 1. row ***************************
               Slave_IO_State: Waiting for master to send event
                  Master_Host: 10.0.0.6
                  Master_User: mmm_replication
                  Master_Port: 3306
                Connect_Retry: 60
              Master_Log_File: node6-binary.000003
          Read_Master_Log_Pos: 98
               Relay_Log_File: node5-relay.000002
                Relay_Log_Pos: 238
        Relay_Master_Log_File: node6-binary.000003
             Slave_IO_Running: Yes
            Slave_SQL_Running: Yes
...
        Seconds_Behind_Master: 0
1 row in set (0.00 sec)
```

The next step is to configure MMM. Unfortunately, MMM requires one Perl package that is not provided in the base or EPEL repositories with CentOS or RHEL, so we must download and install it. The module is Net::ARP (which is used for the IP-takeover) and you can download it from Perl's MCPAN, or use a third-party RPM. In this case, we use a third-party RPM, which can be found from a trusted repository of your choice or Google (in this example, I used `http://dag.wieers.com/rpm/`):

```
[root@node6 ~]# cd mmm
[root@node6 mmm]# wget ftp://ftp.univie.ac.at/systems/linux/dag/redhat/
el5/en/x86_64/RPMS.dries/perl-Net-ARP-1.0.2-1.el5.rf.x86_64.rpm
--18:53:31--
...
18:53:32 (196 KB/s) - `perl-Net-ARP-1.0.2-1.el5.rf.x86_64.rpm' saved
[16582]


[root@node6 mmm]# rpm -ivh perl-Net-ARP-1.0.2-1.el5.rf.x86_64.rpm
warning: perl-Net-ARP-1.0.2-1.el5.rf.x86_64.rpm: Header V3 DSA signature:
NOKEY, key ID 1aa78495
Preparing...                ###########################################
[100%]
   1:perl-Net-ARP           ###########################################
[100%]
```

Now, configure `/etc/mysql-mmm/mmm_agent.conf` with the name of the local node (do this on both nodes):

include mmm_common.conf

this node5

Start the MMM agent on the node:

[root@node6 mysql-mmm-2.0.9]# service mysql-mmm-agent start

Starting MMM Agent daemon... Ok

And configure it to start on boot:

[root@node6 mysql-mmm-2.0.9]# chkconfig mysql-mmm-agent on

Multi Master Replication Manager (MMM): installing monitoring node

In this recipe, we will configure the monitoring node with details of each of the hosts, and will tell it to start monitoring the cluster.

How to do it...

Edit `/etc/mysql-mmm/mmm_common.conf` to change the details for each host and its username and password.

Within this file, define default interfaces, PID and binary paths, and username / password combinations for the replication and MMM agents. For our example cluster, the file looks like this:

```
<host default>
        cluster_interface                eth0

        pid_path                         /var/run/mmmd_agent.pid
        bin_path                         /usr/bin/mysql-mmm/

        replication_user                 mmm_replication
        replication_password             changeme

        agent_user                       mmm_agent
        agent_password                   changeme

        monitor_user                     mmm_agent
        monitor_password                 changeme
</host>
```

We will define these user accounts and passwords here, because in this example we will use the same replication and agent user account and password for both nodes. While it may be tempting to use different details, it is worth remembering that these are relatively "low privilege" accounts and that anyone with access to either server has the same degree of access to all your data!

In this example, we have additionally used one user for both MMM's monitor and agents.

Secondly (in the same `mmm_common.conf` file), define the MySQL hosts involved in the replication. For our example cluster, it looks like this:

```
<host node5>
        ip                              10.0.0.5
        mode                            master
        peer                            node6
</host>

<host node6>
        ip                              10.0.0.6
        mode                            master
        peer                            node5
</host>
```

Define a role for writers and readers; we will have two readers and one writer at any one point (this allows either node to run read-only queries). For our example cluster, it looks like this:

```
<role writer>
        hosts                           node5,node6
        ips                             10.0.0.10
        mode                            exclusive
</role>

<role reader>
        hosts                           node5,node6
        ips                             10.0.0.11,10.0.0.12
        mode                            balanced
</role>
```

If you would like to specify a role to stick to one host unless there is a real need to move it, specify `prefer nodex` in the `<role>` section. Note that if you do this, you will not be able to easily move this role around for maintenance, but this can be useful in the case of widely different hardware.

Finally, tell MMM that you would like the active master to allow write queries:

```
active_master_role      writer
```

Copy `mmm_common.conf` to the MySQL nodes:

```
[root@node4 mysql-mmm]# scp mmm_common.conf node5:/etc/mysql-mmm/
mmm_common.conf
                                       100%   624      0.6KB/s    00:00
[root@node4 mysql-mmm]# scp mmm_common.conf node6:/etc/mysql-mmm/
mmm_common.conf
100%   624      0.6KB/s    00:00
```

Now edit `/etc/mysql-mmm/mmm_mon.conf` on the monitoring node, which controls how monitoring will run.

Include the common configuration (hosts, roles, and so on) defined earlier:

```
include mmm_common.conf
```

Run a monitor locally, pinging all IPs involved:

```
<monitor>
        ip                              127.0.0.1
        pid_path                        /var/run/mmmd_mon.pid
        bin_path                        /usr/bin/mysql-mmm/
        status_path                     /var/lib/misc/mmmd_
mon.status
        ping_ips                        10.0.0.5,10.0.0.6,10.0
.0.10,10.0.0.11,10.0.0.12
</monitor>
```

Finally, start the monitoring daemon:

```
[root@node4 ~]# service mysql-mmm-monitor start
Daemon bin: '/usr/sbin/mmmd_mon'
Daemon pid: '/var/run/mmmd_mon.pid'
Starting MMM Monitor daemon: Ok
```

MMM is now configured, with the agent monitoring the two MySQL nodes. Refer to the next recipe for instructions on using MMM.

Managing and using Multi Master Replication Manager (MMM)

In this recipe, we will show how to take your configured MMM nodes into a working MMM cluster with monitoring and high availability, and also discuss some management tasks such as conducting planned maintenance.

This recipe assumes that the MMM agent is installed on all MySQL nodes, and that a MMM monitoring host has been installed as shown in the preceding recipe.

This recipe will make extensive use of the command mmm_control, which is used to control the hosts inside a MMM cluster.

How to do it...

Within mmm_control, a show command gives the current status of the cluster:

```
[root@node4 ~]# mmm_control show
  node5(10.0.0.5) master/ONLINE. Roles: reader(10.0.0.12)
  node6(10.0.0.6) master/ONLINE. Roles: reader(10.0.0.11),
                                        writer(10.0.0.10)
```

This shows that both node5 and node6 are up, each has a reader role (10.0.0.12 and 10.0.0.11), and node6 has the writer role (10.0.0.10). Therefore, if you need to execute a write query or a read query that must have the latest data, use 10.0.0.10. If you are executing a read-only query that can be executed on slightly old data, you can use 10.0.0.12 in order to keep the load off the active write master.

When your nodes first start, they will appear with a status of AWAITING_RECOVERY:

```
[root@node4 ~]# mmm_control show
  node5(10.0.0.5) master/AWAITING_RECOVERY. Roles:
  node6(10.0.0.6) master/AWAITING_RECOVERY. Roles:
```

This is because MMM needs to be sure that you want to bring them both online.

1. The first step is to configure the nodes to come online using the mmm_control set_online command:

    ```
    [root@node4 ~]# mmm_control set_online node5
    OK: State of 'node5' changed to ONLINE. Now you can wait some time
    and check its new roles!
    [root@node4 ~]# mmm_control set_online node6
    ```

```
OK: State of 'node6' changed to ONLINE. Now you can wait some time
and check its new roles!
[root@node4 ~]# mmm_control show
  node5(10.0.0.5) master/ONLINE. Roles: reader(10.0.0.12),
writer(10.0.0.10)
  node6(10.0.0.6) master/ONLINE. Roles: reader(10.0.0.11)
```

We can now see the MMM has brought both nodes online, giving the writer role to node5.

2. The second step is to check that MMM has successfully configured the read-only node (node6), which we'll do with `show variables like 'read_only';` executed against both the MySQL server with the reader and writer role:

```
[root@node4 ~]# mmm_control show
  node5(10.0.0.5) master/ONLINE. Roles: reader(10.0.0.12),
writer(10.0.0.10)
  node6(10.0.0.6) master/ONLINE. Roles: reader(10.0.0.11)

[root@node4 ~]# echo "show variables like 'read_only';" | mysql -h
10.0.0.10
Variable_name Value
read_only      OFF
[root@node4 ~]# echo "show variables like 'read_only';" | mysql -h
10.0.0.11
Variable_name Value
read_only      ON
```

This shows the same query executed against the writer role (`10.0.0.10`) and the reader role (`10.0.0.11`). As expected, the reader is set to read-only, whereas the writer is not.

If you execute this query against the reader role on the same host as a writer, it will show `read_only` set to off, even though it is a reader role. This is because this parameter is specified on a per-host basis, so if a reader happens to have an active writer role, it will also accept write queries. The important thing is that nodes without a writer are set to read-only, otherwise the replication between the two nodes will break.

3. The next step is to activate the nodes. MMM runs in two modes:

   i. In active mode, the MMM monitoring agent actively takes control of the MySQL nodes, and commands sent to `mmm_control` are executed on the MySQL nodes.

   ii. Passive node is entered in the event of a problem detected on startup (either a problem in communicating with a MySQL node, or a discrepancy detected between the stored status and the detected status on nodes).

4. The fourth step is to check the current status of a node. Do this with the following command on the MMM monitoring node:

```
[root@node4 ~]# mmm_control mode
ACTIVE
```

If a node is in the passive mode, a status report will show this:

```
[root@node4 ~]# mmm_control show
# --- Monitor is in PASSIVE MODE ---
# Cause: Discrepancies between stored status, agent status and
system status during startup.
```

The last step is to turn any inactive node to active. In order to do this, run the following command for each inactive node on the MMM monitoring node:

```
[root@node4 ~]# mmm_control set_active
OK: Switched into active mode.
```

 It is possible to deliberately put MMM into passive mode, make some changes to IP addresses, and then set MMM active, which will have the effect of immediately carrying out all the pending changes (if possible). For more details, see the MMM documentation.

At this point, your MMM cluster is up and running. In the event of failure of a MySQL server, the roles that were running on that server will be migrated off the server very quickly.

How it works...

When MMM moves a role from a node, it uses the functionality provided by the Net::ARP Perl Module to update ARP tables, and rapidly move the IP address from node to node. The exact process is as follows:

On the "current" active writer node:

▸ MySQL server is made read_only to prevent further write transactions (except those executed by a SUPER user)

▸ Active connections are terminated

▸ The writer role IP is removed

On the new writer:

▸ The MMM process running on the slave is informed that it is about to become the active writer

▸ The slave will attempt to catch up with any remaining queries in the master's binary log

> ▸ read_only is turned off
> ▸ The writer IP is configured

There's more...

You will often want to move a role, often the writer role, from the currently active node to a passive one in order to conduct maintenance on the active node. This is trivial to complete with MMM.

Firstly, confirm the current status:

```
[root@node4 ~]# mmm_control show
  node5(10.0.0.5) master/ONLINE. Roles: reader(10.0.0.12)
  node6(10.0.0.6) master/ONLINE. Roles: reader(10.0.0.11),
                                         writer(10.0.0.10)
```

In this example, we will move the active writer role (on node6) to node5, using the move_role command:

```
[root@node4 ~]# mmm_control move_role writer node5
OK: Role 'writer' has been moved from 'node6' to 'node5'. Now you can
wait some time and check new roles info!
```

We can now check the status to see that the role has moved:

```
[root@node4 ~]# mmm_control show
  node5(10.0.0.5) master/ONLINE. Roles: reader(10.0.0.12),
                                         writer(10.0.0.10)
  node6(10.0.0.6) master/ONLINE. Roles: reader(10.0.0.11)
```

Failure detection

If a node fails and MMM is running, MMM will migrate all roles off that node and onto other nodes.

For example, if we have a status with node5 having an active reader and writer, and node6 just a reader:

```
[root@node4 ~]# mmm_control show
  node5(10.0.0.5) master/ONLINE. Roles: reader(10.0.0.12),
                                         writer(10.0.0.10)
  node6(10.0.0.6) master/ONLINE. Roles: reader(10.0.0.11)
```

Here node5 fails, and rapidly `show` will show that all nodes have been migrated:

```
[root@node4 ~]# mmm_control show
# Warning: agent on host node5 is not reachable
  node5(10.0.0.5) master/HARD_OFFLINE. Roles:
  node6(10.0.0.6) master/ONLINE. Roles: reader(10.0.0.11),
                  reader(10.0.0.12), writer(10.0.0.10)
```

When node5 recovers, assuming MySQL is configured to start at boot, it will sit in `AWAITING_RECOVERY` state:

```
[root@node4 ~]# mmm_control show
  node5(10.0.0.5) master/AWAITING_RECOVERY. Roles:
  node6(10.0.0.6) master/ONLINE. Roles: reader(10.0.0.11),
                  reader(10.0.0.12), writer(10.0.0.10)
```

The process for activating this node was covered at the beginning of this section.

 If MySQL does not start at boot, the node will appear in the HARD_OFFLINE state. In this case, investigate the cause on the node before doing anything in MMM.

6
High Availability with MySQL and Shared Storage

In this chapter, we will cover:

- ▶ Preparing a Linux server for shared storage
- ▶ Configuring two servers for shared storage MySQL
- ▶ Configuring MySQL on shared storage with Conga
- ▶ Fencing for high availability
- ▶ Configuring MySQL with GFS

Introduction

In this chapter, we will look at high-availability techniques for MySQL that rely on shared storage. The techniques covered elsewhere in this book have produced highly-available systems while maintaining the independence of each machine involved. Each machine had its own disk drive and the data in the database is synced at application level between the servers using replication or MySQL clustering. With shared storage, the actual database data is not stored on local disk drives, but on a storage array that can be accessed by multiple servers.

It is not possible to just connect a single hard drive to two different servers and use a traditional filesystem, and any attempt to do this will result in almost immediate data corruption.

In this book **GFS** refers to the filesystem open sourced by RedHat
(`http://www.redhat.com/gfs/`), and has nothing to do with the
Google GFS (`http://labs.google.com/papers/gfs.html`),
which is not open source.

Preparing a Linux server for shared storage

Shared storage works by separating the servers that process data from the storage, using
various technologies that are beyond the scope of this book (the most common being Fibre
Channel and iSCSI). The idea is that two servers with the same storage space can easily act
as in active/passive mode (with one node active at any one time), and can quickly fail over
the active node.

The simplified structure of shared-storage cluster is as follows:

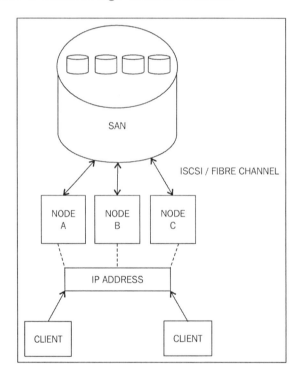

 Note that between the SAN and nodes, there are generally multiple paths for
the storage traffic to take, for both fibre channel and iSCSI based solutions,
these often involve multiple controllers on the storage unit. This book does not
focus on this layer, but multipathing is an essential part of a production setup.

Depending on the solution developed, the service may run on one server at a time (either Node A, Node B, or Node C as shown in the previous diagram) or run on all three nodes with a filesystem specifically designed to allow access from multiple nodes.

In the former case, the active node has a shared IP address listening for clients and mounts the shared-storage volumes. The other two nodes do not mount the storage and do not listen on the shared IP address and the service is stopped. In the event of a failure, the nodes that have not failed detect that a node has failed, forcibly turn off the newly failed node to ensure that it has really died and is no longer writing to the filesystem (a technique called fencing, which we will explore later in this chapter). One of the remaining nodes picks up the virtual IP, mounts the shared storage, recovers the filesystem journal if required, and starts the service so that clients can continue to connect without reconfiguration. In the case of planned maintenance, the service can easily be stopped on one node, the mounted storage unmounted, and virtual IP removed from that node with another node then mounting the storage, taking over the shared IP address, and starting the service.

In the latter case, all the active nodes mount the storage and use a filesystem that is designed to cope with multiple nodes, such as RedHat's **Global File System** (**GFS**). This filesystem uses a **Distributed Lock Manager** (**DLM**) to coordinate access to the shared storage, and includes code to cope with node failures in a clean manner. This solution is often used with only one node active at a time, with the advantage over the former solution of a faster failover time. There is also no risk of accidental mounting of the storage on a non-active node, which would cause corruption. There is a slight overhead in using a clustered filesystem such as GFS.

In either case, each service consists of a set of resources, such as an IP address and an actual process (in our case, MySQL) with a working `init` script, and some shared storage. This service is moved from one server to another by the Cluster Manager which is a user space process, constantly keeping in touch with the other nodes.

> Always use a transactional storage engine such as InnoDB for MySQL instances running on shared storage, except for the `mysql` database which is hardly ever changed. MyISAM has extremely poor recovery characteristics in the event of an unclean shutdown, which is what all unplanned failures are in a shared-storage cluster. In other words, they involve nodes failing hard rather than cleanly unmounting the filesystems.

In this recipe, we will look at some of the design considerations for the storage, and then cover the configuration required for a RHEL or CentOS server to connect to a pre-existing iSCSI volume.

> This is not a book about Linux storage management, but a brief example of iSCSI is included here for completeness in order to allow this book alone to help you configure a shared-storage cluster, even if it is just for testing.

How to do it...

To design a shared-storage architecture, you must consider the performance and storage requirements, and the detail of this is outside the scope of this book. However, to give you a brief idea, you may wish to consider the following in more detail:

- ▸ The type of drives—for I/O intensive loads, fibre channel drives may be required rather than SAS or SATA and an increasing number of storage arrays will allow some Solid State Disks (SSDs) to be used.

- ▸ Many storage networks require detailed designs for storage networking (including the configuration of correct zoning and **Virtual SAN** (**VSAN**) parameters) and storage equipment (including the configuration of LUN masking). Verify at an early stage if this is likely to be a part of your setup, and if so consider it from the start.

- ▸ The RAID configuration—for example, RAID10 provides vastly better write performance when compared with RAID5 and having lots of small disks provides higher I/O operations per second (IOPS), when compared to a few larger ones.

- ▸ The type of protocol—at the time of writing, Fibre Channel storage provides higher throughput and lower latency when compared with iSCSI.

- ▸ The layout of the storage—for example, you may wish to separate data from the logs, or use different block devices with different performance such as SCSI, SATA disks, or SSDs for different **Logical Unit Number**s (**LUN**s).

In storage terminology, a Logical Unit Number (LUN) is the identifier of a SCSI logical unit.

- ▸ The cost of any solution—for example, generally Fibre Channel solutions are more expensive than those based on iSCSI, and SCSI drives are more expensive than SATA.

The increased availability of 10 Gigabit Ethernet may make iSCSI perform better than Fibre Channel (which generally operates at 4 or 8 Gigabit over optical cables—but Fibre Channel over Ethernet is increasing in popularity); be sure to consider all the options!

If you are using a storage system that allows you to export iSCSI volumes, the next part of this section covers getting your Linux nodes to connect to this volume (if you are using software initiators).

There are two ways to connect Linux clients to iSCSI volumes. The first are software initiators that use the existing network cards on a server and present the resulting LUNs to the kernel. The second are hardware initiators that use hardware cards (provided by companies such as QLogic) to connect to the iSCSI disk array. The card then presents the LUNs to the kernel as SCSI devices. Hardware initiators reduce the CPU load on the host, but the configuration generally depends on user space tools specific to the manufacturer and the model, and are not covered in this book.

If you are using Fibre Channel **Host Bust Adapter**s (**HBA**s), iSCSI HBAs ("hardware initiators") or other storage involving hardware such as PCIe cards, it is possible that the cards will not be recognized by the kernel or that the open source driver shipped with RedHat Enterprise Linux and CentOS does not support all of the functionality that you require. In this case, you may have to install a custom driver. It is best to purchase the hardware that is supported without any such drivers, but if such drivers are required refer to your equipment documentation.

The end result must be the same; the same storage volume (**LUN**) must be presented on both nodes in the same place, such that they recognize them (ideally as something conventional such as /dev/sdb).

If you are planning on using iSCSI software initiators, first install the iSCSI initiator package:

If you are using RedHat Enterprise Linux, ensure that the machine has access to a *Clustering* entitlement if you use the RedHat Network. CentOS users can find these packages in the base repository.

```
[root@node2 ~]# yum -y install iscsi-initiator-utils
```

Check your initiator name (which is autogenerated) and use this to configure the iSCSI target (the storage device exporting the iSCSI LUN) to allow access from this node as follows:

```
[root@node2 ~]# cat /etc/iscsi/initiatorname.iscsi
InitiatorName=iqn.1994-05.com.redhat:405646314b4
```

Once you have configured the storage (for which you must refer to the documentation included with your storage), write down the **iSCSI Qualified Name** (**IQN**) of the disk array that you are trying to connect to. It is likely that you will find this given to you when you create the iSCSI volume in the storage management software.

Using the IQN (located earlier) and the IP address of the storage, send a special discovery request to the storage. In the English language, this says "hi, I'm <local initiator name>, what IQNs do you have available for me?"

For the purpose of this book, which is as quick and practical as possible, we have skipped configuring CHAP for authentication, which you should always do in a production setting (CHAP can be configured in `/etc/iscsi/iscsid.conf`). See the main page for `iscsid.conf` for more details.

Do this with the following command (`10.0.0.10` is our storage IP):

```
[root@node1 ~]# iscsiadm -m discovery -t st -p 10.0.0.10
10.0.0.10:3260,1 iqn.1986-03.com.sun:02:bef2d7f0-af13-6afa-9e70-
9622c12ee9c0
```

 The IQN gives you an idea that this is a SUN iSCSI appliance.

Hopefully, you should see the IQN you noted down in the output from the previous command. You may see more, if your storage is set to export some LUNs to all initiators. If you see nothing, there is something wrong—most likely, the storage requires CHAP authentication or you have incorrectly configured the storage to allow the initiator IQN access.

Once you see the output representing the correct storage volume, restart the `iscsi` service to connect to the volume as follows:

```
[root@node1 ~]# /etc/init.d/iscsi restart
Stopping iSCSI daemon:
iscsid dead but pid file exists                          [  OK  ]
Turning off network shutdown. Starting iSCSI daemon:     [  OK  ]
                                                         [  OK  ]
Setting up iSCSI targets:
Logging in to [iface: default, target: iqn.1986-03.com.sun:02:bef2d7f0-
af13-6afa-9e70-9622c12ee9c0, portal: 10.0.0.10,3260]
                                                         [  OK  ]
```

Check that this new storage volume has been mounted in the `kernel` log as follows:

```
[root@node1 ~]# dmesg | tail -1
sd 1:0:0:0: Attached scsi disk sdb
```

Repeat this entire exercise for the other node, which should also mount the same volume as `/dev/sdb`. Do not attempt to build a filesystem on this volume at this stage.

Good! You have successfully prepared your two-node cluster to see the same storage and are ready to run a service from this shared storage.

See also

This book covers some higher level performance tuning techniques in *Chapter 8, Performance Tuning, but will not delve into detailed kernel level performance tuning. For this, I can* recommend *"Optimizing Linux Performance", 2005, Phillip G. Ezolt, Prentice Hall* for an in-depth guide of performance for all the main subsystems in the Linux kernel.

If you are using iSCSI, consider enabling jumbo frames, although consider setting a MTU of 8000 bytes (rather than 9000 bytes), because the Linux kernel is significantly faster at allocating two pages of memory (required for 8000 bytes) as compared to allocating three pages (required for 9000 bytes). See the RedHat Knowledgebase article at: `http://kbase.redhat.com/faq/docs/DOC-3644`

Configuring two servers for shared storage MySQL

In this recipe, we will set up a MySQL service running on two servers, `node1` and `node2`, for sharing a iSCSI volume presented as `/dev/sdb` on both nodes for active/passive clustering. At the end of the recipe, you will see that it will be possible to manually fail over MySQL from one node to the other, but the process is extremely tedious. This recipe is designed as a stepping stone to the next recipe in which the failover process will be automated.

In this recipe, we will:

- ▸ Install the required packages for CentOS
- ▸ Create a logical volume on the shared storage
- ▸ Create a filesystem on this shared-storage logical volume
- ▸ Install MySQL

How to do it...

To follow this recipe, ensure that you have a clean install of CentOS (or RedHat Enterprise Linux with a Cluster Suite entitlement) and your LUNs on your storage array connect to and are visible from both nodes, with both of them seeing this storage device. In this example, we will be using an iSCSI volume, but the steps would be identical for any other shared storage.

Ensure that the preparatory steps discussed in the previous recipe have been completed and that both of your nodes can see the shared LUN (`fdisk -l /dev/sdb` (or `/dev/folder name`)) and show the information for the shared-storage volume.

Carry out the following steps on both the servers:

1. If the Cluster Filesystem package option was not selected in setup, run the following command to install all relevant packages (you can run it to be sure that everything has been correctly installed):

```
[root@node2 ~]# yum groupinstall clustering
```

2. An important early step is to ensure that all servers have time in sync, as some of the cluster work will depend on time being in sync. Install, start, and start on boot the `ntp` service:

```
[root@node2 ~]# yum install ntp
```

```
[root@node2 ~]# chkconfig ntpd on
[root@node2 ~]# service ntpd start
Starting ntpd:                                          [  OK  ]
```

You can specify a NTP server in `/etc/ntp.conf` and restart `ntpd`.

Add the IP addresses for each node involved in the cluster to `/etc/hosts`. In this example, `host1` and `host2` have a private network connected to `eth1` and use IP addresses `10.0.0.1` and `10.0.0.2`, so add these lines to `/etc/hosts` on both nodes:

```
127.0.0.1               localhost.localdomain localhost
10.0.0.1                node1
10.0.0.2                node2
```

 The entire **Fully Qualified Domain Name** (**FQDN**) of the nodes should be added to this file alongside its IP address, along with any aliases. In the previous example, the nodes are not members of a domain. The entire FQDN of the hosts should be added to /etc/hosts, plus any aliases.

Entries for each node in each cluster's `/etc/hosts` file are critical because the cluster processes will execute a large number of name lookups. Many of these will be required to be completed in a certain period of time or the cluster will assume that another node is dead and cause a short period of downtime and some aborted transactions as it fails over. In the event that DNS services are unavailable even for a short period of time and the hosts involved in the cluster are not listed in `/etc/hosts`, its effects on the cluster may be very significant.

3. The next step is to create a partition or logical volume on the shared storage. We will create a logical volume using LVM rather than a simple partition. Using LVM reduces the problems of using partitions (in particular, LUNs from different storage arrays can be presented in a different order after a reboot of a node and be assigned a different device name (for example, /dev/sdd rather than /dev/sdb). These problems can be avoided by assigning persistent device names using either udev or LVM (a third alternative for ext3 and similar filesystems is assigning filesystem labels using e2label, which can cause extremely bizarre problems and potential loss of data).

Carry out the following procedure on only a single node to create a LVM physical volume on the shared storage, build a volume group consisting of that physical volume, and add a logical volume for the data.

Carrying this out on a single node might seem bizarre. The reason is that at this stage, we have not actually installed the cluster daemons (this is part of the next recipe). Specifically, the clvmd daemon is required to automatically sync state across nodes in a cluster. Until this is installed, running, and the nodes are in a cluster together, it is dangerous to make changes to the LVM metadata on more than one node. So we stick to using a single node to create our LVM devices, groups, and volumes, and also our filesystem.

Create a physical volume on the shared disk, /dev/sdb:

```
[root@node1 ~]# pvcreate /dev/sdb
  Physical volume "/dev/sdb" successfully created
```

Now create a volume group (in our example called clustervg) with the new physical volume in it:

```
[root@node1 ~]# vgcreate clustervg /dev/sdb
  Volume group "gfsvg" successfully created
```

Now create a logical volume, 300 MB in size, called mysql_data_ext3 in the volume group gfsvg:

```
[root@node1 ~]# lvcreate --name=mysql_data_ext3 --size=300M  clustervg
Logical volume "mysql_data" created
```

If you have available disk space, it is recommended to leave some storage unallocated in each volume group. This is because snapshots require space, and this space must come from unallocated space in the volume group. When a snapshot is created, it has a size and this size is the amount of data that can be changed (each time a piece of data on the volume that has been *snapshotted* is modified, this change is recorded but obviously does not overwrite the existing data thus increasing the disk space usage. This design is called *copy on write*.

Now that you have a logical volume, you can create a standard `ext3` filesystem on the new logical volume as follows:

```
[root@node1 ~]# mkfs.ext3 /dev/clustervg/mysql_data_ext3
```

We are using a standard filesystem at this point, as this will be mounted on either one node or another node (not both). It is possible to configure a filesystem to exist on both nodes at the same time, using the open source GFS filesystem, but this is not needed for clusters with only one node active. Products such as Oracle RAC (which are active-active) can use GFS extensively, and the final recipe in this chapter demonstrates how to use GFS with MySQL (although still only one node can have MySQL running at a time).

Finally, we need MySQL installed to actually make use of the cluster. We need to get this to install the `mysql` database onto the shared storage, so mount this first. Carry out the following steps on the same single node that you created the LVM logical volume and filesystem on:

```
[root@node1 ~]# mkdir -p /var/lib/mysql
[root@node1 ~]# mount /dev/clustervg/mysql_data_ext3 /var/lib/mysql
[root@node1 ~]# yum install mysql-server
```

Now, start the service (which will run the `mysql_install_db` script automatically to create the `mysql` database):

```
[root@node1 ~]# service mysql start
```

Once completed, stop the service and unmount the filesystem as follows:

```
[root@node1 ~]# service mysql stop
[root@node1 ~]# umount /var/lib/mysql
```

Once you have created the filesystem, there is no reason for you to ever mount it manually again—you should only use cluster tools to bring the service up on a node in order to ensure that there is no risk of data loss. If this concerns you, be sure to use GFS rather than EXT3, as covered in a later recipe.

Finally, install MySQL on the second node as follows:

```
[root@node2 ~]# yum install mysql-server
```

Do not start MySQL.

There's more...

You could, if you wanted, manually fail over the service from `node1` to `node2`. The process would be as follows:

- On `node 1`, stop MySQL, unmount the filesystem on `node 1` then switch to `node 2`.
- On `node 2`, you could manually scan for LVM physical volumes, volume groups, and logical volumes. You would then have to manually enable the shared LVM volume, mount the filesystem on `node 2`, start MySQL on `node 2`, and use it.

If this seems unrealistic and totally useless that is fine, because in the next recipe we will show you how to build on this recipe and install open source software called **Conga** to automate all of this, and do it automatically in the case of server failure.

Configuring MySQL on shared storage with Conga

In this recipe, we will enhance the previous recipe to install open source cluster management software called Conga. Conga consists of two parts—a server called `luci` and a client called `ricci`. Once everything is configured, you will have a highly-available MySQL service which will automatically fail over from node to node.

This recipe will not configure *fencing* as briefly discussed earlier in this chapter; this will be covered in the next recipe. As a result of this limitation, this cluster will not handle all node crashes; for almost all real-world uses, you will use this as a stepping stone towards the next recipe, which adds fencing to the configuration created in this recipe.

How to do it...

In this recipe, we will configure Conga cluster management agent `luci` on a different server, and the client `ricci` on all the nodes (`luci` can be installed on any server, including one of the nodes).

The first step is to install and configure `luci` on a server. In this example, we will use one of the nodes involved in the cluster, `node1`. Run `luci_admin init` as root. Once installed, start the `luci` service as instructed.

If you are using a node on which you have not already installed the clustering package group, you should install `luci` first:

[root@node6 cluster]# yum install luci

This process is shown in the following screenshot:

```
                                                    root@node6:~
File  Edit  View  Terminal  Help
[root@node6 ~]# luci_admin init
Initializing the luci server


Creating the 'admin' user

Enter password:
Confirm password:

Please wait...
The admin password has been successfully set.
Generating SSL certificates...
The luci server has been successfully initialized


You must restart the luci server for changes to take effect.

Run "service luci restart" to do so

[root@node6 ~]# service luci restart
Shutting down luci:                                      [  OK  ]
Starting luci: Generating https SSL certificates...  done
                                                         [  OK  ]

Point your web browser to https://node6:8084 to access luci

[root@node6 ~]# █
```

Ensure that `luci` is configured to start on boot as follows:

[root@node6 cluster]# chkconfig luci on

Ensure that MySQL is not started automatically on boot (as we wish the cluster manager to start it):

[root@node1 cluster]# chkconfig --del mysql

Point your browser at the URL, and log in with the username `admin` and password that you have just created. Select **Cluster** and **Create new cluster**, and enter the details specific to your setup. Ensure that you check **Enable shared storage** and do not select **reboot node**, if (as in our example) `luci` is running on one of the nodes.

After a short wait, you should be redirected to the general tab of the new `mysqlcluster` cluster, which by then should be started.

At time of writing, CentOS had a bug that required a newer version of OpenAIS to be installed for this process to work; if you see an error starting `cman` on a fresh install of CentOS, see CentOS bug #3842 for a description and solution.

With `luci` installed, the next step is to configure some resources in our cluster—an IP address, a service, and a filesystem.

Click on **resources** in the left-hand bar, **Add a resource** and select **IP Address**. Enter the **shared** IP address that will be owned by whichever node is active at that time (this is the IP, that clients will connect to). In our example we use `10.0.0.100`.

Click on **resources | Add a resource | Filesystem** and enter the following details:

- Name—**mysql_data_ext3**
- File system type—**ext3**
- Mount point—**/var/lib/mysql**
- Device—**/dev/clustervg/mysql_data_ext3**

Click on **resources | Add a resource | MySQL** and enter the following details:

- Name—**mysql**
- Config file—**/etc/my.cnf**
- Listen address—**10.0.0.100**
- Shutdown Wait (seconds)—Give a value of at least `15` seconds (otherwise, migrations will almost certainly fail).

Now, we need to add a service which brings together all of the resources under one name. Click on **Services** from the left hand bar, followed by clicking on **Add new service**, and fill in these details:

- Service name—**mysql**
- Automatically start—**yes**
- Recovery policy—**relocate**

Recovery policies basically mean, *what should I do if the service fails?* If you think that it is likely that a service failure may occur normally, select **restart** which simply means run the `init` script with the `restart` parameter. If you think that a service failure is likely to indicate a problem with the server, set it to **relocate** which means fail the service off the current node onto a new node.

You may set the other parameters as you wish, or leave the defaults.

Click on **Add a resource to this service**, and from the second box **Use an existing global resource**. Click on **Submit**, once all three resources (IP address, filesystem, and `init` script) are added.

You should find yourself back at the service main page for the new `mysql` service. Wait a minute, and click on **Services** in the left bar again, to see if this service has started—it should.

From the web interface, you can migrate the `mysql` service from `node1` to `node2` and back again. Each time you migrate the service, the following process is carried out automatically by the cluster services:

- Stop service on source node
- Wait *Shutdown wait* seconds to allow clean exit
- Ensure that service has exited cleanly (if not, leave in disabled state)
- Unmount volume on source node
- Remove virtual IP address
- Mount volume on destination node
- Add virtual IP to destination node, run some Ethernet hacks to update ARP tables
- Start service on destination node
- Check that service has started correctly

You can see from this that at no point is the shared storage mounted on more than one node, and this prevents corruption.

Congratulations! At this point, you have a working shared-storage cluster.

Remember that we do not have any sort of fencing configured, so this setup is not highly available—if you kill the active node, the service may not start on the second node just to ensure that data is not corrupted.

How it works...

While these two processes form a critical part of Conga, it is important to understand that the cluster management system that we used is not involved in the actual cluster processes of failing nodes over and monitoring nodes, but is merely for the configuration of the cluster daemons on each node (which was rather complicated).

The Conga software suite, including `luci` and `ricci`, communicates using SSL as shown in the following diagram:

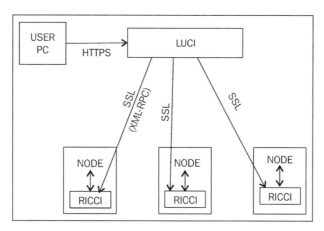

While `luci` is convenient to have, its failure has no effect on the cluster other than removing the ability for you to use a web interface to manage your cluster (the command-line tools, some of which we will explore in this chapter, will however still work). Similarly, a failure of `ricci` on a node simply prevents that node from being managed by `luci`—it will have no effect on the node's actual role in a cluster, once the node is fully configured.

There's more...

For creating your cluster, it is often hard to beat the `luci` / `ricci` combination—the other tools available are not as simple, or in some ways, not as powerful. However, for managing the cluster, it is sometimes easier to stay at the command line of any node. In this section, we briefly outline some of these useful commands.

Obtaining the cluster status

Using the `clustat` command, you can quickly see which nodes in the cluster are up (according to the local node), and which services are running where. It can be shown as follows:

```
[root@node1 lib]# clustat
Cluster Status for mysqlcluster @ Sun Oct 18 19:14:48 2009
Member Status: Quorate
```

```
Member Name                          ID   Status
------  ----                         ----  ------
node1.xxx.com                        1 Online, Local, rgmanager
node2.xxx.com                        2 Online, rgmanager


Service Name                  Owner (Last)              State
-------  ----                 -----  ------             -----
service:mysql                 node1.xxx.com             started
[root@node1 lib]#
```

This shows that service `mysql` is running on `node1`, and the two nodes in the cluster (`node1` and `node2`) are online.

Migration of MySQL from node to node

It is possible to use the `clusvcadm` command to move a service from one node to another. As we are not using a clustered filesystem, this involves stopping the service completely on one node and starting it on the second only after the filesystem has been unmounted from the first node.

For example, have a look at the output of `clustat` command:

```
[root@node1 lib]# clustat
Cluster Status for mysqlcluster @ Sun Oct 18 19:35:02 2009


Service Name                  Owner (Last)              State
-------  ----                 -----  ------             -----
service:mysql                 node1.xxx.com             started
```

From the previous output, we can see that the service `mysql` is currently running on `node1`. We can move this service to `node2` by passing `-e service_name -m preferred_ destination_hostname` to `clusvcadm`, as shown in the following example:

```
[root@node1 lib]# clusvcadm -e mysql -m node2.xxx.com
Member node2.xxx.com trying to enable service:mysql...Success
service:mysql is now running on node2.xxx.com
```

Now, you can confirm the status with `clustat` as follows:

```
[root@node1 lib]# clustat
Cluster Status for mysqlcluster @ Sun Oct 18 19:37:33 2009

 Service Name                      Owner (Last)                    State
 ------- ----                      ----- ------                    -----
 service:mysql                     node2.xxx.com                   started
```

Fencing for high availability

Fencing, sometimes known as **Shoot The Other Node In The Head (STONITH)** sounds pretty dramatic, and at first sight it may seem odd that it is a good thing for high availability. In this recipe, we will discuss why fencing is required in all clusters, and then discuss its implementation using the scripts provided with RHEL and CentOS.

There is only one way to be sure that something is dead—that is, to kill it yourself. For a shared-storage cluster, it is considered good enough to ask something to die—but only if it is able to confirm with absolute clarity that it has indeed successfully died. The reason for this caution is that if a node is considered dead, but is in fact able to consider writing to a shared-storage device (as may occur in the case of a kernel bug for example), the consequences may be total data loss on the shared-storage volume.

What this means in practical terms with shared-storage clusters is that in the event of a controlled movement of a service (for example, either a user asks for a service to be moved from node A to node B, or the service itself fails—but the machine and the cluster is set to relocate failed services), the other nodes in the cluster will ask the node to unmount its storage and release its IP address. As soon as the node confirms that it has done so, this will be considered as sufficient.

However, the most common reason to move a service is that the previously active node has failed (because it had crashed, had a power problem, or had been removed from the network for some reason). In this case, the remaining nodes have a problem—as the node that is being moved away, almost certainly, will not be able to confirm that it has unmounted the storage. Even if it has been removed from the network, it could still quite happily be connected via a separate (fibre) network to a Fibre Channel storage volume. If this is the case, it is almost certainly writing to the volume, and, if another node attempts to start the service, all the data will be corrupted. It is therefore critical that if automatic failover is required, the remaining nodes must have a way to be sure that the node is dead and is no longer writing to the storage.

Fencing provides this technique. In broad terms, configuring fencing is as simple as saying "do x to kill node y", where "x" is a normal script that is run to connect to a remote management card, smart power distribution unit, or to a storage switch to mask the host.

In this recipe, we will show how to configure fencing. Unfortunately, fencing configuration does vary from method to method, but we will explain the process to be followed.

It is possible to configure *manual fencing,* however, this is a bit of a botch—it effectively tells the cluster to do nothing in the case of node failure, and wait for a human operator to decide what to do. This rather defeats many of the benefits of a cluster, and furthermore, due to the problems inherent in manual fencing, namely that it is not sufficient to ensure data integrity and is strongly not recommended, nodes may get stuck while waiting for this man—and not respond to standard reboot commands requiring a physical power boot.

It is also possible to create a dummy fencing script that fools the cluster into thinking that a node has successfully been fenced, when in fact it has not. It goes without saying that doing this is risking data, even if you do get slightly easier high availability. Fencing is an absolute requirement and it is a really bad idea to skip it.

How to do it...

The first step is to add a user on the fencing device. This may involve adding a user to the remote management card, power system, or storage switch. Once this is done, you should record the IP address of the fencing device (such as the iLO card) as well as the username and password that you have created.

Once a user is added on the fencing device, ensure that you can actually connect to the fencing device interface from your nodes. For example, for most modern fencing devices, a connection will run over port 22 on SSH, but it may also involve a telnet, SNMP, or other connection.

For example, testing a SSH connection is easy—just SSH to the fencing user at the fencing device from the nodes in your cluster as follows:

```
[root@node1 ~]# ssh fencing-user@ip-of-fencing-device
The authenticity of host can't be established.
RSA key fingerprint is 08:62:18:11:e2:74:bc:e0:b4:a7:2c:00:c4:28:36:c8.
Are you sure you want to continue connecting (yes/no)? yes
fence@ip-of-esxserviceconsole's password:
[fence@host5 ~]$
```

Once this is successful, we need to configure the cluster to use fencing. Return to the luci page for your cluster and select **Cluster | Cluster List**, select a node, scroll down to **Fencing**, and select **Add an instance**.

Fill in the details appropriate for your specific solution; the fields are fairly self-explanatory and vary from one fencing method to another. But, in general, they ask for an IP, username, and password for the fencing device and some unique aspect of this particular device (for example, a port number).

Once completed, click on **Update main fence properties**.

 In the case of redundant power supply units, be sure to add two methods to the primary fencing method rather than one to the primary and secondary (the secondary technique is only used if the primary fails).

Repeat this exercise for both your nodes, and be sure to check that it works for each node in `luci` (from **Actions**, select **Fence this node**, ideally while pinging the node to ensure that it dies almost immediately).

There's more...

To set up fencing on VMware ESX—a common testing environment—make the following changes to the generic setup explained previously.

 The bundled scripts will only work if you are running the full version of ESX (not the embedded, ESXi, product). However, there are newer scripts available at the Cluster Suite wiki (`http://sources.redhat.com/cluster/wiki/`), that handle pretty much all versions of VMware, but do require you to install the VMware Perl API on all nodes.

Firstly, to add a fence user in VMware, connect directly to the host (even if it is usually managed by vCenter) with the VI client, navigate to the **Users and Groups** tab, right click and select **Add**. Enter a username, name, and password and select **Enable shell access** and click on **OK**.

Secondly, a specific requirement of VMware ESX fencing is the need to enable the SSH server running inside the service console by selecting the **Configuration** tab inside the **host configuration** in the VI client. Click on the **Security Profile**, click on the **Properties** menu, and check **SSH Server**. Click on **OK** and exit the VI client.

When adding your fence device, select **VMware fencing** in `luci` and use the following details:

- Name—`vmware_fence_nodename` (or any other unique convention)
- Hostname—hostname of ESX service console
- Login—user that you created
- Password—password that you have set
- VMWare ESX Management Login—a user with privilege to start and stop the virtual machines on the ESX server, often used for testing `root`
- VMWare ESX Management Password—the associated password for the account
- Port—`22`
- Check—use `SSH`

In my testing, ESX 4 is not supported by the `fence_vmware` script supplied with RHEL/CentOS 5.3. There are two main problems—firstly, detecting node state, and secondly, with the command called.

The hack fix is to simply prevent it from checking that the node is not already powered off before trying to power the virtual machine off (which works fine, although may result in unnecessary reboots); the shortest way to achieve this is to edit `/usr/lib/fence/fence.py` on all nodes to change lines 419 and 428 to effectively disable the check, as follows:

```
if status == "off-HACK":
```

 This change will not just affect VMware fencing operations, and so it should not be used except for testing fencing on VMware ESX (vSphere) 4.

The second problem is the addition of a `-A` flag to the command executed on the VMware server. Comment out lines 94 and 95 of `/sbin/fence_vmware` to fix this as follows:

```
94:        #if 0 == options.has_key("-A"):
95:        #    options["-A"] = "localhost"
```

 This is Python, so be sure to keep the indentation correct. There are also a thousand more elegant solutions, but none that I am aware of that can be represented in four lines!

See also

You can browse the latest available fencing agent scripts for new devices at `http://sources.redhat.com/cgi-bin/cvsweb.cgi/cluster/fence/agents/?cvsroot=cluster`.

Configuring MySQL with GFS

In this recipe, we will configure a two-node GFS cluster, running MySQL. GFS allows multiple Linux servers to simultaneously read and write a shared filesystem on an external storage array, ensuring consistency through locking.

MySQL does not have any support for *active-active* cluster configurations using shared storage. However, with a cluster filesystem (such as GFS), you can mount the same filesystem on multiple servers allowing for far faster failovers from node to node and protecting against data loss caused by accidently mounting on more than one server on a normal filesystem on shared storage. To reiterate—even with GFS, you must only ever run one MySQL process at a time, and not allow two MySQL processes to start on the same data or you will likely end up with corrupt data (in the same way as running two `mysql` processes on the same server with the same data directory would cause corruption).

 GFS2 is a substantially improved version of the original GFS, which is now stable in recent versions of RHEL/CentOS. In this recipe, we use GFS2, and all mentions of GFS should be read as referring to GFS2.

It is strongly recommended that you create your GFS filesystems on top of Logical Volume Manager's (LVM) logical volumes. In addition to all the normal advantages of LVM, in the specific case of shared storage, relying on /dev/sdb and /dev/sdc always being the same is often an easy assumption to make that can go horribly wrong, when you add or modify a LUN on your storage (which can sometimes completely change the ordering of volumes). As LVM uses unique identifiers to identify logical volumes, renumbering of block devices has no effect.

In this example, we will assume that you have followed the earlier recipe showing how to run MySQL on shared storage with Conga, and have a volume group `clustervg` with spare space in it.

How to do it...

Ensure that the GFS utilities are installed as follows:

```
[root@node1 ~]# yum -y install gfs2-utils
```

Check the current space available in our volume groups with the `vgs` command:

```
[root@node1 ~]# vgs
  VG         #PV #LV #SN Attr   VSize    VFree
  clustervg    1   1   0 wz--nc 1020.00M 720.00M
  system       1   2   0 wz--n-   29.41G  19.66G
```

Create a new logical volume that we will use in this volume group to test, called `mysql_data_gfs`, as follows:

```
[root@node1 ~]# lvcreate --size=300M --name=mysql_data_gfs2 clustervg
Logical volume "mysql_data_gfs2" created
```

Now, we will create a GFS filesystem on this new logical volume. We create this with a cluster name of `mysqlcluster` and a volume name of `mysql_data`. The 2 parameter to `-j` is the number of journals; this must be at least the number of nodes (although it can be increased later).

```
[root@node1 ~]# mkfs.gfs2 -t mysqlcluster:mysql_data_ext3 -j 2 /dev/
clustervg/mysql_data_gfs2
```

Now log in to `luci`, select **Cluster** from the top bar, select your cluster name (`mysqlcluster`, in our example). From the left bar, select **Resources | Add a resource | GFS Filesystem** from the drop-down box and enter the following details:

- ▸ Name—a descriptive name (I use the final part of the path, in this case `mysql_data_gfs2`)
- ▸ Mount point—`/var/lib/mysql`
- ▸ Device—`/dev/clustervg/mysql_data_gfs2`
- ▸ Filesystem type— `GFS2`
- ▸ Options—`noatime` (see the upcoming *There's more...* section)
- ▸ Select **reboot host node if unmount fails** to ensure data integrity
- ▸ Click on **Submit** and then click on **OK** on the pop-up box that appears

The next step is to modify our `mysql` service to use this new `GFS` filesystem. Firstly, stop the `mysql` service. In `luci`, click on **Services**, your service name (in our example `mysql`). From the **Choose a task** menu, select **Disable this service**.

At this point, the service should be stopped on whichever node it was active. Check this at the command line by ensuring that `/var/lib/mysql` is not mounted and that the MySQL process is not running, on both nodes:

```
[root@node2 ~]# ps aux | grep mysql
root       6167  0.0  0.0  61184    748 pts/0    R+   20:38   0:00 grep
mysql
[root@node2 ~]# cat /proc/mounts | grep mysql | wc -l
0
```

Now, we need to start MySQL for the first time to run the `mysql_install_db` script to build the `mysql` database. If you have important data on the existing volume, you could, of course, mount that somewhere else and copy the important data onto the new GFS volume.

If you do not need to import any data, you could just start the service for the first time in `luci` and if all goes well, it would work fine. But I always prefer to start the service for the first time manually. Any errors that may occur are normally easier to deal with from the command line than through `luci`. In any case, it is a good idea to know how to mount GFS filesystems manually.

Firstly, mount the filesystem manually on either node as follows:

```
[root@node1 ~]# mount -t gfs2 /dev/clustervg/mysql_data_gfs2 /var/lib/
mysql/
```

Check that it has mounted properly by using following command:

```
[root@node1 ~]# cat /proc/mounts | grep mysql
```

```
/dev/mapper/clustervg-mysql_data_gfs2 /var/lib/mysql gfs2
rw,hostdata=jid=0:id=65537:first=1 0 0
```

Start `mysql` to run `mysql_install_db` (as there is nothing in our new filesystem on `/var/lib/mysql`):

```
[root@node1 ~]# service mysql start
Initializing MySQL database:  Installing MySQL system tables...
OK
Filling help tables...
OK
...
                                                              [  OK  ]
Starting MySQL:                                               [  OK  ]
```

You can enter the `mysql` client at this point if you wish to verify that everything is okay or import data.

Now, stop the `mysql` service by using following command:

```
[root@node1 ~]# service mysql stop
Stopping MySQL:                                               [  OK  ]
```

Unmount the filesystem as follows:

```
[root@node1 ~]# umount /var/lib/mysql/
```

And check that it has unmounted okay by ensuring the exit code as follows:

```
[root@node1 ~]# cat /proc/mounts | grep mysql | wc -l
0
```

There's more...

There are a couple of useful tricks that you should know when using GFS. These are:

Cron job woes

By default, CentOS/RHEL run a cron job early in the morning to update the `updatedb` database. This allows you to rapidly search for a file on your system using the `locate` command. Unfortunately, this sort of scanning of the entire filesystem simultaneously by multiple nodes can cause extreme problems with GFS partitions. So, it is recommended that you add your GFS mount point (`/var/lib/mysql`, in our example) to `/etc/updatedb.conf` in order to tell it to skip these paths (and everything in them), when it scans the filesystem:

```
PRUNEPATHS = "/afs /media /net /sfs /tmp /udev /var/spool/cups /var/
spool/squid /var/tmp /var/lib/mysql"
```

Preventing unnecessary small writes

Another performance booster of a node is the `noatime` mount option. `noatime` is a timestamp for the time the file was last accessed, which may be required by your application. However, if you do not (most applications do not) require it, you can save yourself a (small) write for every read, which can be extremely slow as the node must get a lock on that file. To configure this, in the `luci` web interface, select the **Filesystem resource** and add `noatime` to the options field.

Mounting filesystem on both nodes

In this recipe, we configured the filesystem as a cluster resource, which means that the filesystem will be mounted only on the active node. The only benefit from GFS, therefore, is the guarantee that if for whatever reason the filesystem did become mounted in more than one place (administrator error, fencing failure, and so on), data is much safer.

It is however possible to permanently mount the filesystem on all nodes and save the cluster processes from having to mount and unmount it on failure. To do this, stop the service in `luci`, remove the filesystem from the service configuration in `luci`, and add the following to `/etc/fstab` on all nodes:

```
/dev/clustervg/mysql_data_gfs2 /var/lib/mysql gfs2 noatime_netdev 0 0
```

Mount the filesystem manually for the first time as follows:

```
[root@node2 ~]# mount /var/lib/mysql/
```

And start the service in `luci`. You should find that planned moves from one node to another are slightly quicker, although you must ensure that nobody starts the MySQL process on more than one node!

If you wish to configure active / active MySQL—that is, have two nodes, both servicing clients based on the same storage, see the note at `http://sources.redhat.com/cluster/wiki/FAQ/GFS#gfs_mysql`. It is possible, but not a configuration that is much used.

7
High Availability with Block Level Replication

In this chapter, we will cover:

- ▸ Introduction
- ▸ Installing DRBD on two Linux servers
- ▸ Manually moving services within a DRBD Cluster
- ▸ Using heartbeat for automatic failover

Introduction

Block level replication allows you to keep a highly-available database by replicating data at the hard drive (block) level between two machines. In other words, in two machines, every time a write is made by the kernel on the main server, it is sent to server 2 so as to be written to its disk.

The leading open source software for block level replication is DRBD. **DRBD** stands for **Distributed Replicated Block Device** and describes itself as a "software-based, shared-nothing, replicated storage solution mirroring the content of block devices (such as hard disks, partitions, logical volumes, and so on) between servers".

DRBD works by installing a kernel module on the Linux machines involved in the cluster. Once loaded, this kernel module picks up the IO operations of writes just before they are scheduled for writing by the disk driver. Once the DRBD receives a write, it sends it (via TCP/ IP) to the replica server, which itself sends the write to its local disk. At some stage during this process, the first node sends its write to its disk and reports to MySQL that the write has been completed. There is a consistency versus performance trade-off, and a parameter is specified to state at exactly which point in the process of one node receiving a write the application is told that the write has succeeded. For maximum durability, this will be done only after the write has made it onto the disk on the peer nodes, and this is called a **synchronous mode**.

The process of a single write transaction with this maximum data protection configuration (that is "synchronous" configuration) is illustrated in the following diagram:

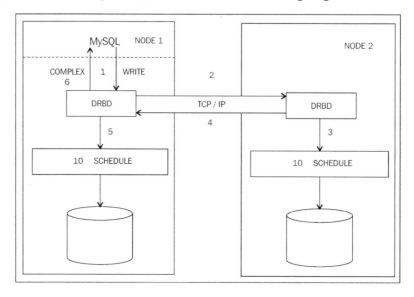

The preceding diagram illustrates the process as follows:

1. The write is committed in MySQL on node1 and sent by the Kernel to the DRBD module.
2. DRBD sends the write to node2.
3. DRBD on node2 sends the write to its drive.
4. DRBD on node2 confirms to node1 that it has received the write and sent it to its disk.
5. DRBD on node1 sends the write to its local disk.
6. The kernel on node1 reports that the write is completed. At this point, the data is almost certainly on the drive in both node1 and node2. There are two possible reasons why it may not be. There may be a cache that is hidden from the Linux Kernel, and there may have been failure on node2 between the time the change hit the scheduler and before it could actually be written to the disk.

As you can probably tell, it is possible for power failures, at unfortunate times, to cause a minute loss of data and / or inconsistency. DRBD recognizes this, and provides a wealth of both automated and manual tools to recover from this situation in a sensible way.

A consequence of DRBD's design is that, as with shared storage devices, if you wish to write to multiple nodes at the same time, a cluster-aware filesystem (for example, GFS) is required. DRBD disables the ability to write to multiple nodes at the same time by default.

Before you start with any of the recipes explained in this chapter, it is worth exploring in slightly more detail the three options for "data availability versus performance" that are available with DRBD. In broad terms, these three are as follows:

1. "Protocol A": Asynchronous—local writes are dealt with as normal (each write only has to make it as far as the local TCP buffer before it is declared as completed to the application). In this example, power loss on the master node will result in consistent but slightly out-of-date data on the slave.

2. "Protocol B": Semi-synchronous—local writes are only declared completed when the write reaches the other node's RAM. In this example, power loss on the master will result in consistent and up-to-date data on the slave, but in the case of power loss to both nodes, the outcome is the same as with Protocol A.

3. "Protocol C": Synchronous—local writes are only declared as completed when the write reaches the other nodes actual disk. In the event of simultaneous power failure, the slave node is both consistent and up-to-date. This is the most common setup if data is valuable.

The obvious benefit to the asynchronous setting (A) is that the performance impact on the master node is minimal—the synchronous option slows down each write by at least an order of magnitude, as it involves two TCP/IP connections which are relatively slow. Unfortunately, this must be balanced with the loss of data that will occur in the event of failure.

 The performance reduction of Protocol C can be partially mitigated through the use of high-speed and low-overhead Dolphin SuperSockets, which are provided by `http://www.dolphinics.com/`.

Installing DRBD on two Linux servers

In this recipe, we will take two freshly installed CentOS 5.3 servers and configure DRBD to synchronize a LVM logical volume on both nodes, running MySQL. We will demonstrate how to manually failover the service.

Getting ready

Ensure that both nodes are freshly installed and, if possible, have a clean kernel. When you install MySQL, ensure that you are not allocating all of the space to the / logical volume (the default in the CentOS / RHEL installer Anaconda). You can either create the LVM logical volume that DRBD will use during setup, or leave the space unallocated in a volume group and create the logical volume later. You can check the space available in a volume group using the vgs command:

```
[root@node3 ~]# vgs
  VG       #PV #LV #SN Attr   VSize  VFree
  system    1   2   0 wz--n- 25.00G 15.25G
```

This shows that the volume group system has just over 15G spare space, which is sufficient for this test.

Ensure that both nodes have the CentOS "Extras" repository installed. If the yum list | grep drbd command doesn't show a package for DRBD, add the following to a .repo file in /etc/yum.repos.d/, such as to the bottom of CentOS-Base.repo:

```
[extras]
name=CentOS-$releasever - Extras
mirrorlist=http://mirrorlist.centos.org/
?release=$releasever&arch=$basearch&repo=extras
#baseurl=http://mirror.centos.org/centos/$releasever/extras/$basearch/
gpgcheck=1
gpgkey=file:///etc/pki/rpm-gpg/RPM-GPG-KEY-CentOS-5
```

If you're using RedHat rather than CentOS, you can still use the CentOS repository.

How to do it...

On both nodes, install the DRBD user-space tools, the kernel module, and the MySQL server:

```
[root@node3 ~]# yum -y install drbd kmod-drbd mysql-server
```

Create the logical volume for DRBD to use on both nodes (ensuring they are identical in name and size); the final parameter in this command is the volume group name, which must have sufficient free extents as shown in the vgs command.

```
[root@node3 ~]# lvcreate --name=mysql_drbd --size=5G system
  Logical volume "mysql_drbd" created
```

Copy the sample configuration file to save typing the entire thing out:

```
[root@node3 ~]# cp /usr/share/doc/drbd-8.0.16/drbd.conf /etc/drbd.conf
cp: overwrite `/etc/drbd.conf'? y
```

Using the text editor of your choice, make the following changes to `/etc/drbd.conf`:

Modify the resource name to `mysql`, that is:

```
resource mysql {
```

Move down to the node configuration (as defined in the hostname). Remove the existing two nodes (`alf` and `amd`) and replace them with the details of your nodes, following the template explained as follows:

 I recommend using the private IP addresses of the nodes here if there is a private network—if not, the public address can be used (but of course, traffic between nodes is insecure and vulnerable).

```
on node3 {
   device      /dev/drbd0;
   disk        /dev/system/mysql_drbd;
   address     IP_OF_NODE3:7788;
   meta-disk internal;
}

on node4 {
   device      /dev/drbd0;
   disk        /dev/system/mysql_drbd;
   address     IP_OF_NODE4:7788;
   meta-disk internal;
}
```

 You should use the hostname as returned by the "hostname" command to replace node3 and node4 in the previous example, and you should ensure that `/etc/hosts` and DNS are correctly set in order to avoid weird problems. It would be possible to configure some sort of encrypted tunnel between nodes in these cases, but performance is likely to be extremely poor.

Remove the final three resources (`r0`, `r1`, and `r2`).

Save your DRBD configuration and copy it to the second node:

```
[root@node3 ~]# scp /etc/drbd.conf node4:/etc/
root@node4's password:
drbd.conf                                  100%    16KB  16.3KB/s
00:00
```

On the first node, initialize the DRBD metadata with the following command: the final parameter is the resource name, which we defined as `mysql` in `/etc/drbd.conf`.

```
[root@node3 ~]# drbdadm create-md mysql
```

 We have selected "internal" metadata option, which means DRBD will take a very small amount of the raw block device and use it for metadata–it is possible (but more complex and with limited benefit) to store metadata in a separate partition.

Repeat this command on the second node.

Now we have DRBD metadata on both nodes, reboot each of them (or restart the `drbd` service) to start the DRBD user space tools and load the kernel module. When the nodes come back up, have a look at the `drbd-overview` information:

```
[root@node3 ~]# drbd-overview
  0:mysql  WFConnection Secondary/Unknown Inconsistent/DUnknown C r---
```

This will show that the local device role is Secondary and the local block device state is Inconsistent. This is because at the moment DRBD has no idea which node is "master" and thus which node has correct and which has incorrect data. To introduce some consistency we must choose a point in time and say that one node is "master"" and one "slave". This is done with the following command:

```
[root@node3 ~]# drbdadm -- --overwrite-data-of-peer primary mysql
```

 The double set of double dashes are not erroneous. - - signals the end of options and disables further option processing. Any arguments after - - are treated as filenames and arguments.

This quote literally says, "take my data and send it to the second node". This process make some time, depending on the network link between the nodes, the configured synchronization speed limits, and the performance of the hardware in each of the nodes. You can use `drbd-overview` to monitor progress:

```
[root@node3 ~]# drbd-overview
  0:mysql  SyncSource Primary/Secondary UpToDate/Inconsistent C r---
  [>...................] sync'ed:  2.2% (5012/5116)M
```

If you see output such as this on the primary node:

```
[root@node3 ~]# drbd-overview

  0:mysql  WFConnection Primary/Unknown UpToDate/
DUnknown C r---
```

Check that the `drbd.conf` file has been synced correctly and restart `drbd` on the second node.

While this is syncing, you can happily use the new filesystem on the first node. Create a ext3 filesystem on it:

```
[root@node3 ~]# mkfs.ext3 /dev/drbd0
```

Mount this filesystem on `/var/lib/mysql`.

In this example cluster we have not installed MySQL yet, so `/var/lib/mysql` is empty. If you already have data in `/var/lib/mysql`, stop MySQL; mount `/dev/drbd0` somewhere else, copy everything in `/var/lib/mysql` to the temporary mount point you selected, unmount it and then remount on `/var/lib/mysql`. Finally be sure to check permissions and ownerships.

```
[root@node3 ~]# mount /dev/drbd0 /var/lib/mysql/
```

Check that it has mounted correctly and with the expected size:

```
[root@node3 ~]# df -h /var/lib/mysql
/dev/drbd0              5.0G  139M  4.6G   3% /var/lib/mysql
```

When the sync has finished, `drbd-overview` should look like this on the primary node:

```
[root@node3 ~]# drbd-overview
  0:mysql  Connected Primary/Secondary UpToDate/UpToDate C r---
```

In other words, "I am the primary node (role) and I am up-to-date (status)". By contrast, the secondary should look like this:

```
 [root@node4 ~]# drbd-overview
  0:mysql  Connected Secondary/Primary UpToDate/UpToDate C r---
```

This shows that it is secondary but also up-to-date.

Congratulations! DRBD is now replicating data on the primary node to the standby, and in a later recipe we will show you how to make use of this standby data.

How it works...

DRBD employs some extremely clever tricks to attempt to minimize the amount of data that is sent between nodes, regardless of what happens while still aiming for 100% data consistency.

The precise details of how DRBD works are beyond the scope of this recipe, but the manual pages at `http://www.drbd.org/docs/more/` are strongly recommended for anyone looking for a detailed yet understandable explanation.

There's more...

While following this recipe almost certainly you will have noticed a message promoting you to make some permission changes. This is to allow the Linux software heartbeat, which is installed with DRBD for automatic failover (the configuration for this can be found in the "Using heartbeat for automatic failover" recipe later in this chapter) to execute some DRBD commands as root in the event of a failure. To eliminate these errors, execute the following commands:

```
[root@node4 ~]# groupadd haclient

[root@node4 ~]# chgrp haclient /sbin/drbdsetup
[root@node4 ~]# chmod o-x /sbin/drbdsetup
[root@node4 ~]# chmod u+s /sbin/drbdsetup

[root@node4 ~]# chgrp haclient /sbin/drbdmeta
[root@node4 ~]# chmod o-x /sbin/drbdmeta
[root@node4 ~]# chmod u+s /sbin/drbdmeta
```

Manually moving services within a DRBD cluster

In this recipe, we will take the DRBD cluster configured in the previous recipe, install a MYSQL server on it, and show how it is possible to move the MySQL service from one node to another quickly and safely.

Getting ready

Ensure that you have completed the previous recipe and that your two nodes are both in sync (`drbd-overview` showing both nodes as `UpToDate`).

In the previous recipe we installed the MySQL server. Now, establish which node is active (which should have `/var/lib/mysql` mounted on top of the DRBD volume during the last recipe) by executing the `df` command on each node and checking to see which has the MySQL volume mounted:

```
[root@node3 ~]# df -h | grep mysql
   /dev/drbd0              5.0G   139M   4.6G    3% /var/lib/mysql
```

On this node only, start MySQL (which will cause the system tables to be built):

```
[root@node3 ~]# service mysqld start
   Initializing MySQL database:  Installing MySQL system tables...
```

Still on the primary node only, download the `world` dataset from MySQL into a temporary directory:

```
[root@node3 ~]# cd /tmp
[root@node3 tmp]# wget http://downloads.mysql.com/docs/world.sql.gz
[root@node3 tmp]# gunzip world.sql.gz
```

Create the world database:

```
[root@node3 ~]# mysql
mysql> CREATE DATABASE `world`;
Query OK, 1 row affected (0.01 sec)Import the world database:
[root@node3 tmp]# mysql world < world.sql
```

The world database, by default, uses the MyISAM storage engine. MyISAM has some problems with DRBD (see the *How it Works...* section) so while in the MySQL client ALTER these tables to be InnoDB:

```
[root@node4 ~]# mysql

mysql> use world;

mysql> show tables;
+-----------------+
| Tables_in_world |
+-----------------+
| City            |
| Country         |
| CountryLanguage |
+-----------------+
3 rows in set (0.00 sec)

mysql> ALTER TABLE City ENGINE=INNODB;
Query OK, 4079 rows affected (0.23 sec)
Records: 4079  Duplicates: 0  Warnings: 0
```

```
mysql> ALTER TABLE Country ENGINE=INNODB;
Query OK, 239 rows affected (0.03 sec)
Records: 239  Duplicates: 0  Warnings: 0


mysql> ALTER TABLE CountryLanguage ENGINE=INNODB;
Query OK, 984 rows affected (0.14 sec)
Records: 984  Duplicates: 0  Warnings: 0
```

How to do it...

With a MySQL server installed and running on the first node (in our example `node3`) it is now time to test a "clean" failover. Before starting, confirm that the secondary is up-to-date:

```
[root@node4 tmp]# drbd-overview
    0:mysql  Connected Secondary/Primary UpToDate/UpToDate C r---
```

Shutdown MySQL on the active node:

```
[root@node3 tmp]# service mysqld stop
    Stopping MySQL:                                      [  OK  ]
```

Unmount the filesystem:

```
[root@node3 tmp]# umount /var/lib/mysql
```

Make the primary node secondary:

```
[root@node3 tmp]# drbdadm secondary mysql
```

Now, switch to the secondary node. Make it active:

```
[root@node4 ~]# drbdadm primary mysql
```

Mount the filesystem:

```
[root@node4 ~]# mount /dev/drbd0 /var/lib/mysql/
```

Start MySQL on the new primary node (previously the secondary):

```
[root@node4 ~]# service mysqld start
```

Check that the world database has some data:

```
[root@node4 ~]# echo "select count(ID) from City where 1;" | mysql world
    count(ID)
    4079
```

How it works...

In this recipe we have shown the most simple technique possible for achieving high availability around where both nodes are still alive (for example, for planned maintenance).

By cleanly stopping MySQL, unmounting the filesystem, and gracefully telling the Primary DRBD node to become Secondary there has been no need to recover anything (either from a filesystem or MySQL perspective). In this case, it would be possible to use MyISAM tables.

Unfortunately, in the next recipe and in the real world DRBD is at its most useful when the primary node fails in a unclean way (for example sudden crash or power outage). In this case, the data on disk may not be in a completely consistent state. In noDB is designed to handle this, and will simply roll back transactions that were not completed to end up with consistent data; MyISAM unfortunately is not to do so, and may do various undesirable things depending on exactly what state the machine was in when it crashed.

Therefore, while not technically required, it is strongly recommended to always use InnoDB for tables stored on DRBD partitions, with the exception of the "MySQL" database which is always left as MyISAM. To change the default table format, add the following to your /etc/my.cnf in the [mysqld] section:

```
default_table_type = INNODB
```

Using heartbeat for automatic failover

In this recipe we will take a already-functioning DRBD setup as produced in the previous recipe, and using the open source software `heartbeat` add automatic failover to ensure that the MySQL service survives the failure of a node. Heartbeat version 2 is included in the EPEL repository for CentOS and RedHat Enterprise Linux, and in this recipe we will use the Cluster Resource Manager which is the recommended technique.

> If you are familiar with heartbeat version 1 clusters, the configuration for CRM-enabled clusters is slightly more verbose, although it has many benefits (not the least of which you no longer need to maintain all configuration files on all nodes manually).

Getting ready

This recipe will start from the point of a configured DRBD setup, with manual failover working (as described in the previous recipe).

Before starting this recipe, stop any services using a DRBD volume and unmount any DRBD filesystems:

```
[root@node4 mysql]# service mysqld stop
umStopping MySQL:                                      [  OK  ]
[root@node4 /]# umount /var/lib/mysql/
```

Ensure that DRBD is fully working, that one node is primary, one node is secondary and both are Up-To-Date. In the following example, node3 is secondary and node4 is primary:

```
[root@node3 ~]# drbd-overview
  0:mysql  Connected Secondary/Primary UpToDate/UpToDate C r---
[root@node4 /]# drbd-overview
  0:mysql  Connected Primary/Secondary UpToDate/UpToDate C r---
```

How to do it...

Start by installing heartbeat. You will find this in the Extra Packages for Enterprise Linux (EPEL) repository we have used elsewhere in this book. Install heartbeat on both nodes:

```
[root@node3 ~]# yum install heartbeat
```

Copy the example configuration to the configuration directory:

```
[root@node3 ha.d]# cp /usr/share/doc/heartbeat-2.1.4/ha.cf /etc/ha.d
```

Modify this file:

```
[root@node3 ha.d]# vi /etc/ha.d/ha.cf
```

At the bottom of the file, add the following:

```
    keepalive 1
    deadtime 30
    warntime 5
    initdead 120
    bcast    eth0
    node     node3.xxx.com
    node     node4.xxx.com
    crm yes
```

Save ha.cf and execute the following bash scriptlet to create a authkeys file, which contains keys to effectively sign traffic between nodes:

```
[root@node3 ha.d]# ( echo -ne "auth 1\n1 sha1 "; \
>    dd if=/dev/urandom bs=512 count=1 | openssl md5 ) \
>    > /etc/ha.d/authkeys
```

```
1+0 records in
1+0 records out
512 bytes (512 B) copied, 0.000161 seconds, 3.2 MB/s
[root@node3 ha.d]# chmod 0600 /etc/ha.d/authkeys
```

Either copy and paste, or SCP this file to the other node (ensuring it keeps permissions of `0600` if you copy and paste):

```
root@node3 ha.d]# scp /etc/ha.d/authkeys node4:/etc/ha.d/
```

Now, we need to produce the Cluster Information Base (CIB). This is in effect the central list of the nodes in the cluster and lists nodes, unique identifiers, resources and any resource constraints. At this point, we only want a super simple configuration listing the two nodes. Firstly, generate unique identifiers for two nodes by running `uuidgen` on each node:

```
[root@node3 ha.d]# uuidgen

7ae6a335-b124-4b28-9e7c-2b20d4f6e5e3
```

Take these two unique IDs with the two node names (full hostnames, check with `hostname -n` command) and insert them into the following template, which should be created in `/var/lib/heartbeat/crm/cib.xml`:

```
<cib>
  <configuration>
    <crm_config>
      <cluster_property_set id="cib-bootstrap-options">
        <attributes/>
      </cluster_property_set>
    </crm_config>
    <nodes>
      <node uname="node3.xxx.com" type="normal" id="7ae6a335-b124-
4b28-9e7c-2b20d4f6e5e3"/>
      <node uname="node4.xxx.com" type="normal" id="3e702838-f41a-
4961-9880-13e20a5d39f7"/>
    </nodes>
    <resources/>
    <constraints/>
  </configuration>
</cib>
```

Start heartbeat on both servers, and configure it to start on boot:

```
[root@node4 ha.d]# chkconfig heartbeat on
[root@node4 ha.d]# service heartbeat start
Starting High-Availability services:

                                                        [  OK  ]
```

Check the status of your new cluster (note that unlike in previous versions, the service start returns very quickly and the cluster then continues to start in the background, so do not be alarmed if it takes a few minutes for your nodes to come alive):

[root@node3 crm]# crm_mon

Output should show like this:

Node: node4.xxx.com (a64f7c5b-096a-4fee-a812-4f9896c69e1d): online

Node: node3.xxx.com (735a8f07-1b29-4a72-a6aa-85e31cbf946e): online

Now we must tell the cluster about our DRBD block device, our ext3 filesystem residing on that, our MySQL service and a virtual IP address to keep on whichever node is "active". This is done by creating a XML file and passing it to the `cibadmin` command. The syntax for this file is provided in the DRBD manual (`http://www.drbd.org/users-guide/s-heartbeat-crm.html`) and the only change that you need to make if you followed the recipes in this book is the IP address. Edit `/etc/drbd.xml` and insert the following:

```xml
<group ordered="true" collocated="true" id="rg_mysql">
  <primitive class="heartbeat" type="drbddisk"provider="heartbeat"
id="drbddisk_mysql">
    <meta_attributes>
      <attributes>
        <nvpair name="target_role" value="started"/>
      </attributes>
    </meta_attributes>
    <instance_attributes>
      <attributes>
        <nvpair name="1" value="mysql"/>
      </attributes>
    </instance_attributes>
  </primitive>
  <primitive class="ocf" type="Filesystem" provider="heartbeat"
id="fs_mysql">
    <instance_attributes>
      <attributes>
        <nvpair name="device" value="/dev/drbd0"/>
        <nvpair name="directory" value="/var/lib/mysql"/>
        <nvpair name="type" value="ext3"/>
      </attributes>
    </instance_attributes>
  </primitive>
  <primitive class="ocf" type="IPaddr2" provider="heartbeat" id="ip_
mysql">
    <instance_attributes>
      <attributes>
```

```
        <nvpair name="ip" value="10.0.0.10"/>
        <nvpair name="cidr_netmask" value="24"/>
        <nvpair name="nic" value="eth1"/>
      </attributes>
    </instance_attributes>
  </primitive>
  <primitive class="lsb" type="mysqld" provider="heartbeat"
id="mysqld"/>
</group>
```

Import this with the following command, and check the exit code of the command to ensure it exits with code 0 (that is successful):

[root@node3 crm]# cibadmin -o resources -C -x /etc/drbd.xml

[root@node3 crm]# echo $?

0

crm_mon now should show these new resources:

Node: node4.xxx.com (a64f7c5b-096a-4fee-a812-4f9896c69e1d): online

Node: node3.xxx.com (735a8f07-1b29-4a72-a6aa-85e31cbf946e): online

Resource Group: rg_mysql

 drbddisk_mysql (heartbeat:drbddisk):   Started node4.xxx.com

 fs_mysql   (ocf::heartbeat:Filesystem):   Started node4.xxx.com

 ip_mysql   (ocf::heartbeat:IPaddr2):   Started node4.xxx.com

 mysqld   (lsb:mysqld):   Started node4.xxx.com

Now, let's check each resource turn by turn. Node4 is the active node.

Verify that this (node4) is the Primary DRBD node:

[root@node4 crm]# drbd-overview

 0:mysql Connected Primary/Secondary UpToDate/UpToDate C r--- /var/lib/mysql ext3 5.0G 168M 4.6G 4%

Check that it has the /var/lib/mysql filesystem mounted:

[root@node4 crm]# df -h /var/lib/mysql

/dev/drbd0   5.0G 168M 4.6G   4% /var/lib/mysql

Check that MySQL is started:

[root@node4 crm]# service mysqld status

mysqld (pid 12175) is running...

Check that MySQL is working and that the `world` database that was imported at the start of this chapter is still present:

```
[root@node4 crm]# echo "SELECT Count(ID) from City where 1;" | mysql
world

Count(ID)

4079
```

Check that the shared IP address is up:

```
[root@node4 crm]# ifconfig eth1:0
eth1:0    Link encap:Ethernet  HWaddr 00:50:56:B1:50:D0
          UP BROADCAST RUNNING MULTICAST  MTU:1500  Metric:1
          Base address:0x2000 Memory:d8920000-d8940000
```

Now, reboot the node (either with a reboot command or by pulling a power plug). In `crm_mon` on `node3` you should notice that it picks up the failure, and then starts by bringing up the DRBD disk:

```
Resource Group: rg_mysql
    drbddisk_mysql  (heartbeat:drbddisk):    Started node3.torn.com
    fs_mysql     (ocf::heartbeat:Filesystem):     Stopped
    ip_mysql     (ocf::heartbeat:IPaddr2):        Stopped
    mysqld    (lsb:mysqld):    Stopped
```

After a short while you should see that all of the services are started, but `node4` is still down:

```
Node: node4.torn.com (a64f7c5b-096a-4fee-a812-4f9896c69e1d): OFFLINE
Node: node3.torn.com (735a8f07-1b29-4a72-a6aa-85e31cbf946e): online


Resource Group: rg_mysql
    drbddisk_mysql  (heartbeat:drbddisk):    Started node3.torn.com
    fs_mysql     (ocf::heartbeat:Filesystem):     Started node3.torn.com
    ip_mysql     (ocf::heartbeat:IPaddr2):        Started node3.torn.com
    mysqld    (lsb:mysqld):    Started node3.torn.com
```

Repeat all of the checks for node3. In addition, verify the MySQL connection to the virtual IP address from a third server.

If all of these checks pass, congratulations—you have a clustered setup.

How it works...

Heartbeat runs in the background and uses one or more communication methods such as unicast (connection from node to node), multicast (sending packets to a multicast address that all nodes are subscribed to) or serial cables (only useful for two node environments but extremely simple).

In the example setup of a two-node cluster with only a single communication method (a single network card), the nodes monitor each other. Unfortunately, if a node fails the only thing that the other node will know with absolute certainty is that the other node is in a unknown state. It can not, for example be sure that it has failed—it may merely have had its network cable cut or a kernel crash.

Having more than one communication method between nodes reduces the chances of split brain—as the most likely cause of a split brain is some sort of network failure adding a serial link into a two-node cluster for example makes this less likely. However, it is still possible to consider a situation where even with two communication links between nodes each considers the other dead (someone could cut both the serial and Ethernet cables, for example).

One solution is to have multiple nodes and use the concept of quorum (discussed in more detail in the context of MySQL Cluster in Chapter 1). However, the detection and failure times from such a setup tend to be fairly slow and it is uncommon (although possible) to have more than two nodes in a DRBD cluster.

It would clearly be bad for DRBD to allow a two-node cluster with DRBD running to become two separate one-node clusters (each thinking that the "other node" has failed) because when the network cable is plugged back in the data is inconsistent and the data updated on one node will be lost. However, this is nothing as bad as the corruption and total data loss that can occur when using shared storage devices as in the previous chapter.

If a split brain is allowed to occur, DRBD does have logic to allow you to choose which nodes data to keep. As soon as the link between two previously split DRBD nodes is resumed, DRBD will look at the metadata exchanged to work out when the last write and the last time both nodes were `UpToDate`. If it detects a split brain (last write is more recent than last sync on both nodes) it immediately stops further writes to the DRBD disk and prints the following to the log:

```
Split-Brain detected, dropping connection!
```

At this point, the first node to detect the split brain will have a connection state of `StandAlone`. The other node will either be in the same state (in the case both nodes discovered the split brain more or less simultaneously) or in state `WFConnection` if it was the slower node.

If this occurs, you need to decide which node will "survive" and you will in effect destroy the data on the other node (the "victim") by resyncing it with the master. Do this with the following command on the victim, replacing `mysql` with the resource name if appropriate:

```
[root@node4 crm]#  drbdadm secondary mysql
[root@node4 crm]#  drbdadm -- --discard-my-data connect mysql
```

If the other node is in `StandAlone` state, enter the following command:

```
[root@node4 crm]#  drbdadm connect mysql
```

At this point the victim will resync from the master, loosing any changes that were made to it since it erroneously became primary.

To avoid this situation, configure multiple communication paths between your two nodes (including a non-ethernet one such as a serial cable if possible in two-node clusters). If it is absolutely vital to prevent split brain situations it is possible to use fencing with DRBD; refer to the DRBD documentation and in particular consider using a Pacemaker (the successor to Heartbeat version 2) cluster.

It is possible to configure DRBD to automatically recover from split brain scenarios. If you value your data, it is not recommended to enable this.

8
Performance Tuning

In this chapter, we will cover:

- ► Tuning the Linux kernel IO
- ► Tuning the Linux kernel CPU schedulers
- ► Tuning MySQL Cluster storage nodes
- ► Tuning MySQL Cluster SQL nodes
- ► Tuning queries within a MySQL Cluster
- ► Tuning GFS on shared storage
- ► MySQL Replication tuning

Introduction

In this chapter, we will cover performance tuning techniques applicable to RedHat and CentOS 5 servers that are used with any of the high-availability techniques covered so far in this book. Some of the techniques in this chapter will only work with some high-availability methods (for example, the "MySQL Cluster" recipes are MySQL Cluster-specific), and some will work on pretty much any Linux server (for example, the discussion of the Linux kernel IO and CPU tuning).

There are some golden rules for performance tuning, which we introduce now:

Make one modification at a time

It is extremely easy, when faced with a slow system, to change multiple things that could be causing the slow performance in one go. This is bad for many reasons, the most obvious being the possibility that one performance tweak could in fact interfere with a negative aggregate effect, when in fact one of the changes on its own could be extremely valuable.

Aim your efforts towards the biggest "bang for buck"

Looking at your entire system, consider the area that makes most sense to optimize. This may in fact not be the database; it makes very little sense to improve your query time from 0.3 to 0.2 seconds if your application takes 2 seconds to process the data. It is extremely easy to continue tuning a system to the point of making changes that are not even noticed except in stress testing—however, such tuning is not only pointless but also damaging, because carrying out performance tuning on a live server is always slightly more risky than doing nothing.

Be scientific in your approach

Never start tuning the performance of a system until you have a performance baseline for the current system, otherwise you will find it very difficult to judge whether tuning has worked.

 Don't always rely on user complaints / reports for response time or availability measurements—they may be a poor measure.

With these rules in mind, read on for the recipes, each of which is targeted at a particular requirement.

Tuning the Linux kernel IO

In this recipe, we will get started by showing the tools that can be used to monitor the **Input/Output (IO)** from a block device. We will then show how to tune the way that the Linux Kernel handles IO to meet your requirements in the best possible manner and finally explain how the Kernel handles IO requests in a little bit more detail.

Getting ready

In this section, we will see how to monitor the IO characteristics of your system using commands that will come installed on a RedHat or CentOS system.

The first command for monitoring IO is a command used most often for other things and it is called top. Running top and pressing *1* to show per-CPU statistics will give you an idea of what your CPUs are doing. Most importantly, in this context, the wa column shows what percentage of time the CPU is spending waiting for IO operations to be completed.

In systems that are very IO-bound, this I/O waiting figure can effectively be 100 percent, which means that the CPUs in the system are doing absolutely nothing but waiting for an IO requests to come back. A value of 0 shows that the logical CPUs are not waiting for IO requests.

The following output from the top command (with the *1* key pressed to show details for each CPU) shows a system under IO load, as is obvious from the wa column—this is high. It is additionally clear that the load falls on a single CPU (therefore, it is likely to be caused by a single process).

```
top - 00:49:34 up 7 min,  4 users,  load average: 1.58, 0.88, 0.37
Tasks:  92 total,   1 running,  91 sleeping,   0 stopped,   0 zombie
Cpu0  :  0.0%us,  3.4%sy,  0.0%ni, 36.7%id, 56.9%wa,  0.7%hi,  2.4%si,  0.0%st
Cpu1  :  0.4%us,  2.8%sy,  0.0%ni, 90.1%id,  6.7%wa,  0.0%hi,  0.0%si,  0.0%st
Mem:   1026868k total,   448072k used,   578796k free,    14624k buffers
Swap:   819304k total,        0k used,   819304k free,   341436k cached

  PID USER      PR  NI  VIRT  RES  SHR S %CPU %MEM    TIME+  COMMAND
  564 root      10  -5     0    0    0 D  1.7  0.0   0:00.05 kjournald
```

By comparison, the following output shows the same system under high CPU usage. In this case, there is no I/O waiting but all the CPU time is spent in `sy` (system mode) and `us` (user mode), with effectively 0 in idle or I/O waiting states:

```
top - 00:48:30 up 6 min,  4 users,  load average: 2.50, 0.81, 0.31
Tasks:  92 total,   6 running,  86 sleeping,   0 stopped,   0 zombie
Cpu0  : 48.3%us, 51.0%sy,  0.0%ni,  0.3%id,  0.0%wa,  0.0%hi,  0.3%si,  0.0%st
Cpu1  : 47.2%us, 52.5%sy,  0.0%ni,  0.3%id,  0.0%wa,  0.0%hi,  0.0%si,  0.0%st
Mem:   1026868k total,   231320k used,   795548k free,    14224k buffers
Swap:   819304k total,        0k used,   819304k free,   136608k cached

  PID USER      PR  NI  VIRT  RES  SHR S %CPU %MEM    TIME+  COMMAND
 3222 root      18   0 68164 1544 1200 R 21.5  0.2   0:34.25 bash
```

A more detailed view of what is going on can be seen with the `vmstat` command. `vmstat` is best launched with the following argument, which will show the statistics every second (the first line of results should be ignored as it is the average for each parameter since the system was last rebooted):

```
[root@node1 ~]# vmstat 1
procs -----------memory---------- ---swap-- -----io---- --system-- -----cpu------
 r  b   swpd   free   buff  cache   si   so    bi    bo   in   cs us sy id wa st
 0  0      0 582656  15804 341940    0    0    74   166  536   73  4  4 91  2  0
 0  0      0 582656  15804 341940    0    0     0     0 1084   40  0  0 100  0  0
 0  0      0 582656  15812 341932    0    0     0    44 1069   58  0  0 99  1  0
 1  0      0 580416  15916 341828    0    0     0     0 1100   62  2 26 72  0  0
 0  0      0 580424  15916 341940    0    0     0     0 1082   50  0  0 100  0  0
 0  0      0 580424  15916 341940    0    0     0     0 1071   37  0  0 100  0  0
 0  0      0 580424  15916 341940    0    0     0     0 1055   41  0  0 100  0  0
 0  0      0 580424  15916 341940    0    0     0     0 1074   45  0  0 100  0  0
 0  1      0 574348  15916 341940    0    0     0 102400 1061   55  0  4 74 22  0
 0  1      0 577944  15916 341940    0    0     0     0 1086   41  0  2 50 48  0
```

 Units in output are kilobytes unless specified otherwise; you can change it to megabytes with the `-s M` flag.

In the output of the previous `vmstat` command, the following fields are particularly useful:

- **Swap**: The two important `swap` values are:
  - `si`: KB/second of memory that is "swapped in" (read) from disk
  - `so`: KB/second of memory that is "swapped out" (written) to disk

In a database server, swapping is likely to be bad news—any significant value here suggests that more physical RAM is required, or the configuration of buffers and cache are set to use too much virtual memory.

▸ **IO**: The two important `io` values are:

 ❏ `bi`: Blocks read from block devices (blocks/s)

 ❏ `bo`: Blocks written to block devices (blocks/s)

▸ **CPU**: The single most important `cpu` value is `wa`, which gives the percentage of CPU time spent waiting for IO.

Looking at the example screenshot, it is clear that there was a significant output of bytes to disk in the 9th second of the command, and that the disk was not able to absorb all the IO immediately (causing 22 percent of the CPU to be in `iowait` state during this second). All the other time, the CPU loads were low and stable.

Another useful tool is the `sar` command. When run with the `-d` flag, `sar` can provide, in Kilobytes, data read from and written to a block device.

 When installed as part of the `sysstat` package, `sar` creates a file `/etc/cron.d/sysstat`, which takes a snapshot of system health every 10 minutes and produces a daily summary.

`sar` also gives an indication of the number of major and minor page faults (see the *There's more...* section for a detailed explanation of these terms). For now, remember that a large number of major faults, as the name suggests, is bad and also suggests that a lot of IO operations are only being satisfied from the disk and not from a RAM cache.

`sar`, unlike the other commands mentioned so far, requires installation and is part of the `sysstat` package. Install this using `yum`:

```
[root@node1 etc]# yum -y install sysstat
```

Look at the manual page for `sar` to see some of the many modes that you can run it in. In the following example, we will show statistics related to paging (the `-B` flag). The number next to the mode is the refresh rate (in the example, it's 1 second) and the second number is the number of values to print:

```
[root@node1 etc]# sar -B 1 2
Linux 2.6.18-164.el5 (node1)      11/22/2009
```

09:00:06 PM	pgpgin/s	pgpgout/s	fault/s	majflt/s
09:00:07 PM	0.00	15.84	12.87	0.00
09:00:08 PM	0.00	0.00	24.24	0.00
Average:	0.00	8.00	18.50	0.00

This shows the number of kilobytes the system has paged in and out to the disk. A detailed explanation of these Page Faults can be found in the There's *more...* section. Now, we look at the general disk IO figures with the lowercase -b flag:

```
[root@node1 etc]# sar -b 1 2
Linux 2.6.18-164.el5 (node1)         11/22/2009
```

08:59:53 PM	tps	rtps	wtps	bread/s	bwrtn/s
08:59:54 PM	0.00	0.00	0.00	0.00	0.00
08:59:55 PM	23.00	0.00	23.00	0.00	456.00
Average:	11.50	0.00	11.50	0.00	228.00

This shows a number of useful IO statistics—the number of operations per second (total (tps) in first column, reads (rtps) in the second and writes (rtps) in the third) as well as the fourth and fifth columns, which give the number of blocks read and written per second (bread/s and bwrtn/s respectively).

The final command that we will introduce in this section is iostat, which is also included in the sysstat package and can be executed with the -x flag to display extended statistics followed by the refresh rate and number of times to refresh:

```
[root@node1 ~]# iostat -x 1 1
Linux 2.6.18-164.el5 (node1)     11/02/10

avg-cpu:  %user   %nice %system %iowait  %steal   %idle
           1.98    0.00    2.16    1.14    0.00   94.71

Device:    rrqm/s   wrqm/s   r/s   w/s   rsec/s   wsec/s avgrq-sz avgqu-sz   await  svctm  %util
sda          3.20    67.12  3.69  3.11   186.79   561.50   110.01     0.79  116.74   3.84   2.61
sda1         0.47     0.00  0.06  0.00     1.06     0.01    17.50     0.00    1.62   1.37   0.01
sda2         0.33     0.00  0.02  0.00     0.78     0.00    36.49     0.00    0.69   0.62   0.00
sda3         2.40    67.12  3.61  3.10   184.82   561.49   111.22     0.79  118.33   3.88   2.60
dm-0         0.00     0.00  3.10 67.56   138.34   540.46     9.61    48.37  684.66   0.19   1.36
dm-1         0.00     0.00  1.37  1.04    10.87     7.89     7.79     0.26  109.42   1.30   0.31
dm-2         0.00     0.00  1.42  1.64    35.47    13.15    15.86     0.03   11.34   4.79   1.47
```

This shows the details of an average CPU utilization (that is, those shown using top/vmstat), but it also shows the details for each block device on the system. Before looking at the results, notice that the final three lines relating to dm-x refer to the Device Mapper in the Linux kernel, which is the technology that LVM is based on. It is often useful to know statistics by physical block device but it can be useful to find statistics on a per LVM volume basis (in this case, sda). To manually translate your LVM logical volumes to the dm-x number, follow these steps:

- Firstly, look at the `/proc/diskstats` file, select out the lines for device mapper objects and print the first three fields:

```
[root@node1 dev]# grep "dm-" /proc/diskstats | awk '{print $1, $2, $3}'
253 0 dm-0
253 1 dm-1
253 2 dm-2
```

- Take the two numbers, mentioned previously (known as a major and minor device number, for example, in the example `dm-0` has major number 253 and minor 0) and check the output of `ls -l` for a match:

```
[root@node1 mapper]# ls -l /dev/mapper/
total 0
crw------- 1 root root  10, 63 Feb 11 00:42 control
brw------- 1 root root 253,  0 Feb 11 00:42 dataVol-root
brw------- 1 root root 253,  1 Feb 11 00:42 dataVol-tmp
brw------- 1 root root 253,  2 Feb 11 00:42 dataVol-var
```

In this example, `dm-0` is `dataVol-root` (which is mounted on `/`, as shown in the `df` command).

 You can pass the `-p` option to `sar` and the `-N` option to `iostat`, which will automatically print the statistics on a per logical volume basis

Looking at the results from `iostat`, the most interesting fields are:

- `r/s` and `w/s`: The number of read and write requests sent to the device per second
- `rsec/s` and `wsec/s`: The number of sectors read and written from the device per second
- `avgrq-sz`: The average size of the requests issued to the device (in sectors)
- `avgqu-sz`: The average queue length of requests for this device
- `await`: The average time in milliseconds for IO requests issued to the device to be served—this includes both queuing time and time for the device to return the request
- `svctm`: The average service time in milliseconds for IO requests issued to the device

Of these, far and away, the most useful is `await`, which gives you a good idea of the time the average request takes—this is almost always a good proxy for relative IO performance.

How to do it...

Now we have seen how to monitor the IO performance of the system and briefly discussed the meaning of the numbers that come out of the monitoring tools; this section looks at some of the practical and immediate things that we can tune.

The Linux kernel comes with multiple IO schedulers, each of which implement the same core functions in slightly different ways. The first function merges multiple requests into one (that is, if three requests are made in a very short period of time, and the first and third are adjacent requests on the disk, it makes sense to "merge" them and run them as one single request). The second function is performed by a disk elevator algorithm and involves ordering the incoming requests, much as a elevator in a large building must decide in which order to service the requests.

A complication is the requirement for a "prevent starvation" feature to ensure that a request, that is an "inconvenient" place, is not constantly deferred in favor of a "more efficient" next request.

The four schedulers and their relative features are discussed in the *There's more...* section. The default scheduler `cfq` is not likely the best choice and, on most database servers, you may find value by changing it to `deadline`.

To check which is the current scheduler in use, read this file using `cat` (replacing `sda` with the correct device name):

```
[root@node1 dev]# cat /sys/block/sda/queue/scheduler
noop anticipatory deadline [cfq]
```

To change the scheduler, `echo` the new scheduler name into this file:

```
[root@node1 dev]# echo "deadline" > /sys/block/sda/queue/scheduler
```

This takes effect immediately, although it would be a good idea to verify that your new setting has been recorded by the kernel:

```
[root@node1 dev]# cat /sys/block/sda/queue/scheduler
noop anticipatory [deadline] cfq
```

Add this `echo` command to the bottom of `/etc/rc.local` to make this change persistent across all reboots.

How it works...

Disks are the slowest part of any Linux system, generally, by an order of magnitude. Unless you are using extremely high performance **Solid State Disk**s (**SSD**s) or your block device has significant amounts of battery-backed cache, it is likely that a small percentage increase in IO performance will result in the greatest "bang for buck" to increase the performance of your system.

Broadly speaking, there are a couple of key things that can be done (in order of effectiveness):

▶ Reduce the amount of IO generated

▶ Optimize the way that this IO is carried out given the particular hardware is available

▶ Tweak buffers and kernel parameters

Virtual memory is divided into fixed-size chunks called "pages". On x86 systems, the default page size is 4 KB. Some of those memory pages are used by a disk cache mechanism of the Linux kernel named "page cache", with the purpose of reducing the amount of IO generated. The page cache uses pages of memory (RAM) that is otherwise unused to store data, which is also stored on a block device such as a disk. When any data is requested from the block device, before going anywhere near a hard disk or other block device, the kernel checks the page cache to see if the page it is looking for is stored in memory. If it is, it can be returned to the application at RAM speeds; if it is not, the data is requested from the disk, returned to the application and, if there is unused memory, stored in the page cache.

When there is no more space in the page cache (or something else requires the memory that is allocated to the page cache), the kernel simply expires the pages in the cache that have the longest time since their last access.

In the case of read operations, this is all very simple. However, when writes become involved, it becomes more complicated. If the kernel receives a write request, it does exactly the same thing—it will attempt to use the page cache to complete the write without sending it to disk if possible. Such pages are referred to as "dirty pages" and they must be flushed to a physical disk at some point (writes committed to the virtual memory, but those that have not made it to disk will disappear if the server is rebooted or crashes). Dirty pages are written to disk by the `pdflush` group of kernel threads, which continually checks the dirty pages in the page cache and attempts to write them to disk in a sensible order.

Obviously, it may not be acceptable for data that has been written to a database to be left in memory until `pdflush` comes around to write it to disk. In particular, it would cause chaos with the entire **atomicity, consistency, isolation,** and **durability (ACID)** concept of databases if transactions that were committed were in fact undone when the server rebooted. Consequently, applications have the option of issuing a `fsync()` or `sync()` system call, which issues a direct "sync" instruction to the IO scheduler, forcing it to write immediately to disk. The application can then be sure that the write has made it to a persistent storage device.

There's more...

The four schedulers mentioned earlier in this section available in RHEL and CentOS 5 are:

Noop: This is a bit of an oddity as it only implements the request merging function, doing nothing to elevate requests. This scheduler makes sense where something else further down the chain is carrying out this functionality and there is no point doing it twice. This is generally used for *fully virtualized* virtual machines.

Deadline: This scheduler implements request merging and elevation, and it prevents starvation with a simple algorithm—each request has a "deadline" and the scheduler will ensure that each request is completed within its deadline (if this is not possible, requests outside of deadline are completed on a first-in-first-out system). The deadline scheduler has a preference for read queries, because Linux can cache writes before they hit the disk (and thus not delay the process) whereas readers for data not in the page cache have no choice but to wait for their data.

Anticipatory: This scheduler is focused on minimizing head movements on the disk with an aggressive algorithm designed to wait for more reads.

CFQ: The "completely fair scheduler" aims to ensure all processes get equal access to a storage device over time.

As mentioned, most database servers perform best with the deadline scheduler except for those connected to extremely high-end SAN disk arrays, which can use the noop scheduler.

While thinking about shared storage and SANs, it is often valuable to check the kilobyte-per-IO figure that can be established by dividing the "kilobytes read per second (rkB/s)" by the "reads per second (r/s)" (and the same for writes) in the output of `iostat -x`. This figure will be significantly lower if you are experiencing random IO (which, unfortunately, is likely going to be what a database server experiences). The maximum number of IOPS experienced is a useful figure for configuring your backend storage—particularly, if using a shared storage, as these tend to be certified to complete a certain number of IOPS.

A database server using a lot of swap is likely to be a bad idea. If a server does not have sufficient RAM, it will start using the configured swap filesystems. Unfortunately, writes to the swap device are just as any other writes (unless, of course, the swap device is on its own dedicated block device). It is possible that a "paging storm" will develop where the IO from the system and the required swap IO contend (endlessly fight) for actual IO, and this generally ends with the kernel **out of memory** (**OOM**) killer terminating one of the processes that is using a large amount of RAM (which unfortunately is likely to be MySQL).

One way to ensure that this does not happen is to set the kernel parameter `vm.swappiness` to be equal to 0. This kernel parameter can be thought of as the kernel's tendency to "claim back" physical memory (RAM) by moving data to disk that had not been used for some time. In other words, the higher the `vm.swappiness` value, the more the system will swap. As swapping is generally bad for database servers, you may find some value in setting this parameter to 0.

To check kernel parameters at the command line, use `sysctl`:

```
[root@node1 etc]# sysctl    vm.swappiness
vm.swappiness = 60
```

`60` (on a scale of 0 to 100) is the default value. To set it to 0, use `sysctl -w`:

```
[root@node1 etc]# sysctl -w vm.swappiness=0
vm.swappiness = 0
```

To make such a change persistent across reboots, add the following line to the bottom of `/etc/sysctl.conf`:

```
vm.swappiness = 0
```

Tuning MySQL Cluster storage nodes

In this recipe, we will cover some simple techniques to get the most performance out of storage nodes in a MySQL Cluster.

This recipe assumes that your cluster is already working and configured, and discusses specific and simple tips to improve performance.

How to do it...

MySQL Cluster supports a conditional pushdown feature, which allows for a significant reduction in the amount of data sent between SQL and storage nodes during the execution of a query. In typical storage engines, a WHERE query is executed at a higher level than the storage engine. Typically, this is a relatively cheap operation as the data is being moved around in memory on the same node. However, with MySQL Cluster, this effectively involves moving every row in a table from the storage nodes that they are stored on to the SQL node where most of the data is potentially discarded. Conditional Pushdowns move this filtering of unnecessary rows into the storage engine. This means that the WHERE condition is executed on each storage node and applied before the data crosses the network to the SQL node coordinating that particular query.

This is a very obvious optimization and can speed up queries by an order of magnitude with no cost. To enable conditional pushdowns, add the following to the [mysqld] section of each SQL node's `my.cnf`:

```
engine_condition_pushdown=1
```

Another useful parameter, `ndb-use-exact-count`, allows you to trade-off between very fast SELECT COUNT(*) queries and slightly slower queries (with `ndb-use-exact-count=1`) and vice versa with `ndb-use-exact-count=0`. Again, add the following to the [mysqld] section of each SQL node's `my.cnf` file:

```
ndb_use_exact_count=0
```

The default value, 1, only really makes sense if you value the SELECT COUNT(*) time. If your normal query scenario is primary key lookups set this parameter to 0 if your normal query scenario is primary key lookups set this parameter to 0. Again, add the following to the [mysqld] section of each SQL node's `my.cnf`:

```
ndb_use_exact_count=0
```

How it works...

Conditional pushdowns broadly work on the following type of query, where x is a constant:

```
SELECT field1,field2 FROM table WHERE field = x;
```

They do not work where "field" is an index (at which point it is more efficient to just look the index up).

They do not work where x is something more complicated such as another field.

They do work where the equality condition is replaced with >, <, IS IN and IS NOT.

To confirm if a query is using a conditional pushdown or not, you can use a EXPLAIN SELECT query, as in the following example:

```
mysql> EXPLAIN select * from titles where emp_no < 10010;
+----+-------------+--------+-------+----------------+---------+---------
+------+------+-----------------------------------+
| id | select_type | table  | type  | possible_keys  | key     | key_len
| ref  | rows | Extra                             |
+----+-------------+--------+-------+----------------+---------+---------
+------+------+-----------------------------------+
|  1 | SIMPLE      | titles | range | PRIMARY,emp_no | PRIMARY | 4
| NULL |   10 | Using where with pushed condition |
+----+-------------+--------+-------+----------------+---------+---------
+------+------+-----------------------------------+
1 row in set (0.00 sec)
```

It is possible to enable and disable this feature at runtime for the current session with a SET command. This is very useful for testing:

```
mysql> SET engine_condition_pushdown=OFF;

Query OK, 0 rows affected (0.00 sec)
```

With conditional pushdown enabled, the output from the EXPLAIN SELECT query shows that the query is now using a simple where rather than a "pushed down" where:

```
mysql> EXPLAIN select * from titles where emp_no < 10010;
+----+-------------+--------+-------+----------------+---------+---------
+------+------+-------------+
| id | select_type | table  | type  | possible_keys  | key     | key_len
| ref  | rows | Extra       |
+----+-------------+--------+-------+----------------+---------+---------
+------+------+-------------+
```

```
|  1 | SIMPLE      | titles | range | PRIMARY,emp_no | PRIMARY | 4
|  NULL |   10 | Using where |
+----+--------------+--------+-------+-----------------+---------+---------
+------+------+-------------+

1 row in set (0.00 sec)
```

Tuning MySQL Cluster SQL nodes

In this recipe, we will discuss some performance tuning tips for SQL queries that will be executed against a MySQL Cluster.

How to do it...

A major performance benefit in a MySQL Cluster can be obtained by reducing the percentage of times that queries spend waiting for intra-cluster node network communication. The simplest way to achieve this is to make transactions as large as possible, subject to the constraints that really enormous queries can hit hard and soft limits within MySQL Cluster.

There are a couple of ways to do this. Firstly, turn off AUTOCOMMIT that is enabled by default and automatically wraps every statement within a transaction of its own. To check if AUTOCOMMIT is enabled, execute this query:

```
mysql> SELECT @@AUTOCOMMIT;
+--------------+
| @@AUTOCOMMIT |
+--------------+
|            1 |
+--------------+
1 row in set (0.00 sec)
```

This shows that AUTOCOMMIT is enabled. With AUTOCOMMIT enabled, the execution of two insert queries would, in fact, be executed as two different transactions, with the overhead (and benefits) associated with that. If, in fact, you would prefer to define your own COMMIT points, you can disable this parameter and enormously reduce the number of transactions that are executed. The correct way to disable AUTOCOMMIT is to execute the following at the start of every connection:

```
mysql> SET AUTOCOMMIT=0;
Query OK, 0 rows affected (0.00 sec)
```

However, applications that are not written to do this can be difficult to modify and it is often simpler to use a trick that disables AUTOCOMMIT for all new connections (this does not include connections made by the superuser). Add the following to the [mysqld] section in my.cnf on each SQL node:

```
init_connect='SET autocommit=0'
```

To achieve the real performance benefits from this change using MySQL, two other changes must be made.

> ▶ Firstly, there is a parameter ndb_force_send that forces a thread to send its part of a transaction to other nodes regardless of other transactions that are going on (rather than waiting and combining the transactions together). Disable the parameter ndb_force_send in the [mysqld] section of /etc/my.cnf on each SQL node:
>
> ```
> ndb_force_send=OFF
> ```
>
> ▶ Secondly, enable the NDB parameter transaction_allow_batching, which allows transactions that appear together when AUTOCOMMIT is disabled to be sent between nodes in one go. Add the following to the [mysqld] section of /etc/my.cnf on each SQL node:
>
> ```
> transaction_allow_batching=ON
> ```

How it works...

When using MySQL Cluster in-memory tables, the weak point from a performance point of view is almost always the latency introduced by a two phase commit—the requirement for each query to get to two nodes before being committed. This latency, however, is almost independent of transaction size; that is to say the latency of talking to multiple nodes is the same for a tiny transaction as for one that affects an enormous number of rows.

In a traditional database, the weak point, however, is the physical block device (typically a hard disk). The time a hard disk takes to complete a random IO transaction is a function of the number of blocks that are read and written.

Therefore, with a traditional disk base MySQL install, it makes very little difference if you have one transaction or one hundred transactions each one-hundredth the size—the overall time to complete will be broadly similar. However, with a MYSQL Cluster, it makes an enormous difference. In the case of a hundred small transactions, you have the latency delay 100 times (and, this is far and away the slowest part of a transaction); when compared to a single large transaction, the latency delay is incurred only once.

There's more...

In the *How to do it...* section, we configured our SQL nodes to batch transactions. There is a maximum batch size, that is, the maximum amount of data that the SQL node will wait for before sending its inter-node communication. This defaults to 32 megabytes, and is defined in bytes with the `ndb-batch-size` parameter in `/etc/my.cnf`. You may find that if you have lots of large transactions, you gain value by increasing this parameter—to do so, add the following to the `[mysqld]` section in `/etc/my.cnf` on each SQL node. This will increase the default setting to four times its value (it is often worth experimenting with significantly higher values):

```
ndb-batch-size=131072
```

Tuning queries within a MySQL Cluster

In this recipe, we will explore some techniques to maximize the performance you get when using MySQL Cluster.

Getting ready

There is often more than one way to obtain the same result in SQL. Often applications take the one that results in either the least amount of thought for the developer or the shortest SQL query. In this recipe we show that, if you have the ability to modify the way that applications use your queries, you can obtain significant improvement in performance.

How to do it...

MySQL Cluster's killer and most impressive feature is its near linear write scalability. MySQL Cluster is pretty much unique in this regard—there are limited other techniques for obtaining write scalability without splitting the database up (of course, MySQL Cluster achieves this scalability by internally partitioning data over different nodegroups. However, because this partitioning is internal to the cluster, applications do not need to worry or even know about it).

Therefore, particularly in larger clusters (clusters with more than one nodegroup), it makes sense to attempt to execute queries in parallel. This may seem a direct contradiction to the suggestion to reduce the number of queries—and there is a tradeoff with an optimum, which can only be discovered with testing. In the case of truly enormous inserts, for example, a million single-integer inserts, it is likely that the following options will both produce terrible performance:

- One million transactions
- One transaction with a million inserts

It is likely that something like 1000 transactions consisting of 1000 inserts each will be most optimal.

If it is not possible for whatever reason to configure a primary key and use it within most queries, the next best thing (it is still a very poor alternative) is to increase the parameter `ndb_autoincrement_prefetch_sz` on SQL nodes, which increases the number of auto-increment IDs that are obtained between statements. The effect of increasing this value (from the default of 32) is to speed up inserts at the cost of reducing the likelihood that consecutive auto increments will be used in a batch of inserts. Add the following to the `[mysqld]` section in `/etc/my.cnf` on each SQL node:

```
ndb_autoincrement_prefetch_sz=512
```

Note that within a statement, IDs are always obtained in blocks of 32.

Tuning GFS on shared storage

In this recipe, we will cover some basic tips for maximizing GFS performance.

Getting ready

This recipe assumes that you already have a GFS cluster configured, and that it consists of at least two nodes and is fully working.

 There are lots of performance changes that can be made if you are running GFS on a single node, but these are not covered in this book.

How to do it...

The single-most effective technique for increasing GFS performance is to minimize the number of concurrent changes to the same files, that is, to ensure that only one node at a time is accessing a specific file, if at all possible.

Ironically, the thing most likely to cause this problem is the operating system itself in the form of the `updatedb` cron job that runs each day on a clean install. The relevant cron job can be seen at `/etc/cron.daily/makewhatis.cron` and should be disabled unless you need it:

```
[root@node4 ~]# rm -f /etc/cron.daily/makewhatis.cron
```

Additionally, for performance reasons, in general all GFS filesystems should be mounted with the following options:

- `_netdev`: This ensures that this filesystem is not mounted until after the network is started.

- `noatime`: Do not update the access time. This prevents a write each time a read is made.

- `nodiratime`: Do not update the directory access time each time a read is made inside it.

An example line in `/etc/fstab` may look like this:

```
/dev/clustervg/mysql_data_gfs2     /var/lib/mysql       gfs2     _
netdev,nodiratime,noatime          0  0
```

GFS2 has a large number of tunable parameters that can be customized. One of the major advantages of GFS2 when compared to the original version of GFS is the self-tuning design of GFS2; however, there are still a couple of parameters worth considering about tuning depending on environment.

The first step to modifying any of them to improve performance is to check the current configuration, which is done with the following command (this assumes that `/var/lib/mysql` is a GFS filesystem, as seen in the examples in *Chapter 6, High Availability with MySQL and Shared Storage*):

```
[root@node4 ~]# gfs_tool gettune /var/lib/mysql
```

This command will list the tunable parameters you can set.

A tunable parameter that can improve performance is `demote_secs`. This parameter determines how often `gfsd` wakes and scans for locks that can be demoted and subsequently flushed from cache to disk. A lower value helps to prevent GFS accumulating too much cached data associated with burst-mode flushing activities. The default (5 minutes) is often higher than needed and can safely be reduced. To reduce it to 1 minute, execute the following command:

```
[root@node4 ~]# gfs2_tool settune /var/lib/mysql demote_secs 60
```

To set `demote_secs` to persist across reboots, there are several techniques; the simplest is to add the previous command to the bottom of the `/etc/rc.local` script, which is executed on boot:

```
[root@node4 ~]# echo "gfs2_tool settune /var/lib/mysql demote_secs 60" >>
/etc/rc.local
```

Another tunable parameter that can improve performance is `glock_purge`. This parameter tells `gfsd` the proportion of unused locks to purge every 5 seconds; the documentation recommends starting testing at 50 and increasing it until performance drops off, with a recommended value of 50-60. To set it to 60, execute these commands:

```
[root@node4 ~]# gfs2_tool settune /var/lib/mysql glock_purge 60
[root@node4 ~]# echo "gfs2_tool settune /var/lib/mysql glock_purge 60" >>
/etc/rc.local
```

It is a good idea to remove the default alias for the `ls` command that includes `--color`. `--color` can be useful, but can cause performance problems. When using GFS, remove this alias for all users by adding the following to the bottom of `/etc/profile`:

```
alias ll='ls -l' 2>/dev/null
alias l.='ls -d .*' 2>/dev/null
unalias ls
```

How it works...

Removing the alias to `--color` deserves more explanation. There are two problems with adding `--color` to `ls`:

- Every directory item listed requires a `stat()` system call when `--color` is specified (to find out whether it is a symbolic link).

- If it is a symbolic link, `ls` will actually go and check if the destination exists. Unfortunately, this can result in an additional lock required for each destination and can cause significant contention.

These problems are worsened by the tendency for administrators to run `ls` a lot in the event of any problems with a cluster. Therefore, it is safest to remove the automatic use of `--color` with `ls` when using GFS.

MySQL Replication tuning

MySQL Replication tuning is generally focused on preventing slave servers from falling behind. This can be an inconvenience or a total disaster depending on how reliant you are on consistency (if you are completely reliant on consistency, of course, MySQL Replication is not the solution for you).

In this chapter, we focus on tips for preventing slaves from "falling behind" the master.

How to do it...

INSERT SELECT is a common and convenient SQL command, however, it it is best avoided by using MySQL Replication. This is because anything other than a trivial SELECT will significantly increase the load on the single thread running on the slave, and cause replication lag. It makes far more sense to write a SELECT and then an INSERT based on the result of this request.

MySQL replication, as discussed in detail in *Chapter 5, High Availability with MySQL Replication*, uses one thread per discrete task. This unfortunately means that to prevent replication "lag", it is necessary to prevent any long-running write transactions.

The simplest way to achieve this is to use LIMIT with your UPDATE or DELETE queries to ensure that each query (or transaction consisting of many UPDATE and DELETE queries—its effect is the same) does not cause replication lag.

ALTER TABLE is very often an enormous query with significant locking time on the relevant table. Within a replication chain, however, this query will lock all queries executed on the slave, which may be unacceptable. One way to achieve ALTER TABLE queries without slaves becoming extremely out of date is to:

> ▸ Execute the ALTER TABLE query on the master prefixed with SET SQL_BIN_LOG=0; and followed by SET SQL_BIN_LOG=1;. This disables binary logging for this query (be sure to have SUPER permissions to execute this or run the query as a superuser).

> ▸ Execute the ALTER TABLE on the slave at the same time.

In situations where the time taken to run ALTER TABLE on a master is unacceptable, this can be taken further to ensure only the downtime involved in failing over from your master to slave and vice versa (for example, using MMM as shown in *Chapter 5*). Carry out the following procedure:

> ▸ Execute the ALTER TABLE with SET SQL_BIN_LOG=0; and with SET SQL_BIN_LOG=1; as above on the slave

> ▸ Move the active writer master to the slave, typically by failing over the writer role virtual IP address

> ▸ Execute the ALTER TABLE with SET SQL_BIN_LOG=0; and with SET SQL_BIN_LOG=1 on the new slave (previous master)

> ▸ If required, fail the master, role back

In the case of extremely large tables, this technique can provide the only viable way of making modifications.

The single-threaded nature of the slave thread means that it is extremely unlikely that your slave can cope with an identical update load if hosted on the same performance equipment as the master. Therefore, loading a master server as far as possible with `INSERT` and `UPDATE` queries will almost certainly cause a large replication lag as there is no way that the slaves single thread can keep up. If you have regular jobs such as batch scripts running in cron, it is wise to spread these out and certainly not to execute them in parallel to ensure that the slave has a chance to keep up with the queries on the master.

There's more...

A open source utility, `mk-slave-prefetch`, is available to "prime" a slave that is not currently handling any queries, but is ready to handle queries in the case of a master failing. This helps to prevent a scenario where a heavily-loaded master, with primed caches at storage system, kernel and MySQL level, fails and the slave is suddenly hit with the load, and crashes due to having empty caches.

This tool parses the entries in the relay log on a slave and transforms (where possible) queries that modify data (`INSERT`, `UPDATE`) into queries that do not (`SELECT`). It then executes these queries against the slave which will draw approximately the same data into the caches on the slave.

This tool may be useful if you have a large amount of cache at a low level, for example, battery-backed cache in a RAID controller and a slave with multiple CPU threads and IO capacity (which will likely mean that the single replication slave SQL thread is not stressing the server). The full documentation can be found on the Maatkit website at `http://www.maatkit.org/doc/mk-slave-prefetch.html`.

 While the query parsing is excellent, it is strongly recommended to run this as a read-only user just to be sure!

Base Installation

All the recipes in this book were completed by starting with a base OS installation shown in the following kickstart file. The same outcome could be achieved by following the Anaconda installer and adding the additional packages, but there are some things that must be done at installation time. For example, if you "click through" the installer without thinking you will create a single-volume group with a `root` logical volume that uses all the spare space. This will prevent you from using LVM snapshots in future without adding an additional storage device, which can be a massive pain. In the following kickstart file, we allocate what we know are sensible minimum requirements to the various logical volumes and leave the remainder of the space unallocated within a volume group to be used for snapshots or added to any logical volume at any time.

When building identical cluster nodes, it is helpful to be able to quickly build and rebuild identical nodes. The best way to do this is to use PXE boot functionality in the BIOS of servers for a hands-off installation. The easiest way to do this is to use something like Cobbler (`https://fedorahosted.org/cobbler/`).

The following kickstart file can be used with Cobbler or any other kickstart system, or using an install CD, by replacing the network line with just the word cdrom. Full documentation on the options available can be found at `http://www.redhat.com/docs/manuals/linux/RHL-9-Manual/custom-guide/s1-kickstart2-options.html`.

The kickstart file used is as follows:

```
install
url --url http://path/to/DVD/files/
lang en_US.UTF-8
keyboard uk
network --device eth0 --bootproto static --ip 0.0.0.0 --netmask
255.255.255.0 --gateway 0.0.0.0 --nameserver 8.8.8.8  --hostname nodex
# If you know the secure password (from /etc/shadow), use
# rootpw -iscrypted $1$....
```

```
rootpw changeme
firewall --disabled
authconfig --enableshadow --enablemd5
selinux --disabled
timezone --utc Europe/London
bootloader --location=mbr --driveorder=sda
# Here, we use /dev/sda to produce a single volume group
# (plus a small /boot partition)
# In this PV, we add a single Volume Group, "dataVol"
# On this VG we create LVs for /, /var/log, /home, /var/lib/mysql and
/tmp
clearpart --all --drives=sda
part /boot --fstype ext3 --size=100 --ondisk=sda --asprimary
part local --size=20000 --grow --ondisk=sda
part swap --size=500 --ondisk=sda --asprimary
volgroup dataVol --pesize=32768 local
logvol / --fstype ext3 --name=root --vgname=dataVol --size=8000
logvol /var/log --fstype ext3 --name=log --vgname=dataVol --size=2000
logvol /var/lib/mysql --fstype ext3 --name=mysql --vgname=dataVol --
size=10000
logvol /tmp --fstype ext3 --name=tmp --vgname=dataVol --size=2000
logvol /home --fstype ext3 --name=home --vgname=dataVol --size=1000


# Packages that are used in many recipes in this book
%packages
@editors
@text-internet@core
@base
device-mapper-multipath
vim-enhanced
screen
ntp
lynx
iscsi-initiator-utils
# If you are using the packaged version of MySQL
# (NB not for MySQL Cluster)
mysql-server


# Install the EPEL repo
# This is used to install some of the packages required for Chapter 5
(MMM)
# rpm --nosignature -Uvh http://download.fedora.redhat.com/pub/epel/5/
i386/epel-release-5-3.noarch.rpm
```

Broadly speaking, this file does the following:

▸ Installs everything apart from /boot onto LVM volumes, leaving some space in the volume group (essential for recipes that involve snapshots and creating additional logical volumes)

▸ Disables SELinux (essential for many recipes)

▸ Installs some useful packages used in each recipe, but otherwise uses a minimal install

▸ Installs the bundled mysql-server package (remove this if you are installing a MySQL Cluster node, as you will install the package from mysql.com)

▸ Installs the Extra Packages For Enterprise Linux (EPEL) packages provided by Fedora, which we use in *Chapter 5, High Availability with MySQL Replication* extensively and provides a large number of open source packages that are built for CentOS / RedHat Enterprise Linux

B
LVM and MySQL

The default installation of RedHat Enterprise Linux and CentOS 5 will create all mount points (including the root mount point, /) on **Logical Volume Manager**'s (**LVM**) **Logical Volume**s (**LV**s).

LVM brings about many benefits. With particular relevance for MySQL high availability is the snapshot feature. This allows you to take a consistent snapshot of a logical volume (for example, the logical volume with the ext3 filesystem mounted on /var/lib/mysql) without affecting the currently mounted volume.

LVM then allows for this snapshot to be mounted somewhere else (/mnt/mysql-3pmtoday) and a backup can then be run against this snapshot without affecting the MySQL instance running on the original logical volume.

The actual process of creating a snapshot takes a very short period of time, normally fractions of a second. Therefore, to take a fully-consistent backup of your MySQL database, you only need to flush all the transactions and caches to disk for that short period of time and then the database can continue as normal.

This is useful for the following reasons:

▶ The time during which your main database is down will be significantly reduced
▶ It is possible to get consistent backups of multiple database servers at the same time easily

While it is possible to carry out this backup process manually, there is a Perl script mylvmbackup available at http://lenzg.net/mylvmbackup/, which carries this out automatically. mylvmbackup was created by Aleksey "Walrus" Kishkin and was released under the GNU Public License.

The definition for `mylvmbackup` from the website at `http://lenzg.net/mylvmbackup/` states:

> *mylvmbackup is a tool for quickly creating backups of a MySQL server's data files. To perform a backup, mylvmbackup obtains a read lock on all tables and flushes all server caches to disk, creates a snapshot of the volume containing the MySQL data directory, and unlocks the tables again. The snapshot process takes only a small amount of time. When it is done, the server can continue normal operations, while the actual file backup proceeds.*

> *The LVM snapshot is mounted to a temporary directory and all data is backed up using the tar program. By default, the archive file is created using a name of the form* `backup-YYYYMMDD_hhmmss_mysql.tar.gz`, *where YYYY, MM, DD, hh, mm, and ss represent the year, month, day, hour, minute, and second of the time at which the backup occurred. The default prefix* `backup`, *date format and file suffix can be modified. The use of timestamped archive names allows you to run mylvmbackup many times without danger of overwriting old archives.*

How to do it...

Installing `mylvmbackup` on a RedHat Enterprise Linux or CentOS 5 system is simple and it is shown in this section:

Firstly, install `perl-Config-IniFiles` and `perl-TimeDate`:

`perl-Config-IniFiles` is available only in the EPEL repository. This was covered earlier in this book in *Chapter 3, MySQL Cluster Management*; you can read the simple install guide for this repository at `http://fedoraproject.org/wiki/EPEL/FAQ#How_can_ I_install_the_packages_from_the_EPEL_software_ repository.3F`.

```
[root@node2 ~]# yum -y install perl-Config-IniFiles perl-TimeDate
Loaded plugins: fastestmirror
Loading mirror speeds from cached hostfile
 * epel: www.mirrorservice.org


Installed: perl-Config-IniFiles.noarch 0:2.39-6.el5 perl-TimeDate.noarch
1:1.16-5.el5
Complete!
```

Download `mylvmbackup` and extract the `tar.gz` file as follows:

```
[root@node2 ~]# cd /usr/src/
[root@node2 src]# wget http://lenzg.net/mylvmbackup/mylvmbackup-0.13.tar.
gz
--18:16:11--  http://lenzg.net/mylvmbackup/mylvmbackup-0.13.tar.gz
Resolving lenzg.net... 213.83.63.50
Connecting to lenzg.net|213.83.63.50|:80... connected.
HTTP request sent, awaiting response... 200 OK
Length: 37121 (36K) [application/x-tar]
Saving to: `mylvmbackup-0.13.tar.gz'


100%[=======================================================================
====================================>] 37,121       --.-K/s   in 0.06s


18:16:11 (593 KB/s) - `mylvmbackup-0.13.tar.gz' saved [37121/37121]


[root@node2 src]# tar zxvf mylvmbackup-0.13.tar.gz
mylvmbackup-0.13/
mylvmbackup-0.13/ChangeLog
mylvmbackup-0.13/COPYING
mylvmbackup-0.13/CREDITS
mylvmbackup-0.13/hooks/
mylvmbackup-0.13/hooks/backupfailure.pm
mylvmbackup-0.13/hooks/logerr.pm
mylvmbackup-0.13/hooks/preflush.pm
mylvmbackup-0.13/INSTALL
mylvmbackup-0.13/Makefile
mylvmbackup-0.13/man/
mylvmbackup-0.13/man/mylvmbackup.pod
mylvmbackup-0.13/man/mylvmbackup.1
mylvmbackup-0.13/mylvmbackup
mylvmbackup-0.13/mylvmbackup.conf
mylvmbackup-0.13/mylvmbackup.pl.in
mylvmbackup-0.13/mylvmbackup.spec
mylvmbackup-0.13/mylvmbackup.spec.in
mylvmbackup-0.13/README
mylvmbackup-0.13/TODO
```

Change to the new directory and install `mylvmbackup` as follows:

```
[root@node2 src]# cd mylvmbackup-0.13
[root@node2 mylvmbackup-0.13]# make install
test -d /usr/local/bin || /usr/bin/install -d /usr/local/bin
test -d /usr/local/man/man1 || /usr/bin/install -d /usr/local/man/man1
test -d /etc || /usr/bin/install -d /etc
test -d /usr/local/share/mylvmbackup || /usr/bin/install -d /usr/local/
share/mylvmbackup
/usr/bin/install -m 755 mylvmbackup /usr/local/bin
/usr/bin/install -m 644 man/mylvmbackup.1 /usr/local/man/man1/
mylvmbackup.1
if test -f /etc/mylvmbackup.conf ; then /bin/mv /etc/mylvmbackup.conf /
etc/mylvmbackup.conf.bak ; fi
/usr/bin/install -m 600 mylvmbackup.conf /etc
for HOOK in hooks/backupfailure.pm hooks/logerr.pm hooks/preflush.pm ; do
if [ ! -f /usr/local/share/mylvmbackup/$HOOK ] ; then /usr/bin/install -m
644 -v $HOOK /usr/local/share/mylvmbackup ; fi ; done
`hooks/backupfailure.pm' -> `/usr/local/share/mylvmbackup/backupfailure.
pm'
`hooks/logerr.pm' -> `/usr/local/share/mylvmbackup/logerr.pm'
`hooks/preflush.pm' -> `/usr/local/share/mylvmbackup/preflush.pm'
```

`mylvmbackup` requires two things to work: the MySQL data directory must be on a logical volume and the volume group that contains this logical volume must have some spare space to hold the snapshot copy for writing. Check these with the following commands:

Firstly, run the `vgs` command to confirm that there is spare space available. In this case, there is 9.66G spare space in the volume group:

```
[root@node1 ~]# vgs
  VG      #PV #LV #SN Attr   VSize   VFree
  system   1   3   0 wz--n- 29.41G 9.66G
```

Secondly, check that there is a logical volume for MySQL with the `lvs` command and note the volume group (`system` in the following example):

```
[root@node1 ~]# lvs
  LV    VG     Attr   LSize  Origin Snap% Move Log Copy% Convert
  log   system -wi-ao  1.94G
  mysql system -wi-ao 10.00G
  root  system -wi-ao  7.81G
```

Finally, check that the MySQL data directory is mounted on this logical volume:

```
[root@node1 ~]# df -h | grep mysql
/dev/mapper/system-mysql
                    9.9G  172M  9.2G   2% /var/lib/mysql
```

With these things verified, you are ready to configure /etc/mylvmbackup.conf file.

Start with the self-explanatory [mysql] section that gives a user the privileges to lock tables.

In the [lvm] section, define the vgname and lvname from the output of vgs / lvs commands used earlier (in our example, the vgname is system and the lvname is mysql). The parameter lvsize determines how much space to keep for the snapshot—the volume group must have that much space free, and this is used to hold the data that is changed while the snapshot is open. The correct setting for this parameter depends on how busy your server is and how long backups take; you can start with 20 percent of the logical volume size.

An example configuration file is as follows:

```
#
# mylvmbackup configuration file
#

[mysql]
user=USER
password=PASSWORD
host=localhost
port=
socket=
mycnf=/etc/my.cnf

#
# LVM-specific options
#
[lvm]
vgname=dataVol
lvname=mysql
backuplv=
# lvsize must be able to cope with differences
lvsize=1G

#
# File system specific options
#
[fs]
xfs=0
```

```
mountdir=/var/tmp/mylvmbackup/mnt/
backupdir=/var/tmp/mylvmbackup/backup/
relpath=

#
# Names of required external utilities
# Make sure the $PATH is set accordingly, especially for cron jobs!
#
[tools]
lvcreate=lvcreate
lvremove=lvremove
lvs=lvs
mount=mount
tar=tar
compress=gzip
rsync=rsync
rsnap=rsnap
umount=umount

#
# Other configuration options
#

[misc]
backuptype=tar
prefix=backup-ibactive
suffix=_mysql
tararg=cvf
tarsuffixarg=
tarfilesuffix=.tar.gz
compressarg=--stdout --verbose --best
rsyncarg=-avWP
rsnaparg=7
datefmt=%Y%m%d_%H%M%S
innodb_recover=0
pidfile=/var/tmp/mylvmbackup_recoverserver.pid
skip_flush_tables=0
extra_flush_tables=0
skip_mycnf=0
hooksdir=/usr/share/mylvmbackup
skip_hooks=0
keep_snapshot=0
keep_mount=0
quiet=0
```

```
#
# Logging options. The Sys::Syslog module is required for syslog
option
# See "perldoc Sys::Syslog" for more information.
#
[logging]
# 'console' (STDOUT, STDERR) or 'syslog' or 'both'.
log_method=console
# 'native', 'tcp', 'udp'. Default is 'native'
syslog_socktype=native
syslog_facility=
# If using remote syslog, don't forget to change the socket type to
tcp or udp.
syslog_remotehost=
```

With the configuration file created, execute `mylvmbackup` to test your backup as follows:

```
[root@node1 ~]# mylvmbackup

20091206 18:39:24 Info: Connecting to database...

20091206 18:39:24 Info: Flushing tables with read lock...

20091206 18:39:24 Info: Taking position record into /tmp/mylvmbackup-
backup-20091206_183924_mysql-mxAD4A.pos...

20091206 18:39:24 Info: Running: lvcreate -s --size=5G --name=mysql_
snapshot /dev/system/mysql

File descriptor 4 (socket:[17769919]) leaked on lvcreate invocation.
Parent PID 20180: /usr/bin/perl

  Logical volume "mysql_snapshot" created

20091206 18:39:25 Info: DONE: taking LVM snapshot

20091206 18:39:25 Info: Unlocking tables...

20091206 18:39:25 Info: Disconnecting from database...

20091206 18:39:25 Info: Mounting snapshot...


20091206 18:39:25 Info: Running: lvremove -f /dev/system/mysql_snapshot

  Logical volume "mysql_snapshot" successfully removed

20091206 18:39:26 Info: DONE: Removing snapshot

[root@node1 ~]# echo $?

0
```

In this case, the tables were locked for less than a second.

Various parts of this procedure can fail for the following reasons:

▸ The MySQL server can be down

▸ The read lock cannot be successfully acquired

▸ Insufficient spare space in the volume group to create the snapshot

▸ The volume group or logical volume name does not exist (that is, a typo in the configuration file)

It is therefore essential in automated scripts to check the exit code (`$?`) and ensure that it is 0—and if it is not, you must schedule a manual look at the backup job.

If the script exits with an exit code of 0, the backup can be found in `/var/tmp/mylvmbackup/backup/`, which is ready for sending to a backup location. For example, you could `scp` or `rsync` it to an offsite location.

How it works...

`mylvmbackup` works by using the following procedure:

1. `FLUSH TABLES`: Forces `MyISAM` buffers to disk as far as possible, but it does not lock the tables.

2. `FLUSH TABLES WITH READ LOCK`: Forces `MyISAM` buffers to disk that have been dirtied since the last `FLUSH TABLES` command. This time, all queries modifying the databases are locked.

3. `lvcreate -s`: This creates a consistent snapshot.

4. `UNLOCK TABLES`: This writes to the database resume.

5. Mount the snapshot to a temporary directory.

6. `tar` and compress the snapshot. If configured (not covered in this appendix), `rsync` this file to another location.

7. Destroy the snapshot.

Be aware that when holding an open snapshot, the "copy on write" architecture of LVM can cause significant performance degradation—one I/O operation without a snapshot may take three to six I/O operations, when there is an open snapshot.

If you only use `InnoDB` tables and the additional activity at block-device level during snapshots causes problems, you can consider the open source `Xtrabackup` project (`https://launchpad.net/percona-xtrabackup`), which aims to achieve zero downtime backups at application level and without this overhead. However, for a database server with cyclical load, it is often possible to schedule backups at a low time where additional I/O will not cause problems.

C
Highly Available Architectures

In this appendix, we will show very briefly some architectures that are worth considering, with some pros and cons for each.

For the purpose of this appendix, a **site** is a single geographical location within which it is possible to have very high-bandwidth and low-latency connections over trusted network infrastructure.

Single-site architectures

There are various single-site architectures available, as described in this section:

MySQL master / slave replication

This replication has two servers—one master and one slave, and an application connecting to an IP address of the master as follows:

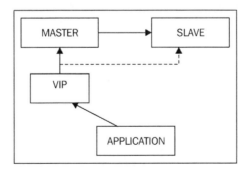

This is the most simple setup; the **Virtual IP address** (**VIP**) can be manually moved. However, in the event of failure of the master, there is a possibility of some data loss and a manual VIP failover can take time. To set this up, go through the recipes *Designing a replication setup, Configuring a replication master, and Configuring a replication slave without synchronizing data* in *Chapter 5, High Availability with MySQL Replication*.

MySQL master / master replication

Two servers, both configured as slaves to the other server, with a management agent such as MMM (which was covered in *Chapter 5* in the recipes *Multi Master Replication Manager* (*MMM*) and *Managing and using Multi Master Replication Manager* (*MMM*)) for automated failover and health checking. It can be shown as follows:

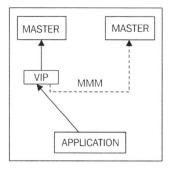

This has the advantage of simplicity (although, it is more complex than master / slave architecture) with automated and faster failover. However, similar to all replication-based high-availability designs, there is a risk of data loss here.

Shared storage

This involves two servers connected either to a redundant shared-storage device such as a shared disk array, which was covered in *Chapter 6, High Availability with MySQL and Shared Storage*, or by using block-level replication such as DRBD and a cluster manager for automated failover, which was covered in *Chapter 7, High Availability with Block Level Replication*. The architecture diagram can be shown as follows:

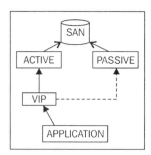

Block level replication

The other type of shared storage is block-level replication—DRBD shown as follows:

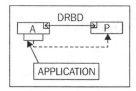

This has the advantage of extremely fast failover and, if configured correctly, there are no lost transactions in the event of a failover. The disadvantage is that it has relatively poor performance. Better performance, which is similar to or greater than the previous two architectures, can be achieved with local storage that requires expensive hardware such as Fibre Channel connectivity to a SAN or Dolphin Interconnects for DRBD.

MySQL Cluster

MySQL Cluster requires a minimum of three servers connected together in a local network as covered in detail in the first four chapters in this book. In the following example, the application is hosted on two servers, which are running SQL nodes that allow the application to connect to the `localhost` MySQL Server. A load balancer is therefore required to distribute users of the application between the two servers and to conduct health checking. It can be shown in the following diagram:

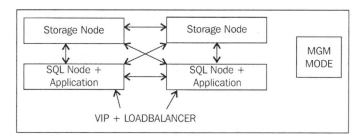

Multi-site architectures

There are two common techniques used for disaster recovery between multiple sites. Such techniques take into account the Internet latency and the overheads of virtual private networks or the other secure systems. The first is MySQL Replication. This can be implemented between MySQL Clusters (which was covered in *Chapter 3, MySQL Cluster Management*) or as standard MySQL Replication (which was covered in *Chapter 5*). Additionally, DRBD can be run in asynchronous mode. DRBD was covered in *Chapter 7*.

Summary of options

Method	Chapter(s)	Advantages	Disadvantages
MySQL Clustering	1-4	▸ Scalable ▸ High performance ▸ Very high uptimes possible	▸ Heavy RAM requirement ▸ Relatively complicated ▸ Heavy reliance on good network links
MySQL Replication	5	▸ Simple ▸ Highly available ▸ Virtually no performance impact	▸ Not scalable ▸ Data can be lost in failure
MySQL Replication between MySQL Clusters	3	All the advantages of MySQL Clustering, with excellent disaster recovery	▸ Extremely expensive ▸ Manual failover
Shared-storage clustering	6	Excellent uptimes possible	▸ Expensive storage required to minimize performance impact ▸ Complexity, limited scalability
Block-level replication	7	Low cost	▸ Performance impact ▸ Scalability

Index

Thank you for buying
High Availability MySQL Cookbook

About Packt Publishing

Packt, pronounced 'packed', published its first book "*Mastering phpMyAdmin for Effective MySQL Management*" in April 2004 and subsequently continued to specialize in publishing highly focused books on specific technologies and solutions.

Our books and publications share the experiences of your fellow IT professionals in adapting and customizing today's systems, applications, and frameworks. Our solution based books give you the knowledge and power to customize the software and technologies you're using to get the job done. Packt books are more specific and less general than the IT books you have seen in the past. Our unique business model allows us to bring you more focused information, giving you more of what you need to know, and less of what you don't.

Packt is a modern, yet unique publishing company, which focuses on producing quality, cutting-edge books for communities of developers, administrators, and newbies alike. For more information, please visit our website: `www.packtpub.com`.

About Packt Open Source

In 2010, Packt launched two new brands, Packt Open Source and Packt Enterprise, in order to continue its focus on specialization. This book is part of the Packt Open Source brand, home to books published on software built around Open Source licences, and offering information to anybody from advanced developers to budding web designers. The Open Source brand also runs Packt's Open Source Royalty Scheme, by which Packt gives a royalty to each Open Source project about whose software a book is sold.

Writing for Packt

We welcome all inquiries from people who are interested in authoring. Book proposals should be sent to author@packtpub.com. If your book idea is still at an early stage and you would like to discuss it first before writing a formal book proposal, contact us; one of our commissioning editors will get in touch with you.

We're not just looking for published authors; if you have strong technical skills but no writing experience, our experienced editors can help you develop a writing career, or simply get some additional reward for your expertise.

MySQL Admin Cookbook

ISBN: 978-1-847197-96-2   Paperback: 376 pages

99 great recipes for mastering MySQL configuration and administration

1. Set up MySQL to perform administrative tasks such as efficiently managing data and database schema, improving the performance of MySQL servers, and managing user credentials

2. Deal with typical performance bottlenecks and lock-contention problems

3. Restrict access sensibly and regain access to your database in case of loss of administrative user credentials

4. Part of Packt's Cookbook series: Each recipe is a carefully organized sequence of instructions to complete the task as efficiently as possible

Creating your MySQL Database

ISBN: 978-1-904811-30-5   Paperback: 108 pages

A short guide for everyone on how to structure your data and set-up your MySQL database tables efficiently and easily.

1. How best to collect, name, group, and structure your data

2. Design your data with future growth in mind

3. Practical examples from initial ideas to final designs

4. The quickest way to learn how to design good data structures for MySQL

Please check **www.PacktPub.com** for information on our titles

Mastering phpMyAdmin 3.1 for Effective MySQL Management

ISBN: 978-1-847197-86-3   Paperback: 352 pages

Create your own complete blog or web site from scratch with WordPress

1. Covers version 3.1, the latest version of phpMyAdmin

2. Administer your MySQL databases with phpMyAdmin

3. Manage users and privileges with MySQL Server Administration tools

4. Get to grips with the hidden features and capabilities of phpMyAdmin

Mastering phpMyAdmin 2.11 for Effective MySQL Management

ISBN: 978-1-847194-18-3   Paperback: 340 pages

Increase your MySQL productivity and control by discovering the real power of phpMyAdmin 2.11

1. Effectively administer your MySQL databases with phpMyAdmin.

2. Manage users and privileges with MySQL Server Administration tools.

3. Get to grips with the hidden features and capabilities of phpMyAdmin

Please check **www.PacktPub.com** for information on our titles

Lightning Source UK Ltd.
Milton Keynes UK
UKOW010102061212

203240UK00003B/65/P